POLICING MAJOR EVENTS

Perspectives from Around the World

International Police Executive Symposium Co-Publications

Dilip K. Das, *Founding President-IPES*

PUBLISHED

Examining Political Violence: Studies of Terrorism, Counterterrorism, and Internal Wars
By David Lowe, Austin Turk, and Dilip K. Das ISBN: 978-1-4665-8820-2

The Evolution of Policing: Worldwide Innovations and Insights
By Melchor C. de Guzman, Aiedeo Mintie Das, and Dilip K. Das, ISBN: 978-1-4665-6715-3

Policing Global Movement: Tourism, Migration, Human Trafficking, and Terrorism
By S. Caroline Taylor, Daniel Joseph Torpy, and Dilip K. Das, ISBN: 978-1-4665-0726-5

Global Community Policing: Problems and Challenges
By Arvind Verma, Dilip K. Das, Manoj Abraham, ISBN 978-1-4398-8416-4

Global Environment of Policing
By Darren Palmer, Michael M. Berlin, and Dilip K. Das, ISBN: 978-1-4200-6590-9

Strategic Responses to Crime: Thinking Locally, Acting Globally
By Melchor de Guzman, Aiedeo Mintie Das, and Dilip K. Das, ISBN: 978-1-4200-7669-1

Police without Borders: The Fading Distinction between Local and Global
By Cliff Roberson, Dilip K. Das, and Jennie K. Singer, ISBN: 978-1-4398-0501-5

Effective Crime Reduction Strategies: International Perspectives
By James F. Albrecht and Dilip K. Das, ISBN: 978-1-4200-7838-1

Urbanization, Policing, and Security: Global Perspectives
By Gary Cordner, Ann Marie Cordner, and Dilip K. Das, ISBN: 978-1-4200-8557-0

Criminal Abuse of Women and Children: An International Perspective
By Obi N.I. Ebbe and Dilip K. Das, ISBN: 978-1-4200-8803-8

Contemporary Issues in Law Enforcement and Policing
By Andrew Millie and Dilip K. Das, ISBN: 978-1-4200-7215-0

Global Trafficking in Women and Children
By Obi N.I. Ebbe and Dilip K. Das, ISBN: 978-1-4200-5943-4

Policing Major Events: Perspectives from Around the World
by James F. Albrecht, Martha C. Dow, Darryl Plecas, and Dilip K. Das, ISBN: 978-1-4665-8805-9

Police Reform: The Effects of International Economic Development, Armed Violence, and Public Safety
By Garth den Heyer and Dilip K. Das, ISBN: 978-1-4822-0456-8

POLICING MAJOR EVENTS

Perspectives from Around the World

Edited by

James F. Albrecht
Pace University
Department of Criminal Justice and Security
New York City, NY, USA

Martha C. Dow
University of the Fraser Valley
Abbotsford, British Columbia, Canada

Darryl Plecas
University of the Fraser Valley
Abbotsford, British Columbia, Canada

Dilip K. Das
International Police Executive Symposium
Guilderland, NY, USA

International Police Executive Symposium Co-Publication

CRC Press
Taylor & Francis Group
Boca Raton London New York

CRC Press is an imprint of the
Taylor & Francis Group, an **informa** business

Cover Top Left: Courtesy of Arindambanerjee / Shutterstock.com

Cover Top Right: Courtesy of Larry Bruce / Shutterstock.com

Cover Bottom Left: Courtesy of Ron Ellis / Shutterstock.com

CRC Press
Taylor & Francis Group
6000 Broken Sound Parkway NW, Suite 300
Boca Raton, FL 33487-2742

© 2015 by Taylor & Francis Group, LLC
CRC Press is an imprint of Taylor & Francis Group, an Informa business

No claim to original U.S. Government works

Printed on acid-free paper
Version Date: 20140923

International Standard Book Number-13: 978-1-4665-8805-9 (Hardback)

Visit the Taylor & Francis Web site at
http://www.taylorandfrancis.com

and the CRC Press Web site at
http://www.crcpress.com

This book is dedicated to the police officials, first responders, volunteers, and innocent victims who have died at the scene of natural disasters, terrorist events, large-scale disorders, and while engaged in rescue and recovery operations.

***

My contribution to this insightful book is the result of the support of my loving family, particularly my son, Jimmy, and my daughter, Kristiana, who have reenergized me through their enthusiasm for life and learning.

James F. Albrecht

I dedicate my contribution to this book to my father, William Dow, as I am deeply grateful that he taught me the importance of living life on the front porch.

Martha C. Dow

I dedicate my contribution to this book to my sons, Ryan and Sean, for giving me a sense of great pride in simply being who they are.

Darryl Plecas

I will again dedicate my efforts to my dear wife, Ana, and my loving daughter, Mintie, for their continuous love and support.

Dilip K. Das

Contents

Prologue

This textbook will closely examine the successes, challenges, and lessons learned from police response to a variety of major events and natural and man-made disasters. The need for comprehensive planning; public dialog; interagency coordination (at the regional, federal, and international levels); effective information and intelligence collection, exchange, and dissemination; the acceptance and implementation of democratic rule of law principles; cultural understanding and appreciation; community involvement; and service through civility are some of the primary considerations that will be analyzed within this informative text.

An impressive complement of experts will provide thoroughly outlined perspectives as seen through the eyes of the practitioner, the academic, the researcher, and the public. Police response to enjoyable global sporting events, such as the World Cup football competition and Olympic Games, will be contrasted to overwhelming natural disasters like Hurricane Katrina in America's South, and tragic and devastating man-made terrorist incidents like those experienced in New York City, London, and Madrid, and those that unfortunately and routinely continue to occur in Nigeria's North Eastern States.

It is anticipated that this book will offer both the student and the policy maker with insight into these phenomena and present viewpoints and understanding that will permit the government, the police, first responders, and the public to better prepare, plan, and respond to future events, whether unforeseen or anticipated.

Foreword

1. To prevent crime and disorder, as an alternative to their repression by military force and severity of legal punishment.
2. To recognise always that the power of the police to fulfil their functions and duties is dependent on public approval of their existence, actions and behaviour and on their ability to secure and maintain public respect.
3. To recognise always that to secure and maintain the respect and approval of the public means also the securing of the willing co-operation of the public in the task of securing observance of laws.
4. To recognise always that the extent to which the co-operation of the public can be secured diminishes proportionately the necessity of the use of physical force and compulsion for achieving police objectives.
5. To seek and preserve public favour, not by pandering to public opinion; but by constantly demonstrating absolutely impartial service to law, in complete independence of policy, and without regard to the justice or injustice of the substance of individual laws, by ready offering of individual service and friendship to all members of the public without regard to their wealth or social standing, by ready exercise of courtesy and friendly good humour; and by ready offering of individual sacrifice in protecting and preserving life.
6. To use physical force only when the exercise of persuasion, advice and warning is found to be insufficient to obtain public co-operation to an extent necessary to secure observance of law or to restore order, and to use only the minimum degree of physical force which is necessary on any particular occasion for achieving a police objective.
7. To maintain at all times a relationship with the public that gives reality to the historic tradition that *the police are the public and that the public are the police,* the police being only members of the public who are paid to give full-time attention to duties which are incumbent on every citizen in the interests of community welfare and existence.
8. To recognise always the need for strict adherence to police-executive functions, and to refrain from even seeming to usurp the powers of

the judiciary of avenging individuals or the State, and of authorita-
tively judging guilt and punishing the guilty.
9. To recognise always that the test of police efficiency is the absence of
   crime and disorder, and not the visible evidence of police action in
   dealing with them. (Lee, 1901)

One does not have to move much from the origins of professional policing
to better comprehend what is needed by government and law enforcement agencies to deal with major events and incidents, whether planned or
unforeseen, in an effective manner. Sir Robert Peel's nine basic principles
for policing highlight the relevance of the role that the public plays in delineating the responsibilities and powers granted to police to accomplish their
tasks. And the police must rely on public input, feedback, and approval to
determine if the police have conducted themselves not only effectively, but
also in line with the community's expectations. These foremost concepts
apply no less to daily crime control and community service responsibilities than they do to the provision of public safety at large-scale events and
disastrous incidents.

Skillful pilots gain their reputations through storms and tempests.
(Epicurus, 4th century BCE)

James F. Albrecht
NYPD Captain (ret.)
September 11, 2001 First Responder

Reference

Lee, W. L. M. (1901). *A history of police in England.* London: Methuan and Company.

Series Editor's Preface

The International Police Executive Symposium (IPES) was founded in 1994 to address one major challenge, that is, the two worlds of research and practice remain disconnected even though cooperation between the two is growing. A major reason is that the two groups speak in different languages. The research is published in hard-to-access journals and presented in a manner that is difficult for some to comprehend. On the other hand, police practitioners tend not to mix with researchers and remain secretive about their work. Consequently, there is little dialog between the two and almost no attempt to learn from one another. The global dialog among police researchers and practitioners is limited. True, the literature on the police is growing exponentially. But its impact upon day-to-day policing, however, is negligible.

The aims and objectives of the IPES are to provide a forum to foster closer relationships among police researchers and practitioners on a global scale, to facilitate cross-cultural, international, and interdisciplinary exchanges for the enrichment of the law enforcement profession, to encourage discussion, and to publish research on challenging and contemporary problems facing the policing profession. One of the most important activities of the IPES is the organization of an annual meeting under the auspices of a police agency or an educational institution. Now in its 17th year the annual meeting, a five-day initiative on specific issues relevant to the policing profession, brings together ministers of interior and justice, police commissioners and chiefs, members of academia representing world-renowned institutions, and many more criminal justice elite from over 60 countries. It facilitates interaction and the exchange of ideas and opinions on all aspects of policing. The agenda is structured to encourage dialog in both formal and informal settings.

Another important aspect of the meeting is the publication of the best papers presented, edited by well-known criminal justice scholars and police professionals who attend the meetings. The best papers are selected, thoroughly revised, fully updated, meticulously edited, and published as books based upon the theme of each meeting. This repository of knowledge under the copublication imprint of IPES and CRC Press/Taylor & Francis Group chronicles the important contributions of the International Police Executive Symposium over the last two decades. As a result, in 2011, the United Nations awarded IPES a *Special Consultative Status* for the Economic and

Social Council (ECSOC) honoring its importance in the global security community.

In addition to this book series, the IPES also has a research journal, *Police Practices and Research: An International Journal* (PPR). The *PPR* contains research articles on police issues from practitioners and researchers. It is an international journal in the true sense of the term and is distributed worldwide. For more information on the *PPR* visit: http://www.tandf.co.uk/journals/GPPR.

In line with the mission of the IPES, this new book will provide both practitioner and academic alike with a realistic and comprehensive overview of the broad array of issues and challenges facing law enforcement leaders, government officials, and community members when dealing with unforeseen disaster, tragedy, or large-scale events and disorder. The experiences and lessons learned from the perspectives presented by the book's authors will highlight the need for a thorough, community-oriented, and transparent process to ensure effective police planning and response to major incidents and events. Collaboration and mutual understanding will prove to be the essential keys to successful performance and will enhance citizen confidence in policing endeavors, particularly as it relates to large-scale and critical challenges that first responders and law enforcement experts routinely or unexpectedly face.

IPES advocates, promotes, and propagates that *policing* is one of the most basic and essential avenues for improving the quality of life in all nations; rich and poor; modern and traditional; large and small; as well as peaceful and strife-ridden. IPES actively works to drive home to all its office bearers, supporters, and admirers that, in order to reach its full potential as an instrument of service to humanity, policing must be fully and enthusiastically open to collaboration between research and practice, global exchange of information between police practitioners and academics, universal disseminations and sharing of best practices, generating thinking police leaders and followers, as well as reflecting and writing on the issues challenging to the profession.

Through its annual meetings, hosts, institutional supporters, and publications, IPES reaffirms that *policing* is a moral profession with unflinching adherence to the rule of law and human rights as the embodiment of humane values.

Dilip K. Das
Founding President
International Police Executive Symposium
www.ipes.info

Book Series Editor for
Advances in Police Theory and Practice
CRC Press /Taylor & Francis Group

Book Series Editor for
Interviews with Global Leaders in Criminal Justice
CRC Press/Taylor & Francis Group

PPR Special Issues as Books
Routledge/Taylor & Francis Group

Founding Editor-in-Chief
Police Practice and Research:
An International Journal, PPR
http://www.tandf.co.uk/journals/GPPR

Acknowledgments

The editors and chapter authors would like to express utmost gratitude to the criminal justice and law enforcement officials and colleagues who provided such a definitive insight into the plethora of issues related to the policing of large-scale events and the response to critical incidents and major disasters. In particular, it is essential to acknowledge police experts in Serbia, Australia, the United Kingdom, Canada, South Africa, Nigeria, and the Netherlands; within the American states of Texas and Louisiana; and within the New York City Police Department, the London Metropolitan Police, and the United Nations Police.

In addition, such a collaborative work could not have been completed without the support of our academic colleagues and mentors, and of course, our work supervisors. And most importantly, our families and loved ones continue to pay the price of our academic and research commitments and clearly deserve the highest levels of appreciation and gratitude.

The International Police Executive Symposium continues to provide the arena for cooperation and exchange of critical information between law enforcement and criminal justice executives, policy makers, researchers, and students of those fields. The IPES founder Dilip Das must be acknowledged for his vision and foresight in developing the initial concepts into the successful organization and network that it has become.

Finally, the success of this book is the result of the guidance of IPES editor Melchor C. de Guzman, and the support and supervision of Carolyn Spence of CRC Press/Taylor & Francis Group.

About the Editors

James "Jimmy" F. Albrecht, is presently working as a professor of criminal justice and homeland security at Pace University in New York City. In addition, Professor Albrecht has 25 years of front-line law enforcement experience, and had previously held a number of executive positions including Police Chief of Criminal Investigations in the joint European Union/U.S. (EULEX) Police in Kosovo (former Yugoslavia). He retired as NYPD Captain and Regional Commander after serving 22 years, which included direct response to the tragic September 11, 2001 attacks on the World Trade Center. Prof. Albrecht served three years as a graduate professor of criminal justice leadership at St. John's University in New York, and is completing his Ph.D. in criminal justice at the University of New Haven (Connecticut). He possesses separate master's degrees in history, human physiology, and criminal justice.

He is the coauthor and editor of three books: *Effective Crime Reduction Strategies: International Perspectives* (CRC Press, 2011); *Policing Major Events: Perspectives from Around the World* (CRC Press, 2014); and a new book, *Police Reserves and Volunteers in Law Enforcement: Global Perspectives* (CRC Press, anticipated publication in 2015). Prof. Albrecht has written many other publications dealing with law enforcement, community policing, emergency incident response, legal history, crime reduction strategies, corruption control, and terrorism. He continues to serve as a special editor of the *Pakistan Journal of Criminology*. He was the recipient of a prestigious Fulbright Fellowship in 1998, where he worked as a professor at the National Police College of Finland; and is the beneficiary of a 2013 IREX Embassy Policy Specialist Fellowship, while currently conducting research and making recommendations to improve law enforcement effectiveness and legitimacy in the Ukraine. Prof. Albrecht continues to highlight the relevance of corruption control and gender equality as it relates to police and democratic reform in developing nations and carries on his service as an expert advisor to the United Nations, the National Institute of Justice, and the U.S. Departments of Homeland Security (DHS), State (DOS), and Justice (DOJ). He has lectured at police facilities and universities in China, Taiwan, Russia, Germany, Austria, Sweden, Norway, Estonia, Finland, Italy, Turkey, Canada, Dubai, Kosovo, Macedonia, Malta, Ukraine, South Africa, and throughout the United States.

Martha C. Dow, Ph.D., is an associate professor in sociology at the University of the Fraser Valley. Dr. Dow has extensive experience working with policing, correctional, and fire service agencies exploring issues related to organizational change and leadership models, recruitment, retention and succession of officers, diversity, and community relations. Many of her research projects explore how public safety agencies, community organizations, schools, and universities might support more progressive professional practices. In addition, Dr. Dow has presented at numerous international conferences and has served on a variety of governmental and community-based committees.

Darryl Plecas, Ed.D., is presently an elected member of the Legislative Assembly of British Columbia in Canada and is serving the Abbotsford South community. Plecas was appointed parliamentary secretary to the Minister of Justice and Attorney General for Crime Reduction on June 10, 2013, shortly after his election to the Legislative Assembly in May 2013. In addition, Dr. Darryl Plecas is professor emeritus at the University of the Fraser Valley in British Columbia, Canada. Most recently, he served as the RCMP University Research Chair and director of the Centre for Public Safety and Criminal Justice Research in the university's School of Criminology and Criminal Justice. He is the author or coauthor of more than 200 research reports and publications addressing a broad range of criminal justice issues. He holds two degrees in criminology from Simon Fraser University, and a doctorate in higher education from the University of British Columbia.

Dilip K. Das, Ph.D., has extensive experience in police practice, research, writing, and education. A professor of criminal justice, former police chief, and founding editor-in-chief of *Police Practice and Research: An International Journal*, Dr. Das is a human rights consultant to the United Nations.

After obtaining his master's degree in English literature, Dr. Das joined the Indian Police Service, an elite national service with a glorious tradition. Following 14 years in the service as a police executive including chief of police, he moved to the United States where he achieved another master's degree in criminal justice as well as a doctorate in the same discipline. Founding president of the International Police Executive Symposium (IPES at www.ipes.info), and founding editor of *Police Practice and Research: An International Journal*, Dr. Das has authored, edited, and coedited more than 30 books and numerous articles. He has traveled extensively throughout the world in comparative police research, as a visiting professor in various universities, for organizing annual conferences of the IPES, and as a human rights consultant to the United Nations. Dr. Das has received several faculty excellence awards and has been recognized as a Distinguished Faculty Lecturer.

About the Contributors

Chapter 1: **Branislav Simonović**, Ph.D., is on the Faculty of Law, University of Kragujevac; **Zoran Đurđević**, Ph.D., is assigned to the Academy of Criminalistics and Police Studies in Belgrade; and **Božidar Otašević**, M.A., works for the Ministry of Interior of the Republic of Serbia.

Chapter 2: **Craig Paterson** is a professor in the Department of Law, Criminology, and Community Justice at Sheffield Hallam University in Sheffield, United Kingdom.

Chapter 3: **Martina Schreiber** is an instructor in the Department of Public Order Management at the Police Academy of the Netherlands in Apeldoorn, Holland; and **Clifford Stott** is a professor in the Department of Applied Psychology at Liverpool University in Liverpool, UK.

Chapter 4: **Sophie Nakueira** is a Ph.D. candidate at the Centre of Criminology, Faculty of Law, University of Cape Town; and **Julie Berg** is a senior lecturer at the Centre of Criminology, Faculty of Law at the University of Cape Town in South Africa.

Chapter 5: **Kesetović Želimir, Sladjana Djurić**, and **Vladimir Cvetković** are on the Faculty of Security Studies at the University of Belgrade in Serbia.

Chapter 6: **Darryl Plecas, Martha C. Dow**, and **Jordan Diplock** are researchers at the Centre for Public Safety and Criminal Justice Research at the University of the Fraser Valley in British Columbia, Canada.

Chapter 7: **Rick Sarre** is a professor at the School of Law and associate head of research at the School of Commerce at the University of South Australia.

Chapter 8: **Dr. A. Oyesoji Aremu** is a professor in the Department of Guidance and Counseling at the University of Ibadan in Nigeria.

Chapter 9: **Dr. Robert D. Hanser** is a criminal justice professor and the director of the Institute of Law Enforcement at the University of Louisiana at Monroe; **Dr. Nathan Moran** is a professor of criminal justice and department chair at Midwestern State University in Texas; and **Professor Anissa Horne** works at the North Delta Human Services Authority and Richwood Correctional Center in Louisiana.

Chapter 10: **Michael R. Sanchez** is a former police director in the UNMIK Police in Kosovo and former regional commander in the United Nations Mission in Haiti, who is pursuing a Ph.D. in business administration at Northcentral University in Arizona.

Chapter 11: **James F. Albrecht** is presently a professor of criminal justice and homeland security at Pace University in New York, and is a retired NYPD Captain and Commanding Officer.

Chapter 12: **Dr. Christiaan Bezuidenhout** is a professor in the Department of Social Work and Criminology at the University of Pretoria in South Africa.

Chapter 13: **Dr. Perry Stanislas** is a professor of criminal justice in the Department of Applied Social Sciences at De Montfort University in Leicester, UK.

Chapter 14: **Dr. Rick Parent** is an assistant professor of police studies at Simon Fraser University, School of Criminology in British Columbia, Canada.

Introduction

Whenever there is a major event that requires police intervention, whether violent or not, there will be questions raised about the appropriateness of the police response. Such questions include whether the police could have prevented the conflict, been better prepared, reacted more quickly, acted more forcefully, and brought the altercation under control more effectively, and are all part of an overall expressed concern that somehow the police did not respond appropriately. These are difficult questions, irrespective of the context, if for no other reason than an assessment of whether events might have escalated or de-escalated had the police prepared or responded differently in the first instance is impossible to answer with certainty. Even attempting to answer such questions is difficult for nonparticipants as it may be difficult to capture the nuances of the mentality of the crowds in any situation. It is with that in mind that this collection hopes to provide food for thought in the consideration of police developing a readiness for policing major events and responding to large-scale disasters across a diverse set of events and sociopolitical contexts.

In Chapter 1, the authors utilize a legislative orientation to examine the efficacy of various police procedures employed in Serbia to respond to major sporting events and the violence that too often accompanies these events. The authors emphasize the necessity of a strong legislative framework to support police as they engage in both preventative and reactive forms of intervention.

In Chapter 2, the author highlights the importance of police/protestor relationships, the media in characterizing those relationships to the general public, and ultimately accountability frameworks in cultivating and maintaining public trust in police. The author argues, using examples of police responding to political protests in the United Kingdom, that effective policing strategies must be attentive to these three factors irrespective of the particular sociopolitical context.

In Chapter 3, the authors employ a qualitative research design to explore the relationship between crowd orientations and the use of low-profile versus high-profile policing strategies. These differences were examined as they manifested themselves in the Portuguese Security Police force's dealing with German football fans at the 2004 European Championship in Portugal.

In Chapter 4, the authors use the 2010 World Cup in South Africa as a model of best practice with respect to the development of collaborative and inclusive governance structures. Most importantly, Chapter 4 emphasizes a more foundational question: how can we ensure that the strategies used to police major events can be emphasized in everyday policy standards and operations.

In Chapter 5, the authors explore the legal, organizational, and practical challenges that inform the theory and the practice of policing football fan violence in Serbia emphasizing the relationships among sports fans, politicians, and organized crime leaders.

In Chapter 6, the security operations of the 2010 Winter Olympic Games in Canada are assessed based on the perceptions of key stakeholders within the unit responsible for securing the Games. Interestingly, given the other chapters in this book is that most critical elements are organizational structure, threat assessment communication, in that there needs to be greater attention paid to the legacy value of these types of events.

Chapter 7 discusses the growing relevance of private security in working with public police forces in a multitude of policing tasks. The author concludes by emphasizing the development of legislative frameworks that guide, regulate, and legitimate this more cooperative approach.

In Chapter 8, the author examines the need to involve community members in any initiatives to curb the terrorist insurgency that is taking place in North Eastern Nigeria. Without public support, direct community involvement, and intelligence-led planning and deployment, law enforcement, military, and government officials will continue to experience difficulties in deterring terrorist attacks and retaliatory violence, and in bringing calm and security to those impoverished regions of the country.

Chapter 9 examines the overall government response to Hurricane Katrina in the American states of Louisiana and Texas, and highlights the tragic and criminal repercussions of the poor planning on the city of New Orleans and other large metropolitan areas that offered to provide housing and assistance to those who were evacuated from those devastated areas. Fortunately this catastrophe and the resulting impacts have been examined in detail to provide recommendations for enhanced and effective disaster response. The tragic lessons learned have led and will continue to lead to saved lives and improved coordination to major critical incidents.

In Chapter 10, a former upper level United Nations police official examines the coordination needed to enhance public safety and develop functional rule of law in post-conflict regions. The responsibilities of the United Nations police are greatly affected (and often restricted) by mandate outlined by the United Nations Security Counsel in their resulting comprehensive resolution. Lessons learned in the United Nations rule of law missions in both Kosovo and Haiti will be comprehensively identified.

In Chapter 11, an experienced New York City Police Department commander outlines the revisions made to the agency's protocols involving critical incident response since the tragic September 11, 2001 terrorist attacks. Proper planning, comprehensive preparation, and regularly conducted and realistic exercise drills have proven to be critical aspects of effective emergency incident response and successful performance at large-scale events in this large metropolis. Procedures, policies, and tactics to enhance emergency incident preparedness and response, and planning for major events will be thoroughly delineated.

Chapter 12 poses an interesting paradox as the South African Police Service has had major success in hosting major global sporting events, as highlighted in Chapter 4, yet continues to struggle in routine policing initiatives across the nation. On the one hand, the police of South Africa have gained international respect, but domestically lack the confidence and support of the local populations. The author reiterates the need for a professional, service-oriented, and modern law enforcement mechanism that, on a daily basis, can rival the successful efforts exhibited while under the international microscope, when coordinating safety and security for significant large-scale events. In addition, the experiences conveyed will support the notion that proper planning and interagency coordination can lead to a successful deployment, enhanced professionalism, and effective performance while dealing with a number of large-scale events, and concludes that the same strategic principles could be applied to routine policing functions on a constant basis.

In Chapter 13, the author presents a bird's eye and front-line perspective of the steps taken to ensure that public safety and security were at their highest levels during the Summer Olympic and Paralympic Games held in London in 2012. Strategies to coordinate interorganizational cooperation to ensure routine police and rescue services across the nation, while enhancing public safety measures at Olympic venue sites and cities, specifically at a time when the terrorist threat was elevated, are concretely outlined, as is the emphasis on the need for continuous professional training for law enforcement leaders and front-line personnel.

The author of Chapter 14 will provide his personal experiences and insight in comprehensively describing the specific policing strategies routinely implemented to address major events that occur on Aboriginal and tribal lands across Canada. Continuously highlighted is the need to involve the community-at-large in the planning, response, and post-event stages. These types of incidents and events require sensitivity and cultural understanding, detailed planning and coordination, and comprehensive and routine training for police personnel of all ranks.

All of the articles highlight the overarching need to understand historical and contemporary examples of the policing of major events in order to effect meaningful change in how future events are policed. Accordingly, this volume seeks not to second guess or question police strategy in any particular circumstance; but rather, to call attention to how changes in law enforcement and sociopolitical uncertainty make it much more difficult for police to prepare, strategize, and respond to such scenarios in general. Even in jurisdictions such as Canada and the United States, with its relatively stable sociopolitical climate and where law enforcement in general is the recipient of high public approval ratings, it has only taken a few high profile events to erode that confidence. Several of the chapters included in this international collection highlight similarly polarizing events.

A critical aspect of these events that is only peripherally mentioned but is arguably becoming more and more important in how police involvement in major events is understood by the public is the use of cell phones and social media to share images, perceptions, and critiques of the police in jurisdictions around the world. Greer and McLaughlin (2010) note that:

> the citizen journalist provides a valuable additional source of real-time information that may challenge or confirm the institutional version of events. However, it is when citizen journalism challenges the "official truth", as portrayed by those powerful institutional sources who have traditionally maintained a relatively uncontested position at the top of the "hierarchy of credibility", that it becomes most potent as a news resource. (p. 1056)

It is our hope that this collection of chapters will illuminate, through a diverse set of international examples, the complex set of factors that shape both the challenges and opportunities of policing major events.

Reference

Greer, C., & McLaughlin, E. (2010). We predict a riot? Public order policing, new media environments and the rise of the citizen journalist. *British Journal of Criminology, 50*(6), 1041–1059.

Violence at Sporting Events

1

The European Standards of Police Procedures and Practice in Serbia

BRANISLAV SIMONOVIĆ, ZORAN ĐURĐEVIĆ,
AND BOŽIDAR OTAŠEVIĆ

Contents

Introduction

Violence at sporting events is an old phenomenon. It was noted even in the texts from the period of ancient Greece and the Roman Empire (Madensen & Eck, 2008). In the recent history of human civilization, violence at football matches has been especially expressed. Although it was not accurately recorded when the first serious incident at a sporting event of this kind happened, a relevant datum is the fact that on July 16, 1916, in Buenos Aires (Argentina), supporters and police came into conflict because the final match of the South American Championships between Argentina and Uruguay had been postponed because the stadium that had room for only 20,000 fans was confronted with 40,000 people (Žužak, 2010). Although England is considered the homeland of modern forms of violent behavior at football matches, this form of violence has quickly spread worldwide (Kozarev, 2007). Violence and indecent behavior at sporting events, particularly at football matches, is an international problem and present in all European countries, both those that are considered traditionally fascinated with football, and those in which this sport is not deeply rooted (Göral, 2008). While Europe is being dominated by various forms of organized football violence, the United States is experiencing more spontaneous, unorganized forms of violence which are prevailing (Madensen & Eck, 2008).

Violence at sporting events, especially in football, became a common phenomenon in the 1980s, culminating in Europe after the tragic events at Heysel Stadium in Belgium on May 29, 1985. This event led to a more severe treatment of this kind of violence and contributed to the adoption of a number of recommendations from international European reports, whose goal was to address the problem in a comprehensive manner and to build international standards that would provide the basis for the improved safety. A primary objective of these efforts is also the development and adoption of international standards of police conduct. The focus of this chapter is to examine key issues in the development and implementation (particularly in Serbia) directed upon building of international standards of police conduct in dealing with the problem of violence at sporting events, especially football matches.

European Standards of Police Procedure: Controlling Violence at Sporting Events

One of the first documents passed in Europe which treats violence in sport is the Recommendation of the Parliamentary Assembly of the Council of Europe in 1983. In that particular recommendation, the prevention of violence in sport is placed within the broader frame of educational and cultural measures in order to reduce violence in society. The recommendations of the Council of Ministers on reducing violence at sporting events followed in 1984 outlining the basic principles, which are applied in the preparation of subsequently enacted documents (Đurđević, 2007).

The first among the conventions of the Council of Europe, which was adopted in the field of penal law, and was related to sport, was the *European Convention on Spectator Violence and Misbehaviour at Sports Events and in Particular Football Matches*. This convention was adopted on August 19, 1985, in Strasbourg and was a response of European countries to the tragedy that occurred at the Heysel Stadium in Belgium.

Article 1 of the convention defines the obligation of member countries, within its constitutional powers, to take necessary measures to implement provisions of the convention. The measures within the convention (Articles 2–6 of the convention) for the reducing and controlling of violence and misbehavior at sporting events can be classified within the following themes: coordination of national policies and measures undertaken by public authorities of the signatory countries; establishment of national coordination bodies; engagement of the police in and around the stadiums and on the roads leading to the stadiums; the adoption and application of regulations that enable the prosecution and punishment of perpetrators of violence at stadiums; police cooperation and information exchange between the signatory countries; organization of appropriate monitoring service; organization of staff out of ranks of fans and cooperation with the fans groups; and measures related to stadiums (e.g., fences, the separation of fans, ticket sales).

The convention classifies the measures for preventing and combating violence and misbehavior at sporting events in three major areas: prevention, cooperation, and the judicial authorities' measures.

Preventive measures include cooperation between the police and sport clubs in the preparatory stage of international matches, organization of consultations of interested parties not later than two weeks before the scheduled match, the actions of physical separation of fans of different teams, the control of access to the stadium, and the prohibition of alcohol and other potentially dangerous items. The convention lays the foundation for greater coordination among various stakeholders through the possibility of establishing coordinating bodies. In addition, the convention outlines a number of measures to deal specifically with the problem of hooliganism.

The convention defines the standards, which for security reasons must be respected during the design and construct phase of new stadiums in order to reduce the probability of aggressive fan behavior. Besides the clear functional scheme, use of appropriate building materials, planning of an appropriate number of entrances and exits, clear marking of the facilities for easier orientation and evacuation in case of emergency, the plan should include the application of technical protection measures, especially sophisticated system of video surveillance, with a fully equipped control room, as well as premises for temporary detention of persons.

Within the framework of cooperation, when playing international matches, the convention highlights the obligation of organizing bodies to establish contacts between the security structures in order to identify and prevent potential hazards and reduce potential risks. As a measure of cooperation of judicial authorities, exchange of information on persons who are registered as perpetrators of criminal offenses with elements of violence is envisaged.

The convention has imposed an obligation on the signatory countries to adopt appropriate laws that should prescribe both criminal offenses and/or misdemeanors that may be committed by engaging in acts of violence and misbehavior at sporting events. For that reason, the European Convention on Spectator Violence and Misbehavior at Sports Events and in Particular at Football Matches is considered to be a source of international penal law in the field of sports. In fact, the convention represents the source of both criminal law and law of torts in the field of sports, since it obliges Member States to develop and enforce relevant criminal offenses and misdemeanors and thus create a mechanism for legal protection of those attending and participating in sporting events (Šuput, 2010).

After the enactment of the European Convention on Spectator Violence and Misbehavior at Sports Events and in particular at Football Matches in 1985, the problem of violence in sport, especially in football, continued to escalate and morphed into new forms. The violence spread beyond sports facilities and was often not even related to specific sports matches. Hooligans developed new ways of organizing and began using a variety of tools to prepare for and engage in violence (e.g., Internet, mobile phones, motorcycles as means of transportation, and both cold and fire weapons) (Kozarev, 2007).

In an effort to develop adequate responses to violence at sporting events, the Council of Europe and its commissions passed a series of resolutions, recommendations, and instructions. In this chapter, the recent European documents that significantly affect the formation of standards of police procedure in solving the problem of violence at sporting events are examined.

The Council Recommendation of 22 April 1996 on Guidelines for Preventing and Restraining Disorder Connected with Football Matches (96/C 131/01) is based on the convention of 1985. The aim of the recommendation is to ensure a consistent, coordinated, and effective response of police and football organizations within EU Member States. The basic recommendations found in this document are: exchange of information (member countries should have a common format for police intelligence reports about the known groups of football hooligans and those who are assumed to be prone to engage in disorderly behavior); cooperation in the field of training (implies exchange and dissemination of information between member countries on the techniques of disorder prevention at football matches, and organization of relevant training intended for police officers of the member countries); police cooperation implies police cooperation between member countries, which includes the exchange of data for at least four weeks before the football match. It was emphasized that a host country should formally contact the responsible authority of the other Member State or States for their police support. Cooperation and supervision implies an obligation of football authorities and clubs to appoint representatives who will attend educational programs and training courses that promote close cooperation and supervision between the clubs and the police in order to achieve secure events.

A key aspect of this document is the recommendation to create a common format for police intelligence reports on football hooligans. Standardized information on fans and fan groups would be entered and categorized into three groups: Group A consists of peaceful supporters; Group B consists of supporters who are prone to confrontation and disorderly behavior, especially under the influence of alcohol; and Group C includes violent supporters or the organizers of violence. The format would include other data important for the control of the fan groups such as means of transportation, event routes, and fan accommodations.

The Council Resolution of 3 June 2010 concerning an updated handbook with recommendations for international police cooperation and measures to prevent and control violence and disturbances in connection with football matches with an international dimension, in which at least one Member State is involved (2010/C 165/01). This document details the procedures that should be applied by police in securing football matches and other sporting events primarily at the international level, but also at national levels. The main focus of the resolution of this document is to optimize international police cooperation, communication, and exchange of information through a multiagency approach and proactive and risk-oriented policing.

The resolution stipulates that all EU Member States must establish a National Football Information Point (NFIP) to act as the central and sole contact point for the exchange of relevant information for football matches with an international dimension, and for developing international police cooperation concerning football matches. The task of this body is to promote cooperation and exchange of information between the police forces of both the organizing country and the visiting countries. In addition, the NFIP should coordinate and supply relevant information to local police in host cities for all national or international football matches. The NFIP should create a national police database relevant to the security of football matches to support risk analysis, security assessments, and the coordination of the work of other stakeholders. NFIPs of the hosting and visiting countries need to exchange *general information* (strategic, operational, and tactical) and *personal information* (fan data including traveling routes of fans, transportation means, accommodation, risk analysis of the visiting team supporters); *information relevant for the police procedure during the sporting event* (tendency toward the use of violence and risks connected directly to the course of football match), and *information relevant to the police procedure after the match* (leaving the stadium, behaving in the host town, returning from the match).

Other sections of the resolution outline a range of issues including: police activities associated with preparing for the event; the interpolice cooperation during the course of a football match; issues of cooperation between the police and organizers of the match; the cooperation between the police and prosecuting authorities; cooperation between police and supporter groups, which represents a necessary condition for the better and timely exchange of information, improvement of safety, creation of a more favorable atmosphere,

---

* *Official Journal of the European Union.* http://eur-lex.europa.eu/LexUriServ/LexUriServ. do?uri=OJ:C:2010:165:0001:0021:EN:PDF

and encouragement of self-organizing of supporters in order to improve the safety; police communication with the media and preparation of media strategy in order to win them over to contribute to the strengthening of security and positive coverage that would not encourage violence, but will contribute to a transparent and timely reporting.

The resolution calls for an analysis of various security aspects of football events, a more comprehensive approach to risk analysis, education and training courses for all participants in the security system, and dissemination of positive practice among states. This document proposes the classification of fans into *Non-Risk Supporters* and *Risk Supporters*, with the second group representing individuals deemed more likely to engage in disorderly behavior and violence. This second group is divided into different subgroups of supporters depending on whether they are prone to disturbing public order and public safety or committing criminal activities.

Within European academic and professional circles, the role of the police in preventing violence in stadiums should be informed by intelligence work, as has been the case in Britain. Informed by the negative experiences in the 1980s when a large number of hooligans were not held accountable due to a lack of evidence and unreliable police records, the British police began to base its work on *intelligence-led policing*, that is, collecting information on supporter groups, their membership, and intentions and protection of the source of information. The precondition for these more proactive police actions is access to full, accurate, timely information on supporters and hooligans, their movements and activities. Information on the number of supporters who will be attending the match, their level of organization, whether their past behavior has been violent, the nature of their relationships with other supporter groups and club management are all very important, because these data are the basis of security evaluation and planning of police force engagement (Spaaij, 2005).

There are numerous methods of obtaining intelligence information on hooligans. One of the possible methods is the use of covert operations, that is, infiltration of police officers into hooligan groups. Information obtained by this method is generally described as the most accurate and most useful in police work.

One of the central methods through which the police obtain information about hooligans is the use of police officers in the jargon known as "spotters." The system of spotters is designed so that every police officer who performs this duty is connected with a particular sports club. His task is to identify and monitor hooligans of a certain club, especially when traveling to guest matches. Those officers enter into close relations with their local clubs, with the leaders of supporter groups, as well as registered hooligans.

This system was developed in Great Britain, where a National Football Intelligence Unit (NFIU) was founded (Spaaij, 2005).

Critical to this approach are information sources such as criminal records and databases. In those databases, all the persons who are involved in violence at sporting events should be recorded. Information from these databases should be shared with other foreign police forces in the preparation phase of securing international matches. Improvement of safety measures at stadiums during sporting events, with the application of modern technical systems, has made the identification of hooligans significantly easier. Coverage of public spaces with cameras, the use of video recordings, and efforts of British police to create comprehensive records proved to be critical in supporting the prosecution of a large number of hooligans who committed acts in the late 1990s (Spaaij, 2005).

Key Recommendations: Establishing Contemporary Standards of Police Conduct in Order to Control Football Hooliganism

Based on international legal regulations adopted in the European Union and various examples of successful practice, the following list represents some key recommendations for police procedure in preventing and controlling violent behavior connected to football matches:

- Establish permanent football intelligence units in each country, and during the preparation of international sports matches intensify regular consultations and exchange of intelligence information between police units from countries whose national teams and/or football clubs will be participating;
- Utilize spotters to monitor hooliganism associated with particular clubs;
- Exchange information and establish national databases on known or suspected troublemakers at football matches including the nature of the security risk they pose, and the travel arrangements and routes of supporters;
- Adopt a common format for police intelligence reports in connection with violence at football matches;
- Introduce and support risk-oriented policing;
- Create and disseminate an annual report on cases of hooliganism at sporting events;
- Develop systems to enhance cooperation and the exchange of information (strategic, operational, and tactical) between various police units, at the national and international level, which are participating in different stages of securing a particular match;

- Enhance cooperation between the police and football clubs' management and organizers of sports events and jointly work on the development and implementation of preventive strategic and operational approaches;
- Develop cooperation between police and supporter groups and their associations through the creation and implementation of programs for the development of a new culture and value of cheering and attitude toward the opposing club and its supporters;
- Divide supporters into several categories (in practice, the most common is the division into three categories) and create and implement different strategies of police procedure in relation to each of them;
- Support more positive and cooperative relationships between the police and the media;
- Develop and disseminate education materials to all stakeholders that will support training opportunities and changes in current practice; and
- Use contemporary technologies of video surveillance and video recording of supporters in policing football matches with an increased risk.

Legislation in Control of Violence at Sporting Events in Serbia

Prior to the passing of special regulations governing the matter of security at sporting events, the Law on Public Order and Peace was employed[*]; however, this legislation provided inadequate measures to address the issues. The former Yugoslavia (including Serbia) ratified the European Convention on Spectator Violence and Misbehaviour at Sports Events and in Particular at Football Matches in 1990.[†] Based on this convention, the Law on Prevention of Violence and Indecent Behaviour at Sports Events was adopted in 2003 and underwent a number of revisions (2005, 2007, 2009) to address implementation problems. This was the first law of its kind in Serbia as it attempted to provide umbrella legislation to address the complexities of the problems associated with fan violence.

Importantly, this legislation precisely defined what should be regarded as misbehavior and violence at sporting events and obligated clubs, sports

---

[*] Official Gazette RS, No. 51, of 30/07/1992.
[†] Law on ratification of European Convention on Spectator Violence and Misbehaviour on Sports Events and in Particular on Football Matches, "Official Gazette SFRY-International Agreements," No. 9/1990.

federations, sports associations, and organizers of sporting events to undertake a series of preventive measures, including:

- The immediate notification of the Ministry of Interior if there is any information which indicates that there is the risk of violence at a sporting event;
- The establishment of relationships with representatives of supporters in order to exchange information;
- The separation of supporter groups by selling numbered tickets for sitting area, at the separated sale points, must be ensured;
- The club is obliged to keep records on ticket sales, and they can only sell tickets to persons with an identification document (the number of tickets that can be sold to one person is limited to seven);
- Prohibiting entry to persons who have no identification and to persons under 16 years, if they are not accompanied by a parent or guardian;
- The visiting sporting team is obligated to take care of their supporters in returning home after the sporting event;
- Prohibiting access to the facility in which the sporting event is held to persons who are under the influence of alcohol or drugs, or their behavior indicates that they are prone to violent or indecent behavior;
- Separating the visiting supporters by directing them to specific entrances and exits of the sporting facility and to a designated section of the grandstand;
- Monitoring spectators to ensure they are sitting in their assigned seat;
- Preventing the entry of spectators onto the playing field and preventing their movement from one part of the grandstand to another;
- Preventing the entry or sale of alcoholic beverages in the sports facility;
- Preventing the entry into the sports facility of items that can be used in violent behavior (e.g., pyrotechnics, poles, bottles), or which may obstruct the course of the match; and
- Warning or removing a spectator whose behavior my cause violence, threaten the safety of participants in the sporting event, or interfere with its course.

As well, the legislation outlines police powers associated with sporting events, including the power to:

- Order all the supporter groups to move by defined route on arrival or departure from the sporting facility during a sports event of increased risk;
- Forbid the entrance to a person whose behavior indicates that he/she is prone to violent and inappropriate behavior;
- Prohibit a sporting event when the safety of the participants is considered to be significantly endangered;

- Order an undertaking of other preventive measures that would contribute to the prevention of violence; and
- Oblige the local community to ban the sale and consumption of alcohol in sports facilities and at a specifically defined distance from the venue during the course of a football match.

The Law on Changes and Amendments to the Criminal Code of the Republic of Serbia came into force in July 2009* and specifically addressed violent behavior at sporting events or public gatherings. Despite the fact that the law details the responsibilities of all participants and the legal consequences for noncompliance, its implementation has been characterized by a number of difficulties. The problem of violence on the sport fields in Serbia remains a major problem for the State and society. The European Football Association, due to numerous incidents at international football matches, is continually faced with the imposition of sanctions against football clubs from Serbia.

Characteristics of Violence at Sporting Events in Serbia

The Period of Profiling of Extremist Football Supporter Groups

During the 1980s, on the territory of the former Yugoslavia, there were major changes in the behavior of supporters: the formation of small clusters of like-minded individuals as well as the development of very large and organized football fan groups; a shift in cheering as an activity related only to matches, to cheering as a subculture. An orientation toward the traditions of the fan group and club, for which they were cheering, became one of the main characteristics of the value system of supporters. At the same time, we should bear in mind that tradition is a set of material, technical, and spiritual knowledge and achievements, values, and behavior patterns. It is maintained through oral transmission upon which continuity and identity of a culture stands (Vidanović, 2006). With respect to the adherence of supporters to these traditions, Clarke notes,

> a sense for history—for great names, great matches, great teams and clubs, had always been important for the football fans. Just like the present, the past was always a part of what football means to its sympathizers.... This history is significant for the discussion about the current issue of football hooliganism, especially because the hooliganism is treated as something new, a problem which has emerged out of nowhere. (1978, p. 38)

* Official Gazette RS, No. 111/09.

In the late 1970s, the first major clashes began between the still underprofiled football fan groups.* During the 1980s, an increasing number of young people in the former Yugoslavia were trying to imitate the behavior of fans from the north of Europe, especially England, by wearing football fan scarves, singing songs, gathering in small groups, and engaging in fights and other forms of violence (Lalić, 1993). During this period, the first indications of what would soon become highly organized football fan groups had appeared, first in Split, Belgrade, and Zagreb, and later in Sarajevo and other major cities. Fan violence is half-symbolic in character as there is a desire to humiliate, but not physically injure opponent's fans.

In the late 1980s and early 1990s, core football fan groups grew into profiled and large organizations with a significant number of members. The Red Star and Partizan supporters established several groups, (e.g., Red Devils, Zulu Warriors, Grave Diggers, Commando), which gradually emerged into the football fan groups "Delije" and "Grobari." Throughout the former Yugoslavia, other football fan groups were also established, including the following: Horde zla [Hordes of Evil] (Football Club [FC] Sarajevo), Armada (FC Rijeka), Varvari [Barbarians] (FC Budućnost). Extreme supporter groups consist mostly of young men and are characterized by antisocial behavior, often without any interest in an actual match, accompanied by elaborated iconography, dominated by symbols typical of the English fan style and violence that had become a part of supporters' subculture. In that period, the first Yugoslav research on "fan tribes" was conducted by Buzov, Magdalenić, Perasović, and Radin (1989) from Zagreb. This research highlighted the need to examine the motivations and behavior of certain fan groups as there appeared to be a growing trend toward an aggressive subculture grounded in a generation of marginalized youth.

At the beginning of the 1990s, interethnic and political animosities began to fuel the already hostile rivalries between the various football supporter groups. Homogenization of football fan groups based on ethnicity became apparent. The disintegration of the former Yugoslavia and the civil war that followed were fueled by political speeches imbued with tremendous hostility toward various ethnic groups, further escalated by the media and ultimately acted out at sporting events as fans engaged in violence.

Some political groups during that time began to manipulate the fans for their own interests. In the early 1990s, football fan groups were targeted in the recruitment of staff for the war volunteer units. Leaders of some football fan groups began providing security staff for various political leaders; some had their own paramilitary units, while others became seriously engaged in politics.

---

* An extreme example was a mass fight during the match "Sarajevo–Hajduk" on June 19, 1979, when around 300 people requested medical help, as well as several serious incidents in the Split, between supporters of "Hajduk" and "Red Star." Quoted from: *The Daily Newspaper Pobjeda* on June 20, 1979.

During this period there was tremendous interplay among extreme supporter groups, clubs, nationalism, politics, and crime, paralleling the situation in Argentina during the rule of Peron and differing from extremist supporter groups in the Netherlands and England, which were apolitical.

> In recent years, the changing character of Argentine political culture has influenced the ways in which groups of soccer fans organize themselves around political and economic goals. Argentine soccer clubs have always had strong ties to local and national politics.... The structure of Argentine soccer allows fans to penetrate the political sphere of soccer clubs. This, in turn, creates an environment where organized groups of fans develop strong ties to club officials. (Paradiso, 2009, p. 65)

Sports Hooliganism in Serbia Since 2001

Riots involving supporters continued after the disintegration of the former Yugoslavia. Contrary to forecasts of those who had in the early 1990s publicly expressed their firm belief that with the resolution of interethnic conflict outbursts of supporters would disappear, these phenomena in fact became more frequent and had more serious consequences. Current violence at sporting events, particularly at football matches in Serbia, has all the characteristics of violence that is encountered in other European countries, with a visible tendency of its relocation from the stadium to the surrounding area, including a wider urban area (European Commission, 2007).

Conflicts of extreme supporter groups in the last 10 years (1999–2009) have resulted in the loss of 10 lives, putting Serbia ahead of all the other countries in Europe. The Ministry of Youth and Sports of the Republic of Serbia, in cooperation with the Association of Sports Journalists of Serbia, conducted a study in 2009 analyzing articles related to violence on and around sports arenas published by the Serbian media in 2008. This research highlighted the fact that every 136 days a fan was killed in Serbia, with all the victims and attackers being between 17 and 25 years of age (Đurđević, 2010, p. 286). In addition, during this period from January 1997 to September 2009, 1561 persons suffered injuries, including 514 police officers. Other consequences of excessive violence of extreme supporter groups in Serbia during that period are shown in Table 1.1 (Department for Analysis of the Serbian Ministry of Interior).

In Figures 1.1 and 1.2, the number of killed and injured in disorders caused by supporters from 1997 to 2009 in the Republic of Serbia is shown (Directorate for Analysis, Ministry of Interior).

It is important to emphasize that almost all serious criminal offenses and misdemeanors were committed outside of sporting grounds, or outside the period in which the law defines a sporting event (90 minutes before and after the sporting event or 120 minutes in cases of "high risk" matches).

Table 1.1 The Consequences of Violence at Sports Events from 1997 to 2009 in the Republic of Serbia

	Consequences of Violent Behavior at Sporting Events							
	Lost Life		Serious Bodily Injury		Minor Bodily Injury		Damaged Vehicles	
	Policemen	Other	Policemen	Other	Policemen	Other	MIA*	Other V.**
Until the Enactment of the Law								
1997			1	1		3		3
1998				4	9	16	3	16
1999	1		1		11	17	3	18
2000			4	24	20	41	18	7
2001			2	2	77	81	3	11
2002	1		1	12	41	94	5	13
Jan–June 2003			1	3	16	17		3
Total	2		10	46	174	269	32	71
After the Enactment of the Law								
July–Dec 2003				6	27	12	9	5
2004		4		10	46	97	5	42
2005	4	3		20	54	110	16	37
2006	2	1		12	51	105	9	44
Jan–Sept 2007	1			20	47	97	3	24
Total	7	8		68	225	421	42	152
After Changes and Amendments to the Law								
Oct–Dec 2007		1		3	2	29		8
2008	1	3		8	53	78	7	26
Jan–Sept 2009	1	2		13	36	112	1	16
Total	2	6		24	91	219	8	50

* Vehicles belonging to the Ministry of Internal Affairs.

** Other vehicles.

While there was violence occurring at other sporting events, without question the most significant number of incidents was occurring at football matches.

Especially important is the fact that in late 2007, violence at sporting events began to spill over into locations that were not directly connected to the event. Thus, in 2008, in addition to 138 serious forms of violence committed before, during, and after sporting events, another 68 cases of violence were recorded on the streets, at public gatherings, in hotels and restaurants and other places outside of the sporting venues and without direct links to specific events.

Almost all of the cases of violent behavior occurring outside of sporting venues were recorded in the area of the Belgrade Police Department (58 of 68); a number significantly higher than those recorded at sports stadiums and nearby facilities where the events were being held (38).

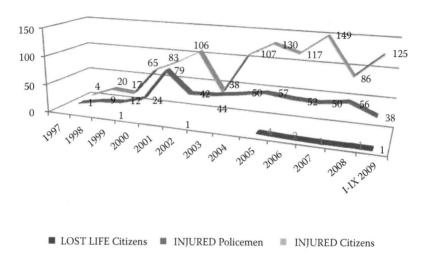

LOST LIFE Citizens ■ **INJURED Policemen** ■ **INJURED Citizens**

Figure 1.1 Number of persons killed and injured in the disorders caused by supporters from 1997 to 2009 in the Republic of Serbia.

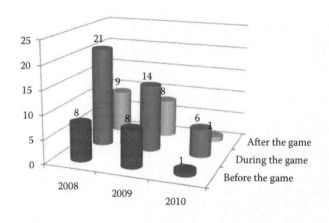

Figure 1.2 Violence at sporting events in the territory of the Belgrade Police Department.

Since the Belgrade Police Department's (BPD) district recorded the highest number of cases of violence (85.29%), an analysis of their operations in 2008, 2009, and 2010 has been conducted.* The first conclusion that can be drawn is the decreasing trend of registered cases of violence in all three years (Figure 1.2), compared to the beginning of the period of analysis: in 2008

---

* Sources of data are records of the Ministry of the Interior of the Republic of Serbia.

there were 38 cases registered, in 2009 there were 30 cases, and in 2010 only eight cases of violence were registered. It seems clear that irrespective of the time period examined, the greatest threat of violence is during the match.

The intensity of the violence appears to have been highest in 2009, when in a fewer number of registered cases (30) compared to 2008 (38), a greater number of individuals were injured (Figure 1.3), including the murder of one fan (not shown in the figure).

In order to obtain a more complete picture of the forms of violence at sporting events, it is necessary to examine the data on the number of reported attacks on sport officials with 19 reported in 2008, 12 reported in 2009, and 24 reported in 2010.

Obviously, a smaller number of cases of violence does not imply that the consequences of violence are reduced. Data that support this conclusion include the incidents of property damage, especially the damage to vehicles. In 2010, in eight cases of reported violence there were 37 vehicles and 11 buildings damaged (Figure 1.4). The largest number of damaged vehicles is public transportation and the Ministry of Interior's vehicles, while damaged buildings, in most cases, are the actual sporting facilities.

Additionally, the number of sporting events interrupted because of violence continues to increase (Table 1.2).

During this three-year period, police detained 1506 persons due to their alleged involvement in violence (misdemeanor and criminal offenses) at sporting events (Table 1.3). The reasons for these arrests, in addition to offenses related to violence at sports events and criminal offenses of violent

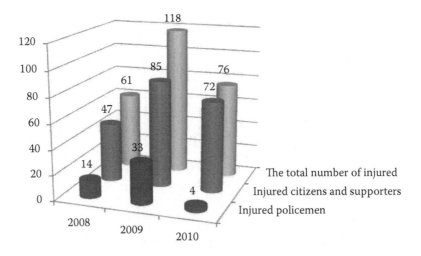

Figure 1.3 The injured persons at sporting events in the territory of the Belgrade Police Department.

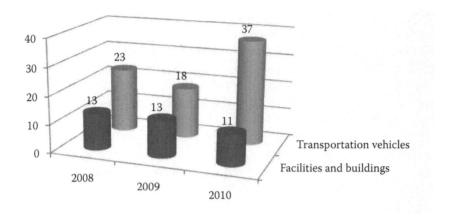

Figure 1.4 Material damage, as a consequence of violence at sporting events in the territory of the Belgrade Police Department.

Table 1.2   Number of Interrupted Sporting Events in the Territory of the Belgrade Police Department

Number of Interrupted Sporting Events		
Year 2008	Year 2009	Year 2010
14	19	22

Table 1.3   Number of Persons Arrested by Police Officers of the Belgrade Police Department

Number of Persons Arrested for Violence at Sporting Events		
Year 2008	Year 2009	Year 2010
406	579	521

behavior at sporting events, included the disruption and prevention of police officers in the performance of security tasks.

The most common means used in carrying out acts of violence are metal rods, wooden sticks, brass knuckles, as well as other similar items used to cause physical injury. The wearing of club colors was often a sufficient enough reason for violence directed toward supporters of other clubs.

The beginning of 2009 was marked by the attempted murder in Belgrade (Municipality of Palilula) of the parent of a boy who was intercepted by seven hooligans on the street. It appeared that they attacked him only because he was wearing a red-white scarf, while his father, who was trying to defend his child, was stabbed with a knife.* Among the perpetrators of this criminal offense were three minors. In addition, there have been reported cases of groups of young men wearing club colors throwing pyrotechnics in public transportation vehicles, intrusions and throwing of tear gas in restaurants, and the interception of students on their way to nearby schools.

The most serious case of hooligan behavior that took place outside of sporting grounds was the murder of a French citizen, a fan of "FC Toulouse," in 2009 in a restaurant located in the very center of Belgrade. While sitting in a cafe in the city center, he was attacked by a large group of football hooligans. After being physically abused and beaten, he was fatally injured when he was thrown from a height of several meters onto the sidewalk.

Although many measures have been effectively employed to combat sport-related violence, new problems are constantly arising. The hooligans are constantly finding new ways of engaging in conflict. In addition, the increasing sophistication of the groups in terms of planning has been enhanced by the use of technology such as mobile phones and the Internet.

The literature states the fact that extreme supporters, in general, are prone to alcohol and drug use and are generally victims of economic disorder, unemployment, and are more likely to be less educated (Göral, 2008). In addition to these factors, the problem of the relative failure of the State in controlling violence at sporting events has its roots in several other factors.

First, in Serbia, a close connection between politicians, clubs, and the fan leaders has existed for decades. Politicians at the national and the local level (depending on the league in which the club competes) hold prominent positions on the boards, in the chairmanship clubs, and in sporting associations. Thanks to political support, the clubs, through their leaders, engage in various illegal activities without facing the scrutiny of police. The financial affairs of football clubs is not a focus of the public authorities and tax institutions (except in extreme cases). Considering the fact that more money is invested in football than in the other sports, and that financial control is weak or nonexistent, football clubs have become a fertile ground for money laundering and various other financial malversations (e.g., manipulation of the sale of players, fixing of match results, etc.). Participation in the management of football clubs enabled politicians to reap financial rewards and achieve political goals by utilizing these supporter groups.

Second, clubs in Serbia were reluctant to support the introduction of preventive and educational programs in order to create new value systems among supporters, even though the law obliged them to do so. Clubs usually protect the fan leaders and provide them with various benefits,

---

* Sources of data are records of the Ministry of the Interior of the Republic of Serbia.

tolerating their aggressiveness by justifying it as dedication to the club. Kozarev (2007) points to the role that football clubs play in perpetuating football hooliganism, football fan extremism, and the associated intolerance.

In 2010, Janković (2010) interviewed 75 police officers of the Intervention Units of the Ministry of Interior of the Republic of Serbia who were engaged in securing sporting events. Interestingly, 89% of these officers indicated that behind the supporters who are committing violence are clubs who almost never condemn their acts of violence.

Third, and related to the observations noted above, these clubs are generally unwilling to cooperate with the police to secure football matches. Fourth, the leaders of hooligan groups in Serbia usually have extensive criminal records and are perpetrators of criminal offenses ranging from drug trafficking to violent and property crimes. To them, football clubs serve as a cover to engage in criminal activities, while fans are potential "soldiers" to commit further criminal actions or simply a market for the distribution of drugs. This connection between hard-core football hooligans and crime, such as cheering activities and close contact with the football clubs serves as a buffer from legal scrutiny, which is highlighted by numerous authors from various parts of the world (Garland & Rowe, 2000; Kozarev, 2007; Paradiso, 2009).

Fifth, there is the inefficiency of the courts during sentencing of cases connected to acts of violence at football matches, especially in the cases of fan leaders. From 2005 to 2010, 289 criminal charges were filed against 25 leaders from the three main fan groups in Belgrade (Red Star, 11; Partizan, 7; Rad, 7).[*] These offenses included murder (5), robbery (13), violent behavior at sporting events (25), violent behavior (40), assault on an official person (33), preventing an official person from performing an official duty (7), illicit production and trade in narcotic drugs (12), extortion (5), and initiating national, racial, and religious hatred and intolerance (17).

Most of the filed charges were never processed, and if they were, there were no final sentencing verdicts. The fan leaders remained "untouchable" and represented a symbol of encouragement for their groups in terms of intergroup cohesion and further violent action (Misić, 2010, p. 116). Perhaps not surprisingly, of the 75 Intervention Unit police officers engaged in securing football matches, 28% indicated that they felt the State was not prepared to respond to sports violence with another 55% saying that the State was only partially prepared to deal with the violence (Janković, 2010).

---

[*] Data from the Belgrade Police Department.

Police Procedure in Serbia

Clearly, the police have a critical role to play in combating fan violence; however, they are only one component of any systemic response to the complex issues that are embedded in this form of violence in Serbia and other places around the world. It is only the reluctance of other state agencies and the wider community to be seriously engaged in the fight against extreme supporter groups that has placed police at the forefront of this problem.

> Law enforcement responses alone are seldom effective in reducing or solving such a problem. Do not limit yourself to considering what police alone can do: carefully consider whether others in your community share responsibility for the problem and can help police better respond to it. In some cases, you may need to shift the responsibility to those who can implement more-effective responses....If we have learned anything from the extreme accounts of spectator violence in Europe, it is that *prevention* is superior to the most effective *response* after fan violence begins. Most experts agree that strategies should emphasize prevention and never confrontation. (Madensen & Eck, 2008, p. 3)

Previous experiences in securing high-risk sporting events have shown that an effective approach to this problem requires a high degree of planning, preparedness, and tactical competence. Securing of these events requires a professional approach, which includes strong operational plans, which are based on sophisticated security assessments.

The mobilization of human and technical resources is essential in order to act effectively if an escalation of violence or disruption of public order and peace on a larger scale occurs.

A special problem in Serbia is the reliance of police on traditional methods of response considered anachronistic at the international level. An important characteristic of this traditional approach, which in academic literature is known as "high profile," is having a large presence of uniformed police officers on the field. This police strategy is based on the separation of fans, that is, prevention of contacts between the football fan groups in order to prevent violence, both at the stadium and outside of it. In planning and making decisions on the number of engaged police officers and the actions of the police, specificities of different football fan groups are often not taken into account (nationality, number of extreme supporters, aims, cultural specificities, etc.). If these differences are not taken into consideration and the police use routine approaches in securing sporting events, the risk of an outbreak of incidents is significantly increased.

Madensen and Eck (2008) point to the dangers of a nonselective approach to policing and an overreliance on police presence:

> It is also important to note that recent findings on crowd behavior suggest that police will instigate or escalate violence if they treat large groups of people as homogenous entities. Assuming that all fans are potentially dangerous will lead to a self-fulfilling prophecy. …People at gatherings have a wide variety of personal agendas, and typically only a small minority of people are willing to engage in violent behaviors. (p. 3)
>
> *Presenting extreme shows of force.* While some police visibility can work as a deterrent to spectator violence, excessive shows of force can create a militaristic and highly hostile atmosphere. Police in riot gear with face shields and batons are usually not necessary to address officer safety concerns, and can stunt efforts to develop a positive rapport with event attendees. Too many uniformed officers may create a hostile atmosphere. (p. 3)

In securing sporting events, the police forces in Serbia undertake physical, traffic, operational, and criminalistic, antidiversion and fire protection security measures. Physical security measures in the sports facility and its perimeter have three phases (before, during, and after the match) with the presence of a significant number of officers. Police officers control the entrance of fans into the stadium, prevent physical contact between fans, maintain public order and peace in the stadium, and monitor fans while they are leaving the stadium. The current approach of having a large number of very visible officers has often led to unnecessary escalation. The current lack of communication and interaction between the police and fans (on the day of the match and during the week) has led, as in many European countries, to the situation of "us against them" on both sides.

Experiences in other countries have shown that it is necessary to establish communication between clubs, police, and organizations of supporters. The goal should be to encourage long-term relationships between the police and fan representatives, to help both sides understand each other and thus search for joint strategies to improve the safety and security at football matches (Đurđević, 2010).

The phenomenon of fan violence dispersion from sports stadiums to other parts of the city is evident in the practice of English supporters. For example, Garland and Rowe (2000) emphasized:

> Interestingly, the disturbances that followed Newcastle United's defeat by Manchester United in the 1999 FA Cup Final occurred in Newcastle city centre, and not in or around Wembley Stadium itself. Newcastle supporters had been watching the match *en masse* in pubs and bars, something that has been a feature of the consumption of "Sky era" 1990s football. This has created the culture of collective participation in crowd-style activity in pubs that was previously confined to the stadium itself. (p. 35)

These authors suggest that the dislocation of violence from stadiums raises two problems. First, it raises a new challenge for police, as they must predict locations where incidents may take place. Second, it raises the question of defining the borders of football hooliganism (Garland & Rowe, 2000). This necessary dispersal of police members to a wider territory requires the involvement of a larger number of police officers, which raises the price of security and requires the involvement of a larger police contingent.

Police officers engaged on the operational-criminalistic security activities identify the perpetrators of criminal offenses, photograph and record events of interest to be used in further operational work, process arrested persons, and bring them to the appropriate judicial authorities. Antidivisional securing includes the counterdiversion search of surroundings and the interior of the stadium and grandstands, in order to find mines, pyrotechnics, and items that may be used in the execution of attacks. Fire protection measures include the counterdiversion inspection of electric and other installations and possible controlling and extinguishing of fires in a sports facility.

These methods of securing sports events consist of the use of common, standardized procedures acquired through practice, without taking into account the specificities of each particular event, and adjusting the methods and tools accordingly. In fact, the police in Serbia base their strategy of combating violence at sporting events on the so-called bang effect. This approach is characterized by dramatic police actions (in the sports facility and its surrounding area on the day of match) and judicial processes that instill a confidence in citizens that the state authorities, in fighting crime, in a concrete, verifiable, and effective manner have achieved significant results (Đurđević, 2010). However, this type of approach has significant drawbacks including: its reactive nature; its insignificant influence on the perpetrators; its failure to reduce the fear and insecurity felt by the public; that it requires substantial human and material resources without long-term benefits.

In a study conducted in Macedonia of police tactics and strategies in the control and prevention of hooligan violence at football matches, the results show that the reactive and necessarily repressive approach dominates with a reliance on the use of batons and physical force and the rare use of preventive measures (Kozarev, 2007).

There is no doubt that new strategies employed by football hooligans require a shift in police responses which emphasizes prevention, enhanced training, and cooperation with other professionals and academics in the development of new strategies, all of which are required by the European Convention for the Prevention of Violence in the Sport and the Resolution of the Council (June 2010). However, in practice, these recommendations are not adequately addressed by policing agencies. For example, Hoggett and Clifford (2010) point out that this more specialized orientation has not replaced the more traditional and more general approaches to training in England and Wales:

> But at present there is not yet any systematic research to determine whether these principles, policies and theories are being incorporated into police training and practice in England and Wales....The current study therefore begins to address these limitations and questions by examining the nature of police training for the policing of football crowds within and across England and Wales....There is currently no training within England and Wales specifically oriented to the policing of public order at football matches. Instead, training for policing football is provided within a framework of courses that deal with the policing of public order more generally. (p. 220)

There is no doubt that new police strategies in controlling violence in sports necessitates the establishment of specialized police units, databases, the introduction of the spotters system, and enhanced criminal intelligence. However, if criminal intelligence activity is not being applied properly, the results will be thin. The best example of this is presented by Garland and Rowe (2000):

> Data relating to those English fans arrested in France during the 1998 World Cup reveal further limitations to the intelligence-led strategy. Of the total number of arrests, 86 per cent were for public order offenses. Yet, given the Home Secretary's claim referred to above, it is revealing to note that only 35 out of the total of 286 arrested (12%) were classed by NCIS as Category C supporters—considered as organised hooligans. A further 16 were recorded as "known Category B" fans, classified as those liable to become involved in disturbances should they occur, and one was Category A, considered non-violent supporters. These totals suggest that 234 of the 286 England fans arrested in France, some 81.8 per cent, were not known to the police. (p. 42)

In this regard, Kozarev's (2007) research examining the Macedonian police is illustrative. In his study survey, he questioned members of extreme supporter groups whether the police had sufficient knowledge of which supporters were the greatest threat to public safety and the overwhelming majority indicated that police did not have sufficient knowledge to make those determinations. If the police are not able to select the right targets, then their actions can only be nonselective and focused on the mass as a homogeneous group, which inevitably leads to a deepening of the gap between the police and the supporters (Otašević, 2010).

Conclusion

As is so often the case, there has been tremendous difficulty in implementing legislative efforts aimed at controlling violence at sporting events. Hasty adoption of various regulations, without consideration of their use in practice and the broad use of penal law repression without clear criteria that would enable compliance of criminal and misdemeanor liability, is one of the reasons behind the poor effects of application of the penal law mechanism for protection of sports in Serbia.

Such experience shows that parallel with the adoption of regulations, professional specialization of employees in the police, prosecution, and the courts is necessary, as they are the main bearers of the function of detection, prosecution, and the sentencing of criminal offenses in the Republic of Serbia. As the problem of violence at sporting events is becoming more complex, there is a greater need for specialized personnel and specialized organizational units within the police, prosecution, and the courts. Specialization in any field is justified only if the subjects (persons) to whom certain specific tasks were assigned, are according to some criteria unique in comparison to their "colleagues," primarily more professional and specially trained. Today, for example, police officers who know little about many things are not wanted anymore, but those who know much about one thing are in high demand.

There is no doubt that Serbia needs to introduce contemporary European standards of police procedure in controlling violence at sports events (e.g., specialization, databases, criminal intelligence). However, as the results of numerous studies show, the introduction of norms and standards is not enough, if their implementation is of poor quality and insufficiently professional.

To address these problems effectively, the Ministry of Interior of the Republic of Serbia is in the process of establishing units for monitoring and preventing violence at sporting events (National Football Information Point), whose tasks will include planning and monitoring of security measures at sporting events, monitoring supporter groups, and exchanging information with key stakeholders. There will also be an operational analytical unit within this unit, whose task will be the analysis of data associated with violence at sporting events, in part through the use of a new software system (*Evidence of Extreme Supporters*).

In order for Serbia to achieve real progress in the field of security in sporting events, it is necessary to change the passivity of clubs and affect their unwillingness to cooperate in improving security. To achieve this, it is necessary to remove the politics from sports clubs and decriminalize clubs, which at this moment represent an impossible mission. However, a journey of a thousand miles begins with a single step.

References

Buzov, Ž., Magdalenić, I., Perasović, B., & Radin, F. (1989). *Fan tribe*. Zagreb: Pitanja.

Clarke, J. (1978). Football and working class fans: Tradition and change. In Roger Ingham (Ed.), *Football hooliganism: The wider context*. London: InterAction Imprint.

Đurđević, N. (2007). *Public authorities and sports*. Kragujevac, Serbia: Faculty of Law in Kragujevac.

Đurđević, N. (2010). Criminal responsibility for the violence and improper behaviour at sporting events in the Republic of Serbia. *Proceedings of the Faculty of Law in Split, 47*(2), 285–308.

European Commission. (2007). White paper on sport. Retrieved from http://ec.europa. eu/sport/white-paper/staff-working-document_en.htm

Garland, J., & Rowe, M. (2000). The "English Disease": Cured or in remission? An analysis of police responses to football hooliganism in the 1990s. *Crime Prevention and Community Safety: An International Journal, 1*(4), 35–47.

Göral, M. (2008). Violence and fair play in sport. *Pakistan Journal of Social Sciences, 5*(6), 502–513.

Hoggett, J., & Clifford, S. (2010). Crowd psychology, public order police training and the policing of football crowds. *Policing: An International Journal of Police Strategies and Management, 33*(2), 218–235.

Janković, B. (2010). Prevencija nasilja na sportskim priredbama, Glasnik prava. Izdavač: Pravni fakultet u Kragujevcu, 1 (3), str. 129–154. [Prevention of Violence at Sporting Events, Herald of Law. Publisher: Faculty of Law in Kragujevac, *1*(3), 129–154.]

Kozarev, A. (2007). *Nasilstvoto i fudbalskiot huliganizam vo Republika Makedonija.* Skopje: Macedonia.

Lalić, D. (1993). *Torcida: pogled iznutra.* Zagreb: AGM.

Madensen, T., & Eck, J. (2008). Spectator Violence in Stadiums. Retrieved from http:// www.popcenter.org/problems/spectator_violence/

Misić, Z. (2010). *Nasilje i nedolično ponašanje navijača kao faktor ugrožavanja bezbednosti.* Beograd: Fakultet Bezbednosti.

Otašević, B. (2010). Urbano okruženje i nasilje u sportu. *Bezbednost, 3,* 267–281.

Paradiso, E. (2009). The social, political, and economic causes of violence in Argentine soccer. *Nexus: The Canadian Student Journal of Anthropology, 21*(July), 65–79.

Spaaij, R. (2005). The prevention of football hooliganism: A transnational perspective. *Amsterdam School for Social Science Research.* Retrieved from http://www. cafyd.com/HistDeporte/htm/pdf/4-16.pdf

Šuput, D. (2010). *Pravni okvir koji uređuje borbu protiv nasilja na sportskim priredbama u evropskim državama.* Institut za uporedno pravo: Strani pravni život.

Vidanović, I. (2006). Rečnik socijalnog rada. *Udruženje stručnih radnika socijalne zaštite Srbije.*

Žužak, M. (2010). Nasilje navijačkih grupa kao vid političkog nasilja u Republici Srbiji. *Pravni Informator časopis za savremene pravnike, 5,* 9–11.

About the Authors

Branislav Simonović, Ph.D., is on the Faculty of Law, University of Kragujevac; Zoran Đurđević, Ph.D., works at the Academy of Criminalistics and Police Studies in Belgrade; and Božidar Otašević, M.A., works for the Ministry of Interior of the Republic of Serbia.

Policing Political Protests in the United Kingdom

2

CRAIG PATERSON

Contents

Introduction

After two decades of relative calm, political protests have returned to the streets of the United Kingdom (UK). The resurgence of political protest since 2009 has seen transnational movements for global justice come together with more localized groups concerned with governmental responses to the economic downturn and their impact in different social policy arenas (HMIC, 2011). Added to this, in August 2011, the Police Service faced a short period of civil disturbances across England which involved protests against police conduct in London, followed by more widespread public disorder in provincial cities. Collectively, this changing social context has presented a new challenge for the service-oriented and community-focused Police Service in the UK (more specifically, England, as neither Scotland, Wales, nor Northern Ireland have experienced similar cases of public disorder). The Police Service in the UK has experienced a 20-year period of community-oriented reform during which there has been a prolonged reduction in crime rates.

Despite this long period of comparative peace and prosperity the memories of the last prolonged period of disorder and social conflict during the 1980s remains deeply embedded in the British psyche. From a policing perspective, this collective social memory takes the form of a decline in police legitimacy (Hall, Critcher, Jefferson, Clarke, & Roberts, 1978), resistance to paramilitary policing strategies (Jefferson, 1990), and deep social divisions generated by the neoliberal governmental agenda of the Thatcher government (1979–1991). While the sustained social disorder and political protest of the 1980s was managed through a paramilitary strategy of escalated force, police reforms since the 1990s have encouraged new approaches, which have been described variously as negotiated management, strategic incapacitation, and strategic facilitation (Waddington, 2011). Similar reforms have been evident internationally (Dow & Plecas, 2011; Perrott, 2011). Yet, the postmodern mix of disparate political agendas that come together within contemporary organized political protests, coupled with a new generation of IT-intelligent protesters versed in the immediate digital language of multimedia communication technologies, has made it more difficult for the Police Service to manage a multitude of increasingly dynamic and flexible protest repertoires.

This chapter looks at recent policing responses to organized political protests in the UK and the broader sociopolitical context influencing changes in police strategy. Three key themes emerge: the importance of police interaction with protest groups; the pivotal role of multimedia reports of police–protester interaction; and the necessity of clear and transparent accountability structures for public order policing. An evolving body of literature has pointed to the resonance in the collective consciousness of "signal" events (Innes, Fielding, & Langan, 2002; Innes, 2010) and the long-term impact on public trust in the police (Hough, Jackson, Bradford, Myhill, & Quinton, 2010) and this knowledge has informed recent police reform. The chapter provides analysis of changes in police strategy within the context of the three themes highlighted above before evaluating the relative strengths and weaknesses of these changes. Some concluding comments are made about changes in strategy and the public debate about the policing of public order that was stimulated by the 2011 civil disturbances in the UK.

A Short History of Protest and Disorder

During the 1970s and 1980s, increased amounts of evidence about police discrimination, malpractice, and corruption became known to the public, which, cumulatively, had an impact on public attitudes toward the police. Sustained concerns about police practice and the policing of public order ultimately led to a program of reform (community policing) that gathered pace in the 1990s and continues today. The public disorder of the 1980s was a core component of the crisis in police legitimacy that became manifest during a period of social upheaval that remains etched in the social psychology of affected communities and neighborhoods. During the 1980s there were problems of civil disorder each year, commencing with the Brixton disturbances of 1981, continuing through the labor disputes in the middle of the decade, and finishing with the poll tax protest in London in 1990.

The "crisis of legitimacy" (Hall et al., 1978) in policing, particularly their poor relations with minority groups, was illustrative of a growing mistrust and malaise among the general public regarding the role of state institutions in civil society. The urban disorder of this period took the form of antipolice and antigovernment protests that exposed fissures between the police and the communities they served. Continued civil unrest highlighted the changing relationship between an increasingly diverse society and unreformed police forces. Initially reported as "race riots," the civil disturbances of the early part of this period initiated a renewed focus upon the police's use of their power, discretion, and position. As Lord Scarman's (1981) report into the Brixton disorders made clear, inner city communities were rejecting a culture within the police that condoned unfair targeting of vulnerable and minority groups as well as the excessive use of force.

The Scarman report (1981) recommended radical reforms. These included the introduction of a new model of police complaints that provided independent supervision of the most serious complaints through the Police Complaints Authority (PCA) to enhance police accountability. Decreased public trust in the police had been generated by a belief that the institution was unrepresentative of society, lacked transparency, and was dominated by an insular culture that protected its own members to the detriment of the wider public. The PCA went on to become the Independent Police Complaints Commission (IPCC) in 2004 following recommendations from the MacPherson Report (1999) that looked at continued tensions between ethnic minority communities and the police in London. This report provided evidence of continued concern about community relations with the police in socially and economically deprived areas although this did not take the form of serious civil disorder. While there were sporadic instances of civil disorder during the 1990s and the 2000s, these incidents were isolated and localized and not linked by the antipolice and antigovernment sentiments of the 1980s.

The contemporary policing of political protest in the UK needs to be understood within the context of the social conflict from the 1980s and subsequent community policing reforms. From 1970 to 1990, UK policing of protest and disorder had drifted toward a paramilitaristic strategy (King & Brearley, 1996). Jefferson takes this further, commenting that, "the paramilitarisation of public order policing strategy and tactics in the UK has led to an institutional reliance on tactics which are primarily based on the use of force" (1990, p. 85). This reliance on coercive force, coupled with the social problems I outlined earlier, contributed to the "crisis of legitimacy" and the subsequent reemergence of a proactive community policing model (Alderson, 1979, 1998; Goldstein, 1979) as a reinvigorated mode of policing disenfranchised communities and rebuilding trust in the police. Following this shift, the 1990s bore witness to a new public order policing strategy of negotiated management, which focused on conciliation and a greater appreciation of the rights of demonstrators and the importance of police legitimacy (Waddington, 1998). This change in police strategy followed similar shifts that had already taken place in Europe and in the United States (della Porta & Fillieulle, 2004).

Police Legitimacy and Political Policing

The coercive powers that police officers hold require them to consistently present themselves to the public as being fair, civil, and accountable in their day-to-day conduct. The most visible consequences of not achieving these high standards are evident in the contact that the police have with the public and are generated by what is perceived to be uncivil, unfair, or discriminatory behavior. This is particularly problematic in the arena of public disorder policing where conflict is inevitable. Over the last 15 years the UK has experienced a period of relative affluence with decreased crime levels but comparatively low levels of public confidence in the police. This has generated a policy focus on police attitudes and behavior, and their influence on public confidence in the police, particularly as this confidence is eroded whenever the public come into contact with the police (Hough et al., 2010).

At the heart of this concern about public confidence is a long-standing debate about the core requirements and functions of the police mission. The aims of policing have been variously interpreted as: peacekeeping (Banton, 1964); the coercive threat of the legal use of force (Bittner, 1980; Waddington, 1998); order maintenance (Wilson & Kelling, 1982); and the social control/governance of perceived problem populations (Cohen, 1985; Stenson, 1993). These different visions of policing, community or otherwise, highlight the complex and contested nature of implementing policing objectives and strategies. This complexity has been augmented by the processes of globalization, enhanced threats to security, and the demands of an increasingly risk-conscious and information-rich public (Beck, 1998).

Because of these realities, social, political, and cultural changes at both the global and local levels have expanded policing functions to meet the demands of societies that place crime and security among their foremost public concerns. Separating, and responding to, the twin threats of security and community safety represents a significant challenge for policing in the UK and is a key driver behind police reform (O'Connor, 2005). Brodeur (1983) characterizes this distinction as a separation between: "high" policing (understood as the policing of national security and political order), and "low" policing (the struggle for community safety at local levels). The policing of public disorder and political protest provides a potential drift between both categories with, according to Brodeur, the core function of police focused upon the maintenance of national security and political order (high policing) while also facilitating the democratic right to protest at the local community level (low policing). An undoubted tension exists between these two functions that can manifest itself in the form of disorder during large protests when individuals expressing legitimate localized concerns are confronted with the strong coercive arm of the state.

The conflict between these two functions becomes manifest during political protests because there is a clear tension between the principles of community policing, the right to democratic protest, and the coercive side of the police role: most obviously, the use of force by police officers; intrusive surveillance; the use of informants; and the protection of key state institutions such as governmental and financial buildings (Brodeur, 2007). Therefore, the late modern emphasis on community engagement and interaction remains a challenge for a police institution founded on modernity's conception of an all powerful state that provides security and order across society. This tension is, at least in part, explained by Brodeur's separate concepts of high and low policing and the undoubtedly political nature of some forms of policing. When political policing takes place, the tension that lies at the heart of the policing condition and the potential use of state-sanctioned force against law-abiding citizens comes to the fore and presents a challenge for both policing strategies and police accountability structures.

Challenging the actions of the police through clear accountability mechanisms is an essential function of democratic societies as this helps maintain the quality of the relationship between the police and civic society. The provision of effective and equitable policing services (or the perception thereof) is a precondition of a democratic political structure as policing in democratic societies takes place within a political landscape that acknowledges the importance of social justice, social cohesion, fairness, equity, and human rights. This makes effective accountability structures essential components of contemporary policing strategies, particularly in the case of the policing of protest. The following section outlines the resurgence of political protest in the UK since 2009 and evaluates the new policing challenges presented in the second decade of the 21st century.

The Resurgence of Political Protest

After two decades of affluence, decreasing crime rates, and sustained social order, the death of Ian Tomlinson during the 2009 G20 protests brought issues of social conflict and the policing of public disorder back to the fore in the UK. The death of Ian Tomlinson coupled with a multitude of complaints about mass containment strategies (more commonly known in the UK as "kettling") and the police use of force reignited old concerns about the policing of protest and public disorder. The public response to this conflict was symbolic of how the UK had changed since the 1980s. Initial police misinformation about the circumstances of Tomlinson's death was counteracted by citizen reporters who provided evidence of a police officer's assault on Tomlinson. Citizen reporters subsequently provided momentum for sustained criticism of police tactics and within days the police response to the G20 protest was subjected to negative national and international media headlines (Greer & McLaughlin, 2010).

The roles of the citizen reporter, social networks, and the broader democratization of media mean that the police can no longer rely on the mainstream media to relay their uncontested version of events directly to the public. During the Miner's strike of 1984–1985, the British Broadcasting Corporation (BBC) notoriously reedited footage of conflict between the miners and the police to make the miners look like protagonists of violent confrontation when the opposite was the case. The reporting of the 2009 protest emphasized the change in role and function of the media during social and political conflict as well as the enhanced role of a range of mobile recording devices and social networking sites in the production and dissemination of user-generated media content. These new media act as modes of communication between disparate yet dynamic protest groups, keeping individuals up to date with developments on the day of the protest, while also providing audio and video records of police actions (Greer & McLaughlin, 2010).

The fallout from the G20 protest confirmed the longstanding view that enhanced transparency of policing strategies was essential to maintain public trust within a hypermediated social-political environment (Mawby, 2002; Greer & McLaughlin, 2010). The necessity of reform of outdated policing strategies to provide a greater emphasis on facilitating protest was supported by the Police Service and the two reviews of public order policing that were produced before the end of 2009 by Her Majesty's Inspectorate of Constabulary (HMIC). It was acknowledged that the Association of Chief Police Officers manual on *Keeping the Peace* gave limited attention to the policing of political protest and that the tactics in the manual placed too much emphasis on the regulation of public order (HMIC, 2009a).

The impact of these police reforms subsequently came under scrutiny during the student protests in London during November and December 2010. Public responses to the protest swayed from concern about the excessive use of police force to concerns about criminal behavior as violence broke out among a small number of protesters. Once again, the oscillation of public opinion over a short period of time demonstrated the difficulties the police face in both managing public order and facilitating peaceful protest, particularly within a socioeconomic context of public expenditure cuts and rising youth unemployment that had engaged young people in a number of political causes. Across Europe, high rates of youth unemployment, recession, and continued financial instability have led to similar, sustained political protests against the failure of political and financial institutions to combat the global recession.

Police Governance, Legitimacy, and Human Rights

In addition to the new socioeconomic context, the policing of public disorder in the 21st century now takes place within an international context that emphasizes the importance of human rights. Public disorder and the policing of political protest frequently becomes a global news story drawing further attention to the actions of a nation's police and military. The introduction of the Human Rights Act in 1998 and the Regulation of Investigatory Powers Act in 2000 fundamentally changed the context in which the policing of protests and disorder in the UK takes place. Respect for human rights, most obviously freedom of expression (article 10) and freedom of peaceful assembly (article 11), came to the fore. Cognizant of the dramatic decline in police legitimacy during the 1980s and the central role of freedom of speech and assembly in ensuring democratic freedoms, much emphasis has subsequently been placed upon the long tradition of protest in British life by senior police officers when speaking publicly about the policing of protests. Therefore, the contemporary public order policing dilemma revolves around how to balance the rights of lawful protesters with the duty to protect property and other citizens from harm (HMIC, 2009b).

The governance structure of the Police Service in England and Wales separates the police from the military (an essential tenet of good democratic governance), although the police retain the constitutional power to call on the military in times of emergency. The police are unarmed and function according to a doctrine of minimal force to maintain as strong links as possible with the communities they police. Threats to social order provide a test of this doctrine and democratic policing more generally, understood as "a form of policing in which the police are accountable to the law and the community, respect the rights and guarantee the security of all citizens in a nondiscriminatory manner" (de Mesquita Neto, 2001, as cited in Haberfeld & Cerrah, 2008, pp. 8–9). The resurgence of political protest in the UK has provided an opportunity to evaluate the evolution of public order policing strategies and police accountability and their application in the community policing era where an enhanced emphasis is placed upon individual democratic rights.

Greer and McLaughlin's (2010) "We Predict a Riot" suggests that the rise in citizen journalism has started to shape the way police formulate their strategy for the policing of democratic political protests and that this is holding the police accountable in new ways. This viewpoint is supported by the two HMIC inquiry reports that were produced in 2009 (*Adapting to Protest* and *Nurturing the British Model of Policing*), and the third report, which was published in 2011 (*Public Order Policing*). Despite this, it is evident that there are additional factors driving strategic developments, not least of which is the policy emphasis on public confidence and the acknowledged importance of procedural justice to police practice. A clear relationship has been identified between the way policing is carried out and experienced by the public (procedural justice) and levels of public trust and confidence in the police (Hough et al., 2010). Her Majesty's Inspectorate of Constabulary acknowledges citizen journalism in their report examining the policing of the G20 but it is essential to place Greer and McLaughlin's focus on digital citizens and social media within its wider context. The next section looks at the impact of the 2009 policy reforms upon police strategy and tactics in 2010 and 2011 to provide a clearer understanding of the continued evolution of protest policing.

Policing Political Protests After 2009

At the height of the social conflict of the 1980s, Jefferson and Grimshaw (1984) commented that policing strategies were formulated with three key audiences in mind: legal audiences (the Home Secretary, the Independent Police Complaints Commission, police authorities); occupational audiences (police management, rank and file officers, the Police Federation, etc.); and democratic audiences (politicians, communities, civil liberties groups). The proliferation and democratization of social media and news reporting has enhanced the power of democratic audiences such as protest groups within this triangular relationship and challenged the dominance of legal and occupational audiences in constructing the news agenda.

This shift in audience power has led to calls for enhanced vertical accountability in addition to previous reforms in horizontal accountability (such as the introduction of the PCA, police performance indicators, HMIC inquiries). It has increasingly been argued that horizontal (or political) accountability does not increase public confidence in the police, but vertical accountability can be seen to be more independent, external, transparent, and ultimately more democratic (Schedler, 1999; Bonner, 2009). Therefore, democratic policing follows the same fundamental principles as community policing, even within the context of public disorder, although with Brodeur's caveat that a shift into the high policing realm may result in a shift in policing objectives. Furthermore, a strategic emphasis on vertical accountability acknowledges the link between public mistrust of government and subsequent mistrust of the police (Ivkovic, 2008). Within the context of contentious political protests the police have to actively demonstrate their independence from the executive arm of government to build and maintain public trust.

These shifting influences over police strategy were evident at the 2010 student protests and 2011 Trade Union Council protest against public expenditure cuts. In the immediate aftermath of the death of Ian Tomlinson in 2009 the importance of transparency and police accountability had been emphasized as an essential means of regulating the conduct of police officers. This emphasis manifested itself in the form of: independent human rights advisors based in police command and control rooms; constant communication with protesters via twitter; the distribution of leaflets directly related to the specific protest; and formally appointed protest stewards who liaised with the police (Joint Committee on Human Rights, 2011). This arrangement was organized in advance and emphasized the mutual responsibility of both the police and (lawful and legitimate) protest groups to facilitate peaceful protest.

This vertical accountability is possible in circumstances where protesters are perceived as legitimate by the police. Legitimacy is attained either through formal negotiation or previous experience of working together to enable the police to make a clear distinction between contained and transgressive protesters (Noakes, Klocke, & Gilham, 2005) and to facilitate the peaceful protest of the "contained" group. The shift in policing strategy from strategic incapacitation and escalated force to negotiated management and ultimately strategic facilitation has been assisted through familiarity between the police and specific protest groups and the establishment of agreed upon rules of engagement (Waddington, 2007) that can help facilitate democratic protest. Where protesters are seen to be democratic, lawful, and legitimate the strength of their position is enhanced although unlawful or disorderly behavior immediately restores the preeminence of legal and occupational positions and the high policing emphasis on the maintenance of security and the restoration of public order.

It is clear that there is a will among senior police in the UK to reform public order strategies and tactics within the context of political protests but the process of translating this commitment into practice is bound to encounter resistance from a front line inculcated in a different myriad of cultures, mentalities, and practices (Lipsky, 1980). HMIC (2011) has stated that better and updated training is required, particularly to educate police officers about evolving social, cultural, and political contexts, yet it seems that the remnants of the paramilitary style of policing public order remains embedded in the officer culture (Hoggett & Stott, 2010). This has been evident in specific problems related to: the use of force; blanket mass containment; and the use of other tactics that have developed informally in police training (HMIC, 2011). More generally, the Human Rights Committee report on Facilitating Peaceful Protests (Joint Committee on Human Rights, 2011, p. 8) emphasizes a lack of understanding of public order policing policy among front-line officers and trainers and this can be evidenced in numerous accounts provided by protesters (Greer & McLaughlin, 2010) as well as HMIC's own review of UK training centers (2011, p. 20).

Furthermore, the continued use of undercover police officers in protest movements remains a barrier to the construction of mutual trust. The collapse of a trial of environmental protesters in 2009 identified a police surveillance officer as a potential agent provocateur and five additional officers were subsequently identified as being embedded in social protest groups. The 2011 Joint Committee on Human Rights report noted that the London Metropolitan Police "refused to confirm or deny" whether undercover police officers were being used more widely in the trade union movement. For many protesters, versed in the narrative of oppressive paramilitary policing from the 1980s, this provided confirmation of their suspicions about continued surveillance and the remnants of a paramilitary policing culture from earlier decades within police management and the "rank and file" (Jefferson, 1990; Hoggett & Stott, 2010).

Once again, connections with Brodeur's (1983) distinction between high and low policing are evident. The freedom to protest in a democratic state is, on the whole, facilitated by the relevant authorities when it is seen to provide no more than a low level threat to social order. Once the context of the protest slips into the terrain of high policing and threats to national security then new and different strategies are enacted. The key area of debate in this continues to be the distinction between the two levels and concern among legitimate democratic protest groups that they are, in certain circumstances, attracting the attention of the intelligence services and a paramilitarized response from the police that retains an emphasis on undercover surveillance, group infiltration, and the unaccountable use of police coercive power.

Looking Forward: Strategic Facilitation?

The controversy surrounding blanket containment strategies and the excessive use of force coupled with the media outcry that followed the 2009 G20 protest has provided further momentum for the shift in police public order strategy to strategic facilitation. HMIC's (2009a) *Adapting to Protest* suggests that this should involve an emphasis on dialog, dynamic risk assessment, communication, facilitation, and differentiation. These views are underpinned by the theory that "the greater the police emphasis on police negotiation and communication with the crowd, the lesser are the chances of violence escalating" (Waddington, 2007, p. 59). Within the postmodern context of multiple protest agendas and repertoires, the Police Service needs to be cognizant of the complex make-up of crowds and avoid treating them as an undifferentiated whole. As Waddington notes (2007, p. 209), the Police Service should, refrain from tactical interventions that fail to differentiate between the guilty and the innocent... this should be achieved by using an interactive approach to crowd management through education (of themselves), facilitation (of the crowd's legitimate protest), communication (effective, clear and to continue as any violence escalates through media and credible representatives), and differentiation (clearly differentiate between those who are culpable and those who are not, when the violence escalates).

This shift to the strategic facilitation (Waddington, 2011) of political protest in the UK has been influenced by the Swedish DIALOGUE model. In the DIALOGUE model (Alven, 2010) the key objectives are to mediate between demonstrators and police departments, to be a link between demonstrators and the police department, and to be a safeguard for all citizens' rights. Alven (2010) notes here that a facilitative approach to policing need not be passive, "everything goes" policing. Strategic facilitation should clearly prioritize the rights of democratic lawful protesters over unlawful protesters to develop and sustain a clear distinction between Noakes et al.'s (2005) contained and transgressive protesters. This is an acknowledgment that democratic policing is a two-way street and that unlawful protesters can undermine democratic protest and potentially trigger public disorder at large protests. Furthermore, the two groups need to be separated to encourage self-policing among peaceful and democratic protesters (Hoggett & Stott, 2009) and the further isolation of trangressive groups.

In order to achieve the above, Hoggett and Stott (2009, pp. 233–234) have argued that,

there is a pressing need to update police education concerning crowd dynamics if support for a "negotiated management" and facilitative approach to public order policing is to become more than tacit... [and] to minimise the circumstances (such as G20) where individual officers are placed in situations where they perceive little option but to use force indiscriminately against people in a crowd as a whole.

Teaching officers how to operationalize their values and beliefs in a way that coexists with the different values and beliefs of other citizens is formidably complex and the momentous challenge that lies at the heart of police training, particularly in an organization that resembles a paramilitary institution when conducting public order operations (Waddington, 1998).

Policing in 21st century democratic societies takes place within a geopolitical landscape that emphasizes the value of social justice, equity, and human rights. These values can be taught to police recruits (Bayley & Bittner, 1984) and applied within a public order and protest context. Roberg and Bonn (2004) take this further and argue that education is necessary for the development of these values and the effective use of discretion that maintains police performance and professionalism, particularly under stressful conditions. Viewed more broadly, there is a clear link between the professional use of discretion, understood as making appropriate situational judgments (Marenin, 2005, p. 109), and their impact upon public accountability and police legitimacy during "signal" events such as large protests.

The findings of the Joint Committee on Human Rights (2011, p. 3) supports this viewpoint:

> There remains considerable room for improving understanding of front line officers of the ACPO guidelines on the use of the tactic (containment) and we look forward to hearing practical proposals for how to ensure the guidance is translated into action on the ground.

More specifically, concerns have been raised about misinterpretations of proportionality in the use of force (see also HMIC, 2011, p. 20) and the absence of specific guidance on the use of the baton against the head. There are similarities here with the problems faced in the policing of football disorder during the 1980s and, to a lesser extent, in the 1990s where only commanders receive training on the specific context of public disorder. The issue of an absence of trained public order officers was raised again in August 2011 after five nights of public disorder and remains an area of dispute at a time of public expenditure cuts.

Conclusion

Between August 6 and August 10, 2011, several cities in England were subject to widespread damage and looting, with the problems originating in Tottenham, London, and spreading out to provincial areas. While the latter days of the riots were characterized by copycat looting the trigger for the initial problems in Tottenham was a product of longstanding police–community tensions. Of most relevance to this chapter was the protest that took place outside Tottenham police station after the shooting of Mark Duggan by the London Metropolitan Police on August 4, 2011. Within a context of widespread rumors in the local community about the exact details of the shooting, the police refused to speak to Duggan's family and other local community and political representatives at an organized peaceful protest on August 6. Added to this, the Independent Police Complaints Commission, the very body set up to ensure transparency and enhance legitimacy, provided inaccurate information about the circumstances of Duggan's death, thus adding further to the frustrations and mistrust of community members. While there are a multitude of factors that led to the disorder of the subsequent days it is clear that the issues of transparency, trust, and police legitimacy in deprived communities were core components of the trigger event.

The policing of protest, political or otherwise, brings the contested nature of policing objectives, strategies, and tactics to the attention of the wider public and highlights the tension at the heart of the police mission in diverse and divided societies: the use of state-sanctioned force against a society's citizens. While the UK has a long history of democratic protest and public disorder it is clear that the resurgence of political protest has presented new challenges for the Police Service. The death of Ian Tomlinson in 2009, amid a plethora of accusations about unacceptable police tactics, provided momentum to a policy agenda that has addressed police engagement with protest groups, the multimedia reporting of this engagement, and the construction of new forms of vertical accountability. HMIC have acknowledged that this is a starting point for reform and that there is still a need to update police training and education if support for new policies and strategies is to be disseminated throughout the Police Service. Further to this, the shift toward enhanced transparency and vertical accountability is challenged by Brodeur's distinction between high and low policing. This conceptual distinction questions the extent to which the shift toward strategic facilitation can take place and points toward intrinsic limitations in the democratic and community models of policing when placed in the context of political protest.

References

Alderson, J. (1979). *Policing freedom: A commentary on the dilemmas of policing in Western democracies*. Plymouth: McDonald and Evans.

Alderson, J. (1998). *Principled policing: Protecting the public with integrity*. Winchester: Waterside Press.

Alven, C. (May 2010). Public order policing in comparative perspective. Paper presented at the Edinburgh knowledge exchange workshop, Edinburgh, UK.

Banton, M. (1964). *The policeman in the community*. London: Tavistock.

Bayley, D., & Bittner, E. (1984). Learning the skills of policing. *Law and Contemporary Problems*, 47(4), 35–59.

Beck, U. (1998). *Risk society: Towards a new modernity*. London: Sage.

Bittner, E. (1980). *The functions of the police in modern society*. Washington, DC: National Institute of Justice.

Bonner, M. D. (2009). Media as social accountability: The case of police violence in Argentina. *The International Journal of Press/Politics*, 14(3), 296–312.

Brodeur, J. P. (1983). High policing and low policing: Remarks about the policing of political activities. *Social Problems*, 30(5), 507–520.

Brodeur, J. P. (2007). High and low policing in post 9/11 times. *Policing: An International Journal of Policy and Practice*, 1(1), 25–37.

Cohen, S. (1985). *Visions of social control*. Cambridge: Polity.

della Porta, D., & Fillieulle, O. (2004). Policing social protest. In D. A. Snow, S. A. Soule, & H. Kriesi (Eds.), *The Blackwell companion to social movements*. Oxford: Blackwell.

Dow, M., & Plecas, D. (June 2011). Policing the 2010 Winter Games. Paper presented at the 2011 International Police Executive Symposium, Buenos Aires, Argentina.

Goldstein, H. (1979). Improving policing: A problem-oriented approach. *Crime and Delinquency, 25*(2), 236–258.

Greer, C., & McLaughlin, E. (2010). We predict a riot? Public order policing, new media environments and the rise of the citizen journalist. *British Journal of Criminology, 50*(6), 1041–1059.

Haberfeld, M., & Cerrah, I (2008). *Comparative policing: The struggle for democratization.* London: Sage.

Hall, S., Critcher, C., Jefferson, T., Clarke, J., & Roberts, B. (1978). *Policing the crisis: Mugging, the state and law and order.* London: MacMillan.

Her Majesty's Inspectorate of Constabulary (2009a). *Adapting to protest.* London: HMIC. Retrieved from http://www.hmic.gov.uk/Inspections/SpecialistInspections/PPR/Pages/home.aspx

Her Majesty's Inspectorate of Constabulary (2009b). *Adapting to protest: Nurturing the British model of policing.* London: HMIC. Retrieved from http://www.hmic.gov.uk/media/adapting-to-protest-nurturing-the-british-model-of-policing-20091125.pdf

Her Majesty's Inspectorate of Constabulary (2011). *Policing public order.* London: HMIC. Retrieved from http://www.hmic.gov.uk/media/policing-public-order-20110208.pdf

Hoggett, J., & Stott, C. (2009). The role of crowd theory in determining the use of force in public order policing. *Policing and Society, 20*(2), 223–236.

Hoggett, J., & Stott, C. (2010). Crowd psychology, public order police training and the policing of football crowds. *Policing: An International Journal of Police Strategies and Management, 33*(2), 218–235.

Hough, M., Jackson, J., Bradford, B., Myhill, A., & Quinton, P. (2010). Procedural justice, trust and institutional legitimacy. *Policing: A Journal of Policy and Practice, 4*(3), 203–210.

Innes, M. (2010). Whatever happened to reassurance policing? *Policing: A Journal of Policy of Practice, 4*(3), 225–232.

Innes, M., Fielding, N., & Langan, S. (2002). *Signal crimes and control signals: Towards an evidence-based framework for reassurance policing.* Guildford: University of Surrey.

Ivkovic, S. (2008). A comparative study of public support for the police. *International Criminal Justice Review, 18*(4), 406–434.

Jefferson, T. (1990). *The case against paramilitary policing.* Milton Keynes: Open University Press.

Jefferson, T., & Grimshaw, R. (1984). *Controlling the constable.* London: Frederick Muller.

Joint Committee on Human Rights. (2011). *Facilitating peaceful protest.* London: HMSO.

King, M., & Brearley, M. (1996). *Public order policing: Contemporary perspectives on strategy and tactics.* Leicester: Perpetuity Press.

Lipsky, M. (1980). *Street-level bureaucracy: Dilemmas of the individual in public service.* New York: Russell Sage Foundation.

MacPherson, Lord. (1999). *The Stephen Lawrence inquiry.* London: Home Office.

Marenin, O. (2005). Building a global police studies community. *Police Quarterly*, *8*(1), 99–136.

Mawby, R. (2002). *Policing images: Policing, communication and legitimacy*. Cullompton: Willan.

Noakes, J. A., Klocke, B., & Gilham, P. F. (2005). Whose streets? Police and protester struggles over space in Washington, DC, September 2001. *Policing and Society*, *15*(3), 235–254.

O'Connor, D. (2005). *Closing the gap: A review of the fitness for purpose of the current structure of policing in England and Wales*. London: HMIC. Retrieved from http://www.hmic.gov.uk/media/closing-the-gap-20050911.pdf

Perrott, S. (June 2011). Not enough force and then too much force by the integrated security unit at Toronto's 2010 G20: A shifting police knowledge and flashpoints model analysis. Paper presented at the 2011 International Police Executive Symposium, Buenos Aires, Argentina.

Roberg, R., & Bonn, S. (2004). Higher education and policing: Where are we now? *Policing: An International Journal of Police Strategies and Management*, *27*(4), 469–486.

Scarman, Lord. (1981). *Report into the inquiry of the Brixton disorders*. London: HMSO.

Schedler, A. (1999). Conceptualising accountability. In A. Schedler, L. Diamond, & M. Plattner (Eds.), *The self-restraining state: Power and accountability in new democracies*. London: Lynne Reinner.

Stenson, K. (1993). Community policing as a governmental technology. *Economy and Society*, *22*(3), 373–389.

Waddington, D. (1998). Controlling protest in contemporary historical and comparative perspective. In D. della Porta, & H. Reiter (Eds.), *Policing protest: The control of mass demonstrations in Western democracies*. Minnesota: Minnesota University Press.

Waddington, D. (2007). *Policing public disorder: Theory and practice*. Cullompton: Willan Publishing.

Waddington, D. (January 2011). Policing contemporary political protest: From strategic incapacitation to strategic facilitation? Paper presented at the CRESR seminar series, Sheffield, UK.

Waddington, P. A. J. (1998). *Policing citizens*. London: UCL Press.

Wilson, J., & Kelling, G. (1982). Fixing broken windows. *The Atlantic Monthly*, *249*(3), 29–38.

About the Author

Craig Paterson is a professor in the Department of Law, Criminology and Community Justice at Sheffield Hallam University in Sheffield, United Kingdom.

Policing International Football Tournaments and the Cross-Cultural Relevance of the Social Identity Approach to Crowd Behavior

3

MARTINA SCHREIBER AND CLIFFORD STOTT

Contents

Introduction

While some classic theorists described crowds as inherently criminal because of the convergence of those predisposed to crime (Allport, 1924; Sighele, 1891) others portrayed them as dangerous because they reverted cultivated individuals to a barbaric level of primitive drive (e.g., Le Bon, 1895). Despite such qualitative difference, the common feature of these explanations was a focus on the crowd itself and its inherent and universal pathology. The decontextualized and reified view of the crowd put forward by classic theory has been supplanted by a large body of research that emphasizes the contextual determination of crowd action, particularly in terms of the dynamics of intergroup interaction.

This view of the crowd as an intergroup process involves a corresponding focus on how the strategies, tactics, and psychology of the police impact on crowd dynamics (Adang, 1998; Björk & Peterson 2006; della Porta & Reiter, 1998, 2006; Drury, Stott, & Farsides, 2003; Jefferson, 1987, 1990, 1993; Kritzer, 1977; McPhail, 1991; McPhail, Schweingruber, & McCarthy, 1998; Peterson, 2006; Reicher, 1996; Stott, 2003; Stott & Reicher, 1998; Waddington, 1987, 1993, 1994; Wahlström, 2007, Wahlstöm & Oskarsson 2006).

The "Friendly But Firm" Low Profile Approach

Questions concerning the effects of different policing strategies on crowd behavior have been further endorsed by research on the policing of football crowds. In their evaluation of the European Championships 2000 in Belgium and the Netherlands, Adang and Cuvelier (2001) found that two different styles of policing were evident across the eight different host cities. According to data collected from a series of structured observations they proposed that a "friendly and firm" or "low profile" concept was successfully carried out in five cities, while a more "high profile" style was recorded in three. A high profile approach was measured in terms of significantly greater visible deployment of uniformed police, riot police, and riot vehicles relative to low profile cities. Moreover, police were deployed in larger groups and were less friendly toward fans. Their study was also able to relate the different styles of policing to the number of "violent" incidents, the highest number of which were at fixtures that had been assessed as "low risk" by the tournament authorities but that were policed in a high profile way. These findings indicated the value of the low profile approach, while suggesting a negative impact of high profile policing. However, Adang and Cuvelier (2001) only demonstrated that the style of policing has a relationship to public order at international tournaments but says nothing about the underlying crowd processes.

A Social Psychological Model

The Elaborated Social Identity Model (ESIM) (Drury & Reicher, 2000; Reicher 1996; Stott & Reicher, 1998) provides an account of the social psychological processes that govern collective action in crowds. The ESIM assumes that people define themselves as members of psychological groups and when these categories are salient, they will conform to that crowd's ideology and norms. Following this, it is suggested that people do not act as an individual within a crowd but rather shift from a personal to a social identity. Collective action then relates to the ideology of the respective category and only those who behave in ways that are consonant with the category "prototype" will be influential (Reicher, 1984, 1987). ESIM regards social identity as a model of self that is embedded in a context of intergroup relations defined by crowd members in terms of legitimacy and power. More specifically, social identity is defined as the perception of the legitimacy of the shared position within a social context along with the collective actions that are possible and legitimate given such a position (Drury & Reicher, 1999, 2000; Reicher, 1996). It is assumed that the participating groups in a crowd event (e.g., police and fans) form the respective context for each other. Therefore, crowd participants' social identity can fundamentally change because intergroup relationships during a crowd event are dynamic. It follows from this that changes in the form and content of a social category lead to changes in the category prototype and therefore to changes in who or what behaviors can become influential (Turner, Oakes, Haslam, & McGarty, 1994).

There are now a number of studies of different crowds that demonstrate how these processes can be involved in the development of "rioting," (e.g., Drury & Reicher, 1999, 2000, 2005; Reicher 1996; Stott & Drury, 2000; Stott & Reicher, 1998). These studies show that where police use indiscriminate force against crowds this can lead to circumstances where crowd participants began to unite psychologically and define their collective relationship with the police as illegitimate. The psychological unity also empowers those wishing to confront the police, who are in turn regarded as "prototypical" in-group members (Stott & Drury, 2000). While negative crowd–police relations are often connected with unnecessary or inappropriate police use of force, such dynamics are also found in situations when crowd members feel insufficiently protected (Stott, Hutchison, & Drury, 2001); findings that correspond with the observations of Spiegel (1969), who sees escalation connected to both police over- and underactivity.

Building upon this early research and theory, Stott and Adang (2003, 2009) examined crowd interaction involving English football supporters attending football matches with an international dimension. Their research suggested that where police managed to maintain legitimate intergroup relations with English fans this corresponded with "self-regulation," avoidance of conflict, and the marginalization of "hooligans." With regard to police practice, the key to this outcome was police understanding of risk as a dynamic process. It was suggested that legitimate relations were created when policing was "balanced" (i.e., police profile matched the actual levels of risk in that specific situation). This implied the need for "dynamic risk assessment" during a crowd event, which then allows for targeted and timely interventions. Their findings led to recommendations for police practice in general (c.f. Reicher, Stott, Cronin, & Adang, 2004; Reicher, Stott, Drury, Adang, Cronin, & Livingstone, 2007) and influenced the security policy of the Portuguese Security Police, PSP, for the UEFA European Championships in Portugal 2004 (Stott & Adang, 2004; Stott & Pearson, 2007).

The European Championships 2004 in Portugal

Similar to the concept for Euro 2000, the Portuguese Security Police, PSP, stated that their policing profile for Euro 2004 was low profile (PSP, 2003). This approach concerned in particular the "tactical depth" of deployment, in which four levels of response provided for targeted and adjustable interventions. In "normal" situations this would concern the deployment of pairs or small teams of officers. Their presence was designed to transmit a feeling of security; their specific tasks involved facilitating fans' enjoyment (e.g., providing directions to local facilities), proactive communication, surveillance, and the resolution of small incidents. In an escalating situation, further intervention units, the "Corpo de Intervenção" that were initially placed out of sight would support them.

A comprehensive analysis of policing and fan behavior at Euro 2004 confirmed the implementation of this form of low profile approach in Portugal's host cities (Stott, Adang, Livingstone, & Schreiber, 2008). A quantitative survey of English fans' perceptions of group relations in PSP areas further revealed that England's fans perceived their relationship with other fans and with the PSP as legitimate. Moreover, in this context fans came to develop an identification with fans from other nations defined in terms of a "positive carnival of football" and as such came to differentiate themselves psychologically from hooligans (Stott, Adang, Livingstone, & Schreiber, 2007). It was also evident that the PSP provided a social context in which self-regulation among England's fans prevented the escalation of violence (Stott et al., 2007; Stott & Pearson, 2007).

The Need for This Study

The existing literature provides substantial evidence that the low profile approach avoids the social and psychological processes necessary for widespread disorder, at least at football tournaments with an international dimension. However, at present the literature focuses exclusively upon the policing and reactions of British fans. There is, as yet, no data on the extent to which the dynamics outlined within ESIM apply to high-risk fan categories from nations attending football matches and tournaments with an international dimension. This absence within the literature is made more acute given the extent to which the ESIM is currently informing updates to international guidelines for police cooperation and pan-European police training with respect to football matches with an international dimension (EU, 2006).

During Euro 2004, German fans were categorized as high risk. Moreover, the organizing authorities classified the fixture between Germany and the Netherlands as the fixture that posed the highest level of risk to public order. Nonetheless the event passed without any major disturbances. Consequently, this study will advance the literature by exploring the policing of German fans and its relationship to their collective psychology and behavior during the tournament. The subsequent analysis will examine if the processes that the ESIM proposes are responsible for the absence of widespread disorder among England's fans and were also evident among German fans attending the same tournament.

Method

The data presented in this chapter was collected as part of a wider research project of which a number of analyses from this broader project have already been published elsewhere (see Reicher et al., 2007; Stott et al., 2007, 2008; Stott & Adang, 2004; Stott & Pearson, 2007). Data was gathered using a variety of techniques.

Semistructured Observations and Interviews

Semistructured observations were carried out for the duration of the tournament by the current authors. This data was obtained while the observers participated in gatherings and events where large numbers of German fans were involved from the beginning to the end of the tournament. Observations were concerned with recording the course of events, the observers' qualitative impressions of fan behavior, fan group interactions, fan–police interaction, and police deployment. Interviews were conducted with fans on an ad hoc basis and the schedule focused on fans' definitions of their group, intergroup relations (with other fan groups, the police, and locals), and fans' attitude toward violent behavior (see Stott et al., 2007). Informed consent was obtained and interviews were digitally recorded and later transcribed. For this aspect of the wider study, 173 interviews with German fans and 12 interviews with Dutch fans were carried out. Unstructured interviews were also held with members of the German fans' embassy, members of FARE (Football Against Racism in Europe), and the Dutch and the Czech fans' embassies. The interview data was also cross-referenced with media reports, such as newspaper and Internet articles.

The authors also conducted a series of semistructured interviews with a variety of police commanders. These included the Deputy Commander of Porto, the Commander of the Corpo de Intervenção (Northern Portugal), Commander of the Central District for Porto, the Senior Commander and the Deputy Commander of the plainclothes police unit in Porto (the NIP), and the Head of the German police delegation in Portugal and members of the police delegation of the Netherlands.

Analytical Strategy

The analytic strategy in this chapter follows that of previous research that is based on the ESIM (e.g., Drury & Reicher, 2000; Reicher, 1996; Stott et al., 2001, Stott et al., 2007). The analysis comprises two sections: an account of the collective behavior and policing of German fans and a phenomenological analysis of German football fans' accounts. The behavioral account provides a chronological description of incidents, police deployment, and behavioral norms among crowds of German fans based primarily upon the semistructured observational data but which also draws from the interview data from fans and police, photographs, and video footage. In particular, the account focuses on those aspects of the events that will be put to further analysis in the subsequent section. Data were triangulated and where only one source provides data related to an event, the source is identified (Drury & Reicher, 2000; Stott et al., 2007). Fans' accounts were analyzed using the principles of thematic analysis (Boyatzis, 1998; Kellehear, 1993) and interpretative phenomenological analysis (Reid, Flowers, & Larkin, 2005; Smith & Osborn, 2004), looking for a form of pattern recognition within the data and to explore the meanings that participants assign to their experiences. The interviews were transcribed and read several times. This process was informed by the theoretical approach and the understandings and perceptions of the specific groups. For the police interviews, the analysis focused on police understandings of their role, their strategy and tactics used to police German fans, and how these relate to those aspects of fan behavior identified as relevant within the behavioral account. The fan data analysis aimed to explore the developing content of fans' social identity and the relationship of this content to the surrounding social context. Again, following the theoretical approach, the analysis focused on the fans' perception of the event and attitudes toward out-groups, the views of in-group behavior, and intergroup relations and any further points of interest and emerging issues that seemed to be relevant.

Analysis: Behavioral Account

The majority of the German fans followed the team from venue to venue during the group phase where they played the Netherlands and Latvia in Porto and the Czech Republic in Lisbon. Eighteen German fans were arrested during this phase, six for public order disturbances and 12 for illegal ticket selling (Presidência do Conselho de Ministros, 2004).* The fixture between the Netherlands and Germany was scheduled for June 15, 2004; the first

---

* 225 persons from different nations were arrested during the group phase in Portugal, 67 of which were for public order offenses. This compares, for example, to 1219 persons arrested due to criminal offenses and 1838 preventive arrests during the World Cup 2006 in the state of Northrhine-Westphalia only (Wolf, 2006), where 16 games were played.

significant mass gathering of fans began on June 14. By midafternoon large numbers of Dutch and German fans had arrived in the pubs, cafes, and in the squares of the city center of Porto. Small numbers of fans from other nations were also present in the city, such as Greeks, English, Danes, and Swedes. The Porto city authorities had assigned official zones to the two fan groups, each set up with a stage and a big video screen. However, fans were not strictly segregated and mixed at these locations and elsewhere in the city center.

According to information from the Dutch and the German police delegations, about 300 German and 60 Dutch hooligans known to them were present in Portugal. The presence of these fans combined with the high-risk classification did not lead the host police to move toward the deployment of riot units. Instead they deployed small teams of officers in normal uniforms[*] that patrolled throughout the city center, in particular in the areas where crowds of fans had gathered. Units from the Corpo de Intervenção were present but according to police commanders were kept deliberately out of sight of gathering crowds.[†] In addition, small teams of approximately five plainclothes officers operated within the crowds. This allowed the officers to monitor for emergent risks within the crowd and if they did so to intervene directly against this threat rather than against the crowd as a whole. A deputy commander of the plainclothes units in Porto at that time pointed out the general approach of their work.

> Our first mission is to look for those situations, but we also act depending on the level of crime or violence or depending on the situation itself … we work undercover, yes, we are spotting. We are looking for the situations, through the fans, always looking for something. To prevent that things happen. When we think that things are going to happen, we act.
>
> **Deputy Commander of NIP**
> *Porto, July 2, 2004*

Despite the official fan zones, the Ribeira, a public square at the banks of the river Douro, is traditionally very popular among visiting football fans. Consequently, on the evening of the 14th, the Ribeira was crowded with fans. We observed about 1000 people gathering there between 10:30 P.M. and midnight. The majority of these were Dutch but according to our observations approximately 20% were German fans and another 10% were a mixed group from England, France, Italy, Denmark, Spain, and local Portuguese. In the center of the Ribeira was a Dutch brass band, playing well-known and

---

[*] This is to say, dark trousers and light blue shirts and baseball hats. Some officers wore fluorescent vests to increase visibility.

[†] Not all officers from these units were completely invisible. Some took up foot patrols but did so without any of their protective equipment.

traditional Dutch songs. The area was densely crowded so groups were in close proximity and our observations recorded many positive interactions between the groups. Around 10:45 P.M. about 10 PSP officers in standard uniforms patrolled the Ribeira; additionally there was a team of plainclothes officers embedded within the crowd.

At around this time a confrontation between a small group of Dutch and German fans took place amid the crowd. Our interview data notes that approximately five German fans had begun to provoke Dutch fans. According to police accounts the group of plainclothes officers noticed the problem and intervened to verbally instruct the German fans to stop, but the German fans then began to physically confront these officers. The five Germans were immediately arrested and removed from the scene.

> The Germans ...started some word and so on and when the police tried to, our guys, tried to react and put a little bit calm, they react against us. And it was against us. Against the police. And they threw a chair and they tried to be a little bit more arrogant and we didn't allow them and we arrested the five.
>
> **Head of NIP in Porto**
> *Porto, July 2, 2004*

Our observational data and interview data with fans that witnessed the incident indicate that the action of his team in making the arrest in the manner that they did had not affected the celebrations of the wider crowd and it was even approved by fans close by.

At around 11:30 P.M., amid this largely Dutch crowd, a group of approximately eight Germans at the river end of the square began singing racist and anti-Dutch chants (e.g., "Holländer Hurensöhne"* or "Zickzack-Zigeunerpack"†). According to a representative from FARE the group included at least two neo-Nazis known to their organization. This behavior went on for at least 30 minutes and tensions began to emerge among Dutch supporters gathered nearby. According to our observations, at around 11:50 P.M., six officers in standard uniform were observed approaching this group, and otherwise showing increased presence in this area of the square. At the same time, as police data reveals, plainclothes officers discreetly placed themselves between the Germans and the main crowd. Shortly afterward, the chanting faded and the officers withdrew.

> ... we had to divide the Germans and the Dutch with ourselves. Few persons... and they know we were not fans and that we were Portuguese and probably police ...We started to move ourselves in between because the Dutch

---

* Dutch sons of a bitch.
† *Zigeuner* = Gypsies.

wanted to have a party, a big party and we saw that ten Germans were not in the mood and then what we saw was they're less and the noise was so loud from the Dutch that they started drinking and enjoying themselves. And they forget that.

Head of the NIP in Porto
July 2, 2004

In line with the stated security concept of providing a festive atmosphere, the PSP commander saw his policing as driven by a strategic intention to protect and to facilitate the Dutch celebrations. Our observations record that throughout these incidents the Dutch brass band continued to play and positive interactions continued elsewhere in the Square. Most of the time people danced and sang, our observations record that a German and a Dutch fan swapped their shirts. At one point a larger group of German fans engaged in a play called *Humpa*, where the whole group sits down and suddenly jumps up and down singing "humpa humpa tataraa," a game where the German fans are making fun of themselves. In the context of this celebration, the head of the German police delegation supposed that the provoking group deliberately withdrew and separated from the crowd because such widespread celebration would undermine their hooligan credibility.

Well there were a couple from which we assumed that they really wanted to cause trouble, who had really liked to, but due to the orange masses they said: Let's make sure that we are not seen on TV so that in the end people at home see us celebrating with the Dutch!" They quickly disappeared from the square and went to a quiet corner.... Under no circumstances they wanted to be linked to the folk that was celebrating there.

Head of German police delegation
Porto, June 17, 2004

The generally positive fan behavior continued on the following match day where prior to the game thousands of Dutch supporters gathered in the Lisboa Square. Information was obtained by the Dutch police delegation that there was an intention of Dutch fans to march to the stadium some five kilometres away, rather than use public transport. Rather than prevent this, Portuguese police made the decision to facilitate the march. Our observations record that at around 6 P.M. a crowd of approximately 6000 Dutch fans moved off en masse behind the Dutch band with the intention of marching to the stadium. The police profile remained very low and no riot police or vehicles were observed in the vicinity. As the crowd proceeded through the streets, traffic police closed the roadways to vehicles. As the march went past, local Portuguese came onto the streets, balconies, and windows to applaud the Dutch fans. At the front and ahead of the march were teams of Dutch and

German police officers (spotters). At times, as the march approached, small groups of German fans came onto the streets and some shouted hostility at the Dutch fans. Those that did were approached by the German and Dutch spotters and verbally instructed to move—which according to our observations, in all of the cases they did. The march eventually arrived at the stadium without incident. The actual game was a 1:1 draw. Following the match, the two fan groups again mixed and celebrated at the Ribeira.

Taken together, the data indicates that a low profile approach was taken to safety and security for this fixture. Though the game had been categorized as high risk there was no obvious sign of riot police or riot vehicles. Instead officers in normal uniforms and plainclothes officers patrolled the crowds. However, it was evident that the police were ready for and engaged in relatively rapid, differentiated interventions in situations where risks to public order began to emerge. The behavior of fans that was broadly in line with lawful behavior was facilitated—even where this posed considerable problems for the police, as was the case with the march. Where problematic fans were present their attempts of provocations and violent action were identified at an early stage and controlled. This form of policing coincided with peaceful encounters between fans from Germany and the Netherlands and the absence of any widespread conflict.

Fan Psychology

With regard to the historically more negative relations between the two countries, some German fans had actually anticipated high profile policing and described feeling rather surprised by the PSP's low profile deployment.

> G48: Especially because there are, say, there are many Dutch, many Germans here, the rivalry had always been particularly big, therefore I had expected much more police.

Interview with German fan
Porto City Center, June 14, 2004

While the German fans we interviewed described their relations with the Dutch fans in Porto as legitimate some reported the presence of fans they knew to be hooligans. The presence of these violent fans combined with the history of disorder between the two nations led some to expect disorder at the Netherlands match.

> G56: ... just a minor little thing and it will go off. That is the problem, I think ...
> G57: Some people I met in Porto only came because of that.
> MS: Because of the match.
> G57: Yes, yes and because of the trouble.

MS: What do you reckon? Do you think it will go off tomorrow?
G57: Yes. Not in the stadium. Afterwards here in Porto maybe, in small groups.

Interview with German fans
Porto City Center, June 14, 2004

Many of the fans arriving in Porto for the opening match described that what united them was their national identity. If conflict with the Dutch fans occurred it would also involve ordinary fans expressing their solidarity with one another, in terms of the historically embedded conflict between nations.

G59: I think if really something happens there will be many who will join in, who are usually not like that.
MS: Why is that?
G59: Just to support the own people. Because everybody is prepared against the Dutch.
MS: And that refers to the opponent?
G59: They still talk about the war. Van Nistelrooy said in the paper today that we still have to work something out from 60 years ago. Why does he say that?
G58: Yes, but that was in the tabloid.
G59: So? But the Dutch are like that. They are all like that.... They just hate us more than we hate them.

Interview with German fans
Porto City Center, June 14, 2004

Despite these expectations, German fans we spoke to immediately noticed the differentiated manner of PSP policing in the Ribeira. Some explicitly contrasted it from the more hostile and undifferentiated forms of policing that they had experienced with other police forces at previous tournaments.

G35: ... it is very friendly, the police is very much holding back, I think, not overwhelmingly present, for example where it was really bad was in France or Belgium. They [the PSP] don't show this dominant appearance. They are standing there, but somehow unobtrusively in the corner.

Interview with German fan
Porto City Center, June 14, 2004

Some even contrasted the PSP with the hostile policing they experienced within their own nation.

G60: ... I just saw, well the Germans [police] are really mad, they just bang into it no matter if it is you or him or me who is standing beside it. Here they [the Portuguese officers] have observed precisely, many plain clothes, watched: who is it? And whoosh, arm on the back,

into the car, off they go. All was clear. In Germany you're finished
because it is taken out on all of you, that is the problem.

Interview with German fan
Porto Ribeira, June 14, 2004

It is also evident that subsequent to this experience of legitimacy in policing category, boundaries were redefined by some fans, no longer in terms
of nationality but now in terms of violent versus nonviolent behavior. Both
German and Dutch fans that had witnessed the incidents of hostility and
police intervention described those involved not as fellow nationals but as differentiated from a broader categorization defined in terms of nonviolent collective action.

> G66: ... there was this bunch of idiots, three, four Germans who were throwing
> beer glasses and things.
> MS: So you regard people who do stuff like that as idiots?
> G66: Yes, of course.
> MS: Not everybody thinks like that, some think that that is really great...
> G66: Actually I do not care at all if somebody is a Croat or English or whatever.
> We are here to have a party – for three weeks.

Interview with German fan
Porto Ribeira, June 14, 2004

> MS: What do you think about the way that the police reacted? Was that
> appropriate?
> H2: Very good, yes, it is appropriate, they were very fast and it was good, yeah.
> They immediately took one down and carried him away. This time
> it was a German, it could also have been a Dutch guy, that doesn't
> matter he is gone and we should think of this as a big party. And
> this is nice. Loud music and this is good...

Interview with Dutch fan
Porto Ribeira, June 14, 2004

Fans we interviewed described how these attempts of provocation from
German fans rather than representing them actually set them apart from the
majority.

> MS: What happened to this group of people who engaged in singing these
> more aggressive songs?
> G91: They dissolved in the end... this was a bit, I think, well I did not join in their
> chanting, for me this is, not everybody joined in there, maybe five
> guys started to sing "Scheiss Holland" many did not like this a lot.

Interview with German fan
Porto camping site, June 18, 2004

Even fans that were interviewed later in the tournament referred to the positive context that they perceived during their stay in Portugal and linked this specifically to a sense of unity between fans from different nations that arose directly from the PSP's approach to security.

> G91: It really is so peaceful! Well, you always see some rivalry of course but... Well I was down there in Porto at the harbour, where really: There were English together with Italians, Swedes, Danes, Portuguese, Germans, Latvians, all together, there was a mega party, absolutely peaceful! All united by football and keen on having a big football feast. And this is what the hosts definitely achieved: To make a football party for the fans! Not overdoing security, or putting merchandise upfront but organising a football feast for the fans who came down here. Respect Portugal, really!

> **Interview with German fan**
> *Lisbon, City Center, June 23, 2004*

Discussion

The aim of this chapter was to provide a cross-cultural analysis of fans' psychology in order to explore if the social psychological processes underpinning dynamics among England's fans during Euro 2004 in Portugal (e.g., Stott et al., 2007, 2008) were also evident among German fans. The analysis suggests that the policing around German fans was low profile, in line with the stated security concept of the Portuguese police. From this context a form of fan identity was apparent in which category boundaries were not defined by nationality but by nonviolence and good relations with fans from other nations. Fans saw the unobtrusive behavior of police officers as contributing to the overall positive atmosphere, partly because it contrasted with the hostile policing they experienced elsewhere. However, the impact of the policing was even more evident during a situation of emerging conflict at the Ribeira. Low profile policing tactics allowed for the police to work within crowds and therefore to identify problems as they emerged. It may be that as a consequence the quick and targeted arrest of confrontational fans may have prevented further escalation. In this context of the ongoing positive intergroup relations between Germans and Dutch during the first major crowd event within which they were involved, German hooligans were either seen to merge with the peaceful crowd or to be marginalized from it. These processes have a great deal of correspondence with those that Stott and colleagues (2007, 2008) argue underpinned the absence of disorder among England's fans that attended the tournament.[*]

[*] Similar processes have recently been described by Schreiber and Adang (2010a, 2010b) around the 2006 World Cup in Germany.

However, while the experience of legitimate policing instigated processes of self-regulation among England's fans, this was not as evident in our data. However, a connection was evident between low profile policing and the support of nonviolent group norms among crowd participants along with the apparent disempowerment and marginalization of confrontational groups. The present study therefore provides support for the ESIM. Our analysis suggests, tentatively at least, that the social and psychological processes that the model proposes underpin effective public order management are not limited to a single cultural group. Of course the current study is far from conclusive but it does suggest the pressing need for further research on how ESIM dynamics cross cultural boundaries.

Implications for Policing and Research

The positive atmosphere of Euro 2004 has been widely praised (e.g., Deutsche Welle, 2004; Klemm, 2004) and considering the relatively small arrest numbers, it can be regarded as the most peaceful major football tournament in Europe in the last 30 years. In line with previous research (Stott et al., 2007, 2008; Stott & Pearson, 2007), our study adds further weight to the argument that this success can be attributed in large part to the low profile approach that was adopted by the Portuguese Security Police. Our study suggests that a key feature of their approach was the fact that police officers (both plainclothed and uniformed police) were embedded within the crowd, enabling them to monitor for and react to emerging problems at an early stage. As such, they were able to deal with events before they escalated and therefore potentially to avoid initiating the group level dynamics known to be responsible for rioting in previous international tournaments in Europe (Stott & Reicher, 1998; Stott et al., 2001).

A further factor for the success of Euro 2004 can be seen in the effective cooperation between research and police practice. It was the case that the security policy for this tournament was informed by scientific research (Stott & Pearson, 2007). Moreover, our ability to advance understanding in this context has arisen precisely because the PSP supported our research endeavors during the tournament. Consequently, we contend that science and research are also part of an effective armory in the policing of major international tournaments.

Acknowledgments

This research was made possible by grants from the Economic and Social Research Council (RES-000-23-0617) and from the U.K. Home Office. Data collection was made possible through the long-term cooperation of the

U.K. Home Office, especially David Bohannon and Martin Goodhay; the Portuguese Public Security Police, especially José Leitão, Paulo Pereira, José Neto, Luis Simões, and João Pires; the British Consulate in Portugal, especially Gary Fisher and Glynne Evans; the Euro 2004 Organising Committee, especially Paulo Gomes and Luís Trindade Santos; the German police delegation for Euro 2004, especially Andreas Morbach, the German fan embassy, particularly Thomas Schneider and Michael Gabriel; the Dutch police delegation, especially Henk Groenenvelt, the Dutch fan embassy, especially Ilya Jongeneel. Thanks should also be extended to Klaus Boehnke from Jacobs University Bremen and Otto Adang from the Police Academy of the Netherlands, for their comments on an earlier version of this chapter. Otto Adang was also cosupervisor of the broader research project and provided some additional observations. And finally, we would like to give our thanks to all the anonymous fans that attended Euro 2004 and contributed greatly to this research.

References

Adang, O., & Cuvelier, C. (2001). *Policing Euro 2000*. Beek-Ubbergen: Tandem Felix.

Adang, O. M. J. (1998). *Hooligans, autonomen, agenten. Geweld en politie-optreden in relsituaties*. Alphen aan den Rijn: Samsom.

Allport, F. H. (1924). *Social Psychology*. Boston: Houghton Mifflin Co.

Björk, M., & Peterson, A. (2006). *Policing contentious politics in Denmark and in Sweden*. Maastricht: Shaker Publishing.

Boyatzis, R. E. (1998). *Transforming qualitative information: Thematic analysis and code development*. Thousand Oaks, CA: Sage.

della Porta, D., & Reiter, H. (1998). The policing of protest in western democracies. In D. della Porta & H. Reiter (Eds.), *Policing protest: The control of mass demonstrations in Western democracies* (1–32). Minneapolis: University of Minnesota Press.

della Porta, D., & Reiter, H. (2006). The policing of transnational protest: A conclusion. In D. della Porta, A. Peterson, & Herbert Reiter (Eds.), *The policing of transnational protest* (175–189). Aldershot, Burlington: Ashgate.

Deutsche Welle. (2004). Fans, not Hooligans the Story of Portugal. Retrieved from http://www.dw-world.de/dw/article/0,1564,1254575,00.html

Drury, J., & Reicher, S. (1999). The intergroup dynamics of collective empowerment: Substantiating the social identity model. *Group Processes and Intergroup Relations, 2*, 381–402.

Drury, J., & Reicher, S. (2000). Collective action and psychological change: The emergence of new social identities. *British Journal of Social Psychology, 39*, 579–604.

Drury, J., & Reicher, S. (2005). Explaining enduring empowerment: A comparative study of collective action and psychological outcomes. *European Journal of Social Psychology, 35*, 35–58. doi: 10.1002/ejsp.231

Drury, J., Stott, C., & Farsides, T. (2003). The role of police perceptions and practices in the development of public disorder. *Journal of Applied Social Psychology, 33*, 1480–1500.

EU. (2006). Updated handbook with recommendations for international police cooperation and measures to prevent and control violence and disturbances in connection with football matches with an international dimension, in which at least one Member State is involved. (2006/C 322/01). Retrieved from http://eur-lex.europa.eu/LexUriServ/LexUriServ.do?uri = OJ:C:2006:322:0001:0039:EN:PDF

Jefferson, T. (1987). Beyond paramilitarism. *The British Journal of Criminology, 27*, 1, 47–53.

Jefferson, Tony. (1990). *The Case Against Paramilitary Policing.* London: Milton Keynes. Open University Press.

Jefferson, T. (1993). Pondering paramilitarism: A question of standpoints? *The British Journal of Criminology, 33*, 374–381.

Kellehear, A. (1993). *The unobtrusive researcher: A guide to methods.* St. Leonard's: Allen & Unwin.

Klemm, T. (July 1, 2004). *Apfelsinenkulturen an der Algarve: Stimmung statt Randale.* Frankfurter Allgemeine Zeitung.

Kritzer, H. M. (1977). Political protest and political violence: A nonrecursive causal model. *Social Forces, 55*, 630–640.

Le Bon, G. (1895). *The crowd: A study of the popular mind.* London: Ernest Benn.

McPhail, C. (1991). *The myth of the madding crowd.* New York: Aldine de Gruyter.

McPhail, C., Schweingruber, D., & McCarthy, J. (1998). Protest policing in the United States, 1960–1995. In D. della Porta & H. Reiter (Eds.), *Policing protest: The control of mass demonstrations in Western democracies* (49–69). Minneapolis: University of Minnesota Press.

Peterson, A. (2006). Policing contentious politics at transnational summits: Darth Vader or the keystone cops? In D. della Porta, A. Peterson, & Herbert Reiter (Eds.), *The policing of transnational protest* (43–73). Aldershot, Burlington: Ashgate.

Presidência do Conselho de Ministros. (2004). Euro 2004: Ponto de Situação de 19 a 25 de Junho. Retrieved from the Portuguese Cabinet's Web site http://www.portugal.gov.pt/pt/GC15/Governo/Ministerios/PCM/MinistroAdjuntoPM/Documentos/Pages/20040625_MAPM_Doc_Euro2004_Situacao.aspx

PSP. (2003). *Níveis Intervenção Policial.* Confidential document of the Portuguese Security Police. Lisbon: Home Office.

Reicher, S. (1984). The St. Paul's riot: An explanation of the limits of crowd in action in terms of a social identity model. *European Journal of Social Psychology, 14*, 1–21.

Reicher, S. D. (1987). Crowd behaviour as social action. In J. C. Turner, M. A. Hogg, P. J. Oakes, S. D. Reicher, & M. S. Wetherell (Eds.), *Rediscovering the social group: A self-categorization theory.* Oxford: Blackwell.

Reicher, S. D. (1996). "The Battle of Westminster": Developing the social identity model of crowd behaviour in order to explain the initiation and development of collective conflict. *European Journal of Social Psychology, 26*, 115–134.

Reicher, S., Stott, C., Cronin, P., & Adang, O. (2004). An integrated approach to crowd psychology and public order policing. *Policing: An International Journal of Police Strategies & Management.* 24, 4, 558–572. doi: 10.1108/13639510410566271

Reicher, S., Stott, C., Drury, J., Adang, O., Cronin, P., & Livingstone, A. (2007). Knowledge based public order policing: Principles and practice. *Policing, 1*, 403–415. doi: 10.1093/police/pam067

Reid, K., Flowers, P., & Larkin, M. (2005). Exploring lived experience. *The Psychologist, 18,* 20–23.

Schreiber, M., & Adang, O. (2010a). The Poles are coming! Fan behaviour and police tactics around the World Cup match Germany vs. Poland. *Sport in Society, 13,* 487–505.

Schreiber, M., & Adang, O. (2010b). Fiction, facts and a summer's fairy tale—Mixed messages at the World Cup 2006. *Policing and Society, 20,* 2, 237–255.

Sighele, S. (1891). *La foule criminelle. Essai de psychologie collective.* Paris: Alean.

Smith, J. A., & Osborn, M. (2004). Interpretative phenomenological analysis. Chap. 2. In G. M. Breakwell (Ed.), *Doing social psychology research* (229–253). Oxford: Blackwell.

Spiegel, J. P. (1969). Hostility, aggression and violence. In A. D. Grimshaw (Ed.), *Racial violence in the United States* (331–339). Chicago: Aldine.

Stott, C. J. (2003). Police expectations and the control of English soccer fans at "Euro 2000." *Policing: An International Journal of Police Strategies and Management, 26,* 640–655.

Stott, C. J., & Adang, O. M. J. (2003). Policing Football Matches with an International Dimension in the European Union: Understanding and Managing Risk. Unpublished report to the U.K. Home Office.

Stott, C., & Adang, O. (2004). Crowd dynamics, policing and "hooliganism" at "Euro 2004." Research Report for the Economic and Social Research Council. Retrieved from http://www.esrcsocietytoday.ac.uk/ESRCInfoCentre/ViewAwardPage.aspx?AwardId=3336

Stott, C., & Adang. O. (2009). *Understanding and managing risk.* Slagelse: Bavnebanke Press.

Stott, C. J., Adang, O., Livingstone, A., & Schreiber, M. (2007). Variability in the collective behaviour of England fans at Euro 2004: Policing, intergroup relations, social identity and social change. *European Journal of Social Psychology, 37,* 75–100. doi: 10.1002/ejsp.338

Stott, C. J., Adang, O., Livingstone, A., & Schreiber, M. (2008). Tackling football hooliganism: A quantitative study of public order, policing and crowd psychology. *Psychology, Public Policy, and Law, 14,* 2, 115–141. doi: 10.1037/a0013419

Stott, C., & Drury, J. (2000). Crowds, context and identity: Dynamic categorization processes in the "poll tax riot." *Human Relations, 53,* 247–273.

Stott, C., Hutchison, P., & Drury, J. (2001). "Hooligans" abroad? Inter-group dynamics, social identity and participation in collective "disorder" at the 1998 World Cup Finals. *British Journal of Social Psychology, 40,* 359–384.

Stott, C., & Pearson, G. (2007). *Football "hooliganism."* London: Pennant Books.

Stott, C. J., & Reicher, S. D. (1998). How conflict escalates: The inter-group dynamics of collective football crowd "violence." *Sociology, 32,* 353–377.

Turner, J., Oakes, P., Haslam, S., & McGarty, C. (1994). Self and collective: Cognition and social context. *Personality and Social Psychology Bulletin, 20,* 454–463.

Waddington. P. A. J. (1987). Towards paramilitarism? Dilemmas in the policing of public order. *The British Journal of Criminology, 27,* 37–46.

Waddington, P. A. J. (1993). The case against paramilitary policing considered. *The British Journal of Criminology, 33,* 353–373.

Waddington, P. A. J. (1994). *Liberty and order: Policing public order in a capital city.* London: UCL Press.

Wahlström, M. (2007). Forestalling violence: Police knowledge of interaction with political activists. *Mobilization: The International Quarterly, 12*(4), 389–402.

Wahlström, M., & Oskarsson, M. (2006). Negotiating political protest in Gothenburg and Copenhagen. In D. della Porta, A. Peterson & H. Reiter (Eds.), *The policing of transnational protest* (117–143). Aldershot: Ashgate.

Wolf, I. (2006). Rede von Innenminister Dr. Ingo Wolf anlässlich der Pressekonferenz zur endgültigen WM-Bilanz. Retrieved from the Northrhine-Westphalia Home Office's Web site http://www.im.nrw.de/pm/100706_919.html

About the Authors

Martina Schreiber is an instructor at the Department of Public Order Management, Police Academy of the Netherlands in Apeldoorn, the Netherlands; and Clifford Stott is a professor in the Department of Applied Psychology at Liverpool University in Liverpool, UK.

Innovations in the Governance of Security

4

Lessons from the 2010 World Cup in South Africa

SOPHIE NAKUEIRA AND JULIE BERG

Contents

Introduction

Today's increasingly globalized world has brought about a New World Order that calls for reconceptualizing the Hobbesian or Westphalian notion of viewing the state as a monopolist on power. Indeed, in today's world, which is sometimes referred to as the "Age of Governance," the centrality of the state as the primary figure of authority has been challenged not only by the "decreasing relevance of formal models of administrative hierarchy [but also by] the recognition of interdependence among private and public actors" (Schmidt, 2004).[*]

The role of non-state actors as auspices of security governance[†] has increased to the point that in some areas they are seen to be in competition with the state as sources of authority (Muellerson, 2000). Innovations in new governance have illustrated new functions for the state and non-state actors. Moreover, the proliferation of "private governments" and how they operate only affirms the increasing importance of "non state as both auspice and provider of governance" (Burris, Kempa, & Shearing, 2008, p. 59).[‡] Also, the hybrid and plural nature of the auspices of security governance at times encompasses both public and private sectors not only on the domestic level but also supranational entities at the international and transnational level (Bayley & Shearing, 2001). However, despite the increasingly complex web of fragmentation and decentralization, a "collective capacity to govern" has been prevalent (Muellerson, 2000, p. 138). This collective capacity to govern has been facilitated by auspices of governance that are located in local and international communities, civil societies, nongovernmental organizations, "social movements, sub national governments, political parties, professional societies, multinational corporations and not only in nation states" (Rosenau, 1997, as cited in Muellerson, 2000, p. 138).

In this chapter, we posit that both the scholarship on the governance of security and empirical studies that have concentrated on new governance has shown a more nuanced and interwoven relationship than the narrowly defined "state as auspice and non state as provider" neo-liberal lens. This highly complex realm of governance needs an in-depth exploration other than through the general neo-liberal lens through which changes in governance have been prevalently interpreted (Berg & Shearing, 2010). Thus, by examining the security

---

[*] Also see Strange, S. (1996). *Retreat of the state: Diffusion of power in the world economy.* Cambridge: Cambridge University Press.

[†] For the purposes of this chapter, governance is defined as "organised efforts to manage the flow of events in a social system" (Burris et al., 2008). We thus define the governance of security, in particular, as "actions designed to shape events so as to create [safe] 'spaces' in which people can live, work and play" (Wood & Shearing, 2007).

[‡] Also see Macaulay, S. (1986). Private Government. In Lipson, L. & S. Wheeler (Eds.), *Law and the social sciences.* New York: Russell Sage Foundation.

arrangements of the 2010 World Cup in Cape Town, the chapter illustrates how *Fédération Internationale de Football Association* (FIFA), a non-state actor, orchestrates a web of collaborative governance, or a collective capacity to govern, that is nuanced by non-state and state actors both engaging as auspices and providers of security for the hosting of the 2010 World Cup. This chapter thus illustrates the "pervasive role of (non-state) supranational normative orders" in the governance of relations that penetrate into the territorial boundaries of South Africa hence challenging the traditional concept of nation state sovereignty (Braithwaite & Drahos, 2000).

We thus use the security governance of mega events as a lens by which to explore the interface between the different auspices in their provision of security governance and to shed further light on the complexities of polycentric security arrangements. Mega event spaces are particularly relevant sites to observe security governance arrangements as they are regulated by special legislation and guidelines which significantly impact the role of both state and non-state actors.[*] These spaces are important to study for a number of reasons of which we will highlight two that are critical to this chapter. First, because these events draw large crowds and have a venue capacity of between 10,000 and 250,000 people they are useful sites to explore how the "rituals of public space are played out" (Palmer & Whelan, 2007, p. 402).[†] Second, because they are unique spaces where large crowds experience security as a public good, they become crucial sites for the exploration of negotiations between private and public and state and non-state actors in securing these spaces in terms of policing arrangements and provision of safety (Palmer & Whelan, 2007).

Thus the 2010 World Cup venues in Cape Town were crucial venues for our study as they provided important sites for investigating who was involved in policing and providing security in the mega event spaces and how these entities engaged with each other to achieve the collective goal of safety during the event.

The Legal Mandate

In order to have a proper appreciation for the overlapping arrangements that facilitated the securing of the 2010 World Cup, it is important to understand the legal obligations that had to be fulfilled by South Africa in general and the city of Cape Town more specifically.

---

[*] For the hosting of the World Cup matches in Cape Town these legislations and guidelines included the 2010 Special Measure Acts, 2010 FIFA World Cup South Africa Official World Cup Fan Parks Event Manual, and the Host City Agreement. The venues covered by these laws and rules included Public Viewing Areas, the Fan Parks, and Stadiums.

[†] See 2010 FIFA World Cup South Africa Official World Cup Event Fan Parks Event Manual (Hereinafter, "Fan Parks Event Manual").

The first step before a country can be awarded the right to host the World Cup is for the national government to support FIFA's guarantees. FIFA expects this of all countries aspiring to host the World Cup. To this end, the South African government promised to deliver a total of 17 guarantees*: the Ministry of Safety and Security pledged to provide safety and security; the Ministry of Health pledged to provide medical care; the Ministry of Trade and Industry promised to protect FIFA from having its marketing rights exploited; the Ministry of Transport pledged to provide transport to all hotels, major event venues, and public viewing areas; and the Ministry of Communications guaranteed that there would be telecommunications and information technology. Although these are only a few of the guarantees made by various ministries to FIFA, this chapter will illustrate how the cooperation between these different agencies in delivering these guarantees according to FIFA's requirements was instrumental in securing the 2010 World Cup in general.

After the country has won the right to host the World Cup, the host cities have to sign a Host City Agreement with FIFA and the Local Organising Committee (LOC), which spells out the legal obligations as required of them for hosting the event. The city of Cape Town thus had to sign a Host City Agreement with FIFA and the Local Organising Committee.[†]

It is under the ambit of the host city fulfilling its mandate under the Host City Agreement and the Ministry of Safety and Security's attempt to fulfill its contractual obligations to provide safety and security that we witness an overlap and interplay of several state and non-state actors as they engage with each other in the complex game of security governance.[‡]

Security Governance Structure for Cape Town

In fulfilling their obligations to FIFA, host cities were mandated to work together with all levels of government (national, provincial, and local). Hence for the security arrangements for Cape Town, operation centers were divided into various levels to collaborate with the relevant levels of government in case of an incident. The nature of the incident dictated the necessary level of government that would deal with any particular incident. At the operational level, Venue Operation Centres (VOCs) were expected to deal locally with any incident and then advise the City Joint Operation Centres (City JOCs)

---

* These guarantees are contained in the original bid book in support of the South African Football Association (SAFA) in its bid to host the 2010 FIFA World Cup. See "Governments 2010 Guarantees" available at http://www.sa2010.gov.za/guarantees (November 4, 2010).

† See Host City Agreement of March 15, 2006 between FIFA, the LOC, and the city of Cape Town. (Hereinafter, "the Host City Agreement").

‡ The above legislation was to operate with other laws such as the 2010 Cape Town by-laws.

and the Provincial Joint Operation Centres (Prov JOCs). At the tactical level, when an incident required citywide coordination, the City JOCs and Prov JOCs were to be notified. At the strategic level when a matter necessitated province-wide coordination, the matter was reported to the Prov JOCs and any response would have to be supported by the Disaster Management structures.[*] All these arrangements were integrated into a "Command and Control Communications" structure for the city of Cape Town with the National Joint Operation Centre being the highest government level of intervention.[†]

Thus from this governance structure it is apparent that there was a broad framework for support for the city of Cape Town for any incident that might happen during the World Cup and the overall arrangement ensured that such incidents would be dealt with immediately by the appropriate governmental levels. However, at the operational level of policing the tournament, security governance was more nuanced than the state and private security (SAPS) governance that would ordinarily secure the various spaces.

Using the conceptual framework of nodal governance, we examined the various entities, institutions, and actors that were involved in the policing of the World Cup without assuming that SAPS would be *a priori* the central provider of security governance (Shearing, 2006).

Despite the fact that FIFA had made SAPS the lead actor for securing the event, SAPS was expected to collaborate with other departments to deliver on its guarantee of securing the event. This meant that an empirical exploration was necessary to investigate the roles played by the various auspices and providers of security at the event. Moreover, in order to maximize on any security legacy beyond the 2010 World Cup, it was vital that an empirical exploration of the orientations of the different actors be carried out.

While acknowledging that our concept of security is very broad,[‡] we concentrate on the major security "nodes" that were involved in securing the 2010 World Cup in the city of Cape Town and illustrate how they engaged with each other to secure the tournament.

Safety and Security Work Streams

To respond to the challenges associated with securing the World Cup, tasks were allocated to the relevant role-players and the projects were to be executed according to the needs of the work stream. For the policing of the World Cup, the major nodes, as defined by the safety and security work stream, included Fire services, Metro Police, Law Enforcement, Disaster and

---

[*] LOC Presentation (July 2010).
[†] Ibid.
[‡] We define security governance as "actions designed to shape events so as to create [safe] 'spaces' in which people can live, work and play" (Wood & Shearing, 2007).

Risk Management, and CCTV.* However, because of the overlapping nature of security, the Safety and Security work stream had synergies with other work streams such as Transport, Health, Tourism, and Informal Trading.†

These work streams met on a weekly basis before and during the World Cup. Hence these various work streams, which integrated all of the role-players, acted as a monitoring tool to ensure that tasks were on schedule and were being implemented according to plan.

According to the interviews conducted, the overall success of securing the World Cup was attributed to the Transport work stream and Cape Town had to collaborate with the Transport work stream to fulfill its obligations under the Host City Agreement. The Host City had to ensure that transport structures took the Official Fan Park into consideration so that fan mobility between various mega event venues was easily facilitated.‡ The Transport work stream anticipated the spaces within which fans would commune and mapped out an overflow structure to and from the various mega event spaces. Various modes of transport from all the different venues were taken into consideration in the plans. The Transport department made sure that the rail system ran an expanded schedule during the tournament and that there were shuttles from various venues. To avoid congestion in the city center, there were Park and Ride stations at several venues and rail stations.§ The Transport work stream was instrumental in encouraging the Safety and Security work stream and Traffic work stream among others, to appreciate the overall structure that was required to secure the event.

Volunteers

Volunteers played a significant role in ensuring safety during the tournament. There were 489 volunteers, who were managed by 77 Host City Volunteers.¶ They were deployed at various mega event spaces including at the Park and Ride stations. Depending on the needs of the venue, the volunteers played various roles such as transport consultants, giving directions to fans on where to access certain services, and participating in crowd management. They were also trained to identify infringements on FIFA's marketing rights and those of its commercial affiliates. When interviewed on how they would react if they saw someone committing a crime, volunteers said that they would report the matter to the police to promote the safety and security

---

* LOC Presentation (July 2010).
† The 2010 Observer Programme.
‡ Fan Parks Event Manual version 1 (January 2008).
§ More than 130,000 people used the Park and Ride and for the eight matches more than 1 million football fans used the rail system to get to the city for the festivities. See the 2010 Observer Programme.
¶ The 2010 Observer Programme.

of the event. A critical part of the success of the volunteer program was the clear command and control structure, which enabled communication and specified tasks for the volunteers.[*]

Fire and Rescue Services

Fire and Rescue Services played a critical role in securing the World Cup. Before the World Cup, Fire and Rescue Services had mapped out what they thought to be potentially dangerous areas in terms of inaccessible spaces and fire hazards. They trained SAPS on how to handle explosives and declared maximum numbers for the various mega event venues to facilitate evacuation in case an emergency occurred. Fire and Rescue Services had a meticulous communication and deployment plan mapping out numbers of persons needed and their responsibilities in case an emergency occurred at any venue. Additionally, they had a state-of-the-art "Control Bus," which was equipped with the latest technology that allowed it to access data in real time from all the local Venue Operation Centres.[†] This strategy was instrumental in ensuring safety and security of the tournament as the resources to respond to an emergency were readily available.

Private Security

SAPS was hesitant to work with private security as they felt that they had enough personnel to secure the tournament; however, FIFA insisted that private security be included in the plan to secure the event. Their responsibility during the World Cup was to ensure that property was not damaged and that unruly people were not allowed in venues. At the Fan Parks and public viewing areas the role of private security was to ensure that people did not enter with prohibited items. Several private security companies were deployed at various mega event spaces and public viewing areas and their services contributed greatly to securing the tournament.

Cleaning Companies

Due to the large crowds that are attracted to partake in festivities, it was anticipated that the spaces would be littered with various potentially problematic items brought into the mega event venues and then discarded. The host city was obliged under the city beautification clause to ensure that all mega event spaces were clean and kept. Hence cleaning companies were hired to care for all mega event areas and large streets near the event sites. The cleaning of these spaces contributed to the feeling of safety and security as the findings in the interviews revealed.

---

[*] Ibid.
[†] Ibid.

To secure the World Cup a spatial mapping of mega event sites was drawn and spatial manuals articulating FIFA's requirements were implemented accordingly. The policing of every mega event site was implemented according to a manual which specified integrated project teams and their responsibilities, thereby ensuring safe spaces for enjoying the World Cup activities. Below is an illustration of how the main sites in Cape Town were secured for the successful hosting of the tournament.

How Mega Event Sites in Cape Town Were Secured in 2010

Fan Fest

Following the success of the Fan Fest at the 2006 World Cup in Germany, it was decided that host cities would create Fan Parks where fans without tickets would enjoy the 2010 World Cup free of charge. So under the "No ticket, No problem" slogan, the host city embarked on a marketing campaign[*] to promote these fan parks and the city of Cape Town made sure that it followed FIFA's Fan Park Event manual to construct the Grand Parade Fan Park. It is posited that the design, the staff that were deployed, and other arrangements made at the Fan Park were the main reasons that the fan park was a safe space in part by securing the site with 210 private security personnel. The main safety and security nodes such as SAPS, Traffic, Disaster and Risk management, Fire and Rescue, Metro Police and Law Enforcement were deployed in and around the fan park all with varying roles, which contributed to securing the fan park. These roles were articulated in the FIFA 2010 Grand Parade Fan Park Emergency and Contingency Plan.[†] Additionally, the Venue Operation Control Centres had representatives from each department that were deployed including Event Management and Event Security.[‡] All public viewing areas were expected to follow the same design and were to be implemented as mandated by the Host City Agreement and the FIFA Fan Park Manual irrespective of whether or not they were official fan parks.

Fan Walk

"Never before have so many people walked so far with so few tickets."[§] This phrase appeared along the fan walk, which was a 2.5 mile route designed as an alternative to other transportation modes and passed through major

---

[*] LOC Presentation (July 2010).
[†] FIFA 2010 Grand Parade Fan Park Emergency and Contingency Plan, p. 6.
[‡] Ibid.
[§] LOC Presentation (July 2010).

historical sites contributing to a "carnival-type" feel (Berg & Nakueira, 2011). Various forms of entertainment en route to the stadium, SAPS on horseback and other nodes such as transport consultants, medical services, and security guards all contributed to the feeling of safety on the fan walk. The design of the fan walk, which included input from various nodes, ensured that people moved swiftly while enjoying the two-mile walk to the stadium. The positive attitude created by the fan walk made policing of the fans and the area an easy task.[*]

The Cape Town Stadium

The SAPS had input into the design of the stadium, thus they knew where the potentially problematic locations were, facilitating proactive measures to minimize both the likelihood of an incident occurring and the consequences of any situation that did arise.[†] The design of the stadium had sufficient exit points that could evacuate a crowd of 65,000 in as little as 15 minutes.[‡] Additionally the volunteers had been trained to ensure that they were familiar with the stadium to fans irrespective of their need. The Cape Town stadium had various nodes securing the space in addition to a Venue Operation Control Centre, which had representatives from all the various nodes that were securing the stadium and surrounding area.

Lessons Learned

There were a number of key elements that made the security strategy employed at the 2010 World Cup a success. First, the city of Cape Town Safety and Security Strategy model was a "product of international best practice."[§] It was crowd-friendly, it was based on proven risk management principles, it was supported by world class best practice training programs, every possible and necessary resource was available, and it was based on "multiple concentric rings of security strategy."[¶] Additionally, it was "successfully piloted and refined" and most important of all, the integrated approach that included every aspect of the tournament made it work.[**] However, qualitative and quantitative research conducted during the duration of the event revealed some noteworthy findings that were significant to securing the World Cup. Below are some of the key elements that made the 2010 World Cup a success.

[*] This was revealed in an interview with a private security company (August 2010).
[†] Interview with SAPS officer.
[‡] Ibid.
[§] The 2010 Observer Programme.
[¶] Ibid.
[**] Ibid.

Fulcrum Capacity

The World Cup event was successfully secured primarily because there was a fulcrum institution to ensure that the obligations of all of the key stakeholders were being met. FIFA was that institution as it had the capacity to orchestrate and ensure that the various nodes collaborated to meet the single goal of delivering a safe World Cup. The incentives created and the threat of sanctions if the need arose ensured that all role players participated, which in the end was "to the benefit of their organisations, whether it is faster or bigger [crime] reductions; cheaper compliance; or smarter hence implementable and enforceable programs" (Weber, 2007).

Common Vision and Incentive to Succeed

The common vision of having a successful and safe World Cup cannot be underestimated. The sharing of a common purpose, a clear and unwavering deadline(s), and significant incentives to succeed, paved the way for cooperative relations among all role-players:

> ...there was a common vision and a common desire to see the success of the World Cup in no uncertain terms from everyone around. I mean, there are a large euphoria and that kind of fuelled people to work together in a way that perhaps we have not seen in the last 10 [years]. And so that kind of gave impetus for us to work together.*

What was also vital is the fact that this common vision was formalized through the signing of contracts at a very early stage of the process at all levels of government and thus facilitated the creation of a "complex web of accounting players," legally accountable to each other and the laws governing the event.†

"Whole-of-Government" and "Whole-of-Society" Approach to Crime Prevention

The integration of nodes involved both directly and indirectly in securing the World Cup reflects a "whole-of-government" approach to safety (involving all government departments). But the incorporation of non-state actors (including the public) reflects a broader "whole-of-society" approach to safety (Johnston & Shearing, 2003). The integrated approach to crime

---

* Metro Police representative, personal communication, July 2010.
† SAPS representative, personal communication, August 2010.

prevention by all stakeholders—both state and non-state—was an important element as it helped all parties address common problems. Joint meetings played a significant role in helping the different state and non-state agencies to understand each other's issues and how their different roles were critical to achieving the joint goal of safety and security for the event. The public was also, in many respects, enrolled in the joint vision of creating a safe World Cup experience and thus they were important stakeholders in the safety of the event. Due to the collective capacity that was well utilized to deliver on the safety and security measures of the event, it is critical to have integrated plans with all role-players and not simply rely on SAPS alone to provide security.

Preventative Mentality Versus Reactive Mentality

The mentality of the security model was preventative rather than exclusively reactionary; therefore, the loopholes for the "opportunity offender" were greatly minimized. The creation of safe spaces that were clean and well maintained with visibility and the presence of various agencies reduced the likelihood for would-be offenders to engage in disruptive and/or criminal behavior. Also the integrated approach that involved all relevant players in the 2010 work streams was critical to making the event successful. Not only did the key role-players know what was at stake and what their roles were, they were able to cooperate effectively and utilize resources efficiently. This approach can be taken forward in the future as it ensures that the different agencies with overlapping interests of synergies can provide the requisite services without wasting resources.

Reliable Institutions

The law was implemented vigorously in particular for those who infringed on FIFA's marketing rights and those of its sponsors. Additionally, the fact that there were 24-hour dedicated courts to prosecute individuals who were charged, greatly contributed to reducing the crime rate, as people knew that the legal system was responsive when people broke the law.

Planning, Decision Making, and Leadership

A collaborative approach to decision making was facilitated through regular meetings involving the different work streams that were aimed at checking compliance and setting deadlines to achieve any outstanding goals. The Volunteer Management Structure was based on a model that ensured proper leadership and included one city staff supervisor. Regular motivational exercises were significant in boosting the morale of the volunteers. This issue was also stressed when commenting on making decisions at work stream meetings. Ensuring that people did not leave work stream meetings until a consensus on an issue was reached helped streamline duties and the responsibilities between the different agencies.

Visibility and Friendly Attitude of Security Providers

The visibility of the police was an important factor in and around venues. Members of the general public commented that seeing the police presence made them feel safer. Additionally, the friendly demeanor of SAPS was a critical component in making people feel secure as they participated in the events. Although there were many security providers, many individuals indicated that they felt reassured simply by the visibility of SAPS, while some were happy to see that there were clearly identifiable authorities present to deter and respond to any disruptive or criminal behavior. This visibility has been credited as a contributing factor to crime aversion as would-be offending and opportunities were greatly reduced in the presence of so many police officers.

Training

The World Cup was a success because the different role-players had skills that were relevant to securing the event. Each role-player or node had special skills to fulfill its particular mandate. There is a need for proper briefing and training of staff so that each of them is clear on their specific role and has the skills necessary to fulfill their responsibilities. Commitment to the training necessary to provide professional and responsive services ensured that the World Cup was safe and there is a need to maintain this commitment beyond 2010 by the different role-players.[*]

Sensitizing the Public About Crime

Marketing the event and communicating to the public on how to keep safe and encouraging them to be at their best behavior made them "own" the event. With the exception of a few, most people were at the festivities to enjoy themselves and were not there to engage in disruptive behavior. This marketing and communication strategy greatly influenced the attitudes of the public and thus helped create a safe environment.

---

[*] The 2010 Observer Programme.

Challenges Beyond 2010

The presence of a fulcrum was critical in securing the World Cup. Collaboration and partnership worked well because of the incentives and various goals that had to be met. Beyond 2010, the story changes. Even though the goal for securing South Africa is an ongoing one, the motivations for collaboration have changed.

Security governance as it has been described above highlights some noteworthy elements that have been described by other empirical findings. The institutions through which the state and non-state actors engage each other depends on the objectives that each of them deems appropriate to achieving their own goals. The implications of this reality are many and will often determine which node is more influential in certain areas than others. This is evidenced by the examples given above, which show that in some areas some nodes are more prevalent than others and the reverse is true.

While generally SAPS performed well in fulfilling its legal mandate to head security operations in fulfillment of the state's guarantee to FIFA to provide, in some areas other security providers played an equally important and sometimes stronger role in making people feel safe and securing the World Cup event as a whole. For future events it will be critical to understand and recognize that given the plurality of security providers, it is important to cultivate the collective capacity of all role-players. Even though SAPS was theoretically and legally the lead agency, there were times when other security providers were more prominent and more efficient in the fulfillment of their responsibilities.

> I had more of a relationship with Metro; I found they're more user friendly for us. Metro, many times when we had issues of illegal traders and stuff, they were always available. When I always found that we looked for SAPS I could never find that, to be quite honest. I mean there was times when I would have to phone the main JOC and say... "Listen, you know, this is happening on the ground, we need SAPS assistance now and then he would have to phone somebody who would have to phone somebody and then they would appear.[*]

Having said that, in response to the role that SAPS played in securing the event, an interviewee commented:

> So I think across the board we were pleasantly surprised at the SAPS delivery particularly at the end of the day. And of course you have Metro Police, who come to the fore, but our Achilles heel we thought was going to be SAPS and it wasn't.[†]

---

[*] Private security company, personal communication, August 2010.
[†] Cape Town Partnership, personal communication, September 2010.

Only by analyzing what made the security governance arrangements for the World Cup successful can one begin to address how local resources can be properly coordinated beyond the 2010 World Cup. In the study conducted, the primary incentive that drove all the role-players to achieve the common goal of securing the major event venues was the aspiration to meet FIFA's requirements as stipulated in the Host City Agreement.

Conclusion

In this chapter, although we propose that collaboration should continue beyond 2010 in order to secure South Africa, we understand the challenges that are ahead. For collaboration to happen there needs to be a fulcrum to ensure that all goals are being met. This fulcrum need not be the state as was evidenced by the role FIFA played in securing the World Cup.

The question left to ask ourselves is a simple one which paradoxically has no simple solution. Knowing what we know now, given the skills and capacities that we have to provide security, what is necessary to motivate key stakeholders in South Africa to secure the country beyond 2010?

References

Bayley, D. H., & C. Shearing. (2001). *The new structure of policing: Description, conceptualisation, and research agenda.* Washington, DC: National Institute of Justice.

Berg, J., & C. Shearing. (November 1–2, 2010). New Authorities: Relating State and Non-State Security Providers in South African Improvement Districts. Paper presented at the Danish Institute for International Studies Conference: Access to Justice and Security: Non-State Actors and the Local Dynamics of Ordering, Copenhagen, Denmark.

Berg, J., & S. Nakueira. (2011). *Best principles of collaborative security governance: Lessons from the 2010 Soccer World Cup.* Centre of Criminology: University of Cape Town.

Braithwaite, J., & P. Drahos. (2000). *Global business regulation.* Cambridge: Cambridge University Press.

Burris, S., M. Kempa, & C. Shearing. (2008). Changes in governance: A cross disciplinary review of current scholarship. *Akron Law Review*, 41(1):1–66.

Johnston, L., & C. Shearing. (2003). *Governing security: Explorations in policing and justice.* London: Routledge.

Muellerson, R. (2000). *Ordering anarchy: International law in international society.* The Hague: Kluwer International Law.

Palmer, D., & C. Whelan. (2007). Policing in the "communal spaces" of major event venues. *Police Practice and Research*, 8(5): 401–414.

Schmidt, P. (2004). Law in the age of governance: Regulation, networks and lawyers. In Shearing, C. D. (2006). Reflections on the refusal to acknowledge private governments. In Strange, S. (1996). *Retreat of the state: Diffusion of power in the world economy.* Cambridge: Cambridge University Press.

Shearing, C. (2006). Reflections on the refusal to acknowledge private governments. In Jennifer Wood & Benoit Dupont (Eds.), *Democracy, society and the governance of security* (11–32). Cambridge: Cambridge University Press.

Weber, E. P. (2007). *Pluralism by the rules: Conflict and cooperation in environmental regulation*. Washington, DC: Georgetown University Press.

Wood, J., & C. Shearing. (2007). *Imagining security*. Collumpton: Willan Publishing.

About the Authors

Sophie Nakueira is a Ph.D. candidate at the Centre of Criminology, Faculty of Law, University of Cape Town, and can be contacted at: sophienakueira@hotmail.com. Julie Berg is a Senior Lecturer at the Centre of Criminology, Faculty of Law, University of Cape Town, who can be contacted at: julie.berg@uct.ac.za.

Sports Fan Violence in Serbia

5

Shadow of Turbulent Sociopolitical Circumstances*

KESETOVIĆ ŽELIMIR, SLADJANA DJURIĆ, AND VLADIMIR CVETKOVIĆ

Contents

Introduction

Violence among sports fans has been a constant, running alongside the development of sport as one of the oldest human activities. As a uniquely human activity, sports have a complex and ambivalent nature that is expressed through the parallels of homogenizing (integrative) and antagonizing (disintegrative) potential (Armstrong & Giulianotti, 1999), so it, on the one hand, stimulates the cooperation/amalgamation of different groups, nations, and cultures, but, on the other hand, leads to various kinds of violence and conflict being associated with the sport. Taking into account this information, authors who put forward the argument that sport is the universal

* This text is the result of the realization of the scientific research project entitled *Security and protection of functioning of the educational system in the Republic of Serbia (basic precepts, principles, protocols, procedures and means)*. The project is financed by the Ministry of Education and Science of the Republic of Serbia (No. 47017), and carried out by the faculty of Security Studies in Belgrade and partner institutions (2011–2014).

anticriminal agent might be considered rather naïve; one should make the distinction between professional and amateur sporting activities, especially given that professional sports have been exposed to diverse kinds of criminals and crime-related activities (Ignjatović, 1998).

The sporting audience is growing more and more, and within this huge following, certain groups have been formed that are passionately engaged in supporting their respective clubs. At sporting events, fans often cause serious disturbances, which can be almost impossible for police to control and manage. Thus, these groups can pose significant problems for the authorities and also to the safety of the community. Violence of fan groups within sport is perhaps a manifestation of widespread violence in the modern world, including as it does youngsters that accept this violence as a form of communication. As it becomes more serious, often resulting in fatalities, material losses, and damage, sporting violence provides a significant challenge for police and other public and private security agencies, medical services, local, regional, and national government, thus emphasizing the need for a serious and systematic holistic approach.

Supporting a club and being affiliated to a group of sports fans is becoming a modern behavioral feature among youngsters who have developed a strong sense of belonging to a particular group, and who also directly participate in the sporting event, thus turning the supporting of a team into a spectacle or ritual, and, sometimes, transferring the violence from the social milieu to the stadium. This kind of behavior is not exclusive to football fans and football matches, but can also occur at basketball, handball, ice hockey, and various other sporting gatherings.

Fan Violence in Serbia—Overview

In the region of Serbia and the former Yugoslavia, violence among fans of sport became a serious social, security, and political problem in the 1980s, especially among nationalist-oriented fan groups in Bosnia-Herzegovina, Croatia, and Serbia. It culminated with TV-broadcasted scenes of violence in May 1990, at the stadium of Dinamo Zagreb (Croatia), when the football team from Croatia was involved in a match with Crvena Zvezda Belgrade (Serbia). Some analysts state that this event, on a symbolic level, indicated the end of the federal state and was a precursor to the bloody dissolution of the SFR Yugoslavia (Žugić, 1996), while other analysts believe that the history of the disintegration of Yugoslavia could be described as being the story of the evolution of violence in Yugoslav sport, particularly among football fans–hooligans, and the gradual transfer of that violence, in the late eighties and early nineties, to the field of interethnic conflict, the "big national" policy, and, hence, to the battlefield.

Sport is one of the most powerful catalysts of mass expressions of emotions and the valve that enables vehement manifestation of basic instincts, so it could be used as an indicator of forthcoming crisis in Yugoslav society. Sport matches were less an opportunity to enjoy the sport itself, but more an opportunity for gathering of extremists who used supporting the team as a cover for expressing their political opinion and/or social discontent (Harnischmacher & Ingo, 1989). What was not allowed to be expressed in public discourse was voiced in the stadium stands.

Sports fan violence and hooliganism in Serbia have escalated in the last two decades, in accordance with world trends. The most important contributing factors were increasing aggressiveness and politicization of sports fans and transformation of sports into interethnic conflicts (Mihajlović, 1997). In addition to these factors, researchers in England highlight the following causes of extremist behavior: social crisis, dissolution of social values, crisis of big ideas, loss of the meaning of life, unemployment and lack of perspective, the situation in football (criminalization, match-fixing, parlay, withdrawal of the best players, and cadre), institutionalization of hooliganism through sports fan organizations, patronizing attitude of clubs toward fans, and general benevolence toward inappropriate behavior. Fans are becoming instruments of sport organizations (clubs, management, coaches) and political and other organizations (Mišić, 2010, p. 87). It is well known in Serbia that the fans of the most renowned clubs are showered with various privileges resulting in their support becoming a sort of profession. They influence "their beloved club's" policy along with the club management. If necessary, and when provoked by a certain decision, they threaten with boycott.

Sports Fan Groups in Serbia

Theoretical explanations of sports fan violence exploring concepts such as anomie, subculture models of collective behavior, imitation, the purifying catharsis model, the model of imperative victory and, finally, models of understanding professional supporters (Koković, 2001) provide important possibilities for research. Mihajlović has created a synthetic index of aggression that he used to classify the spectators at football matches in the following manner: 14% tolerant, 46% mildly aggressive (e.g., wrangles, but do not participate in fights), 23% moderately aggressive (verbal aggression with sporadic participation in fights and throwing objects onto the field of play), 12% fairly aggressive (verbal aggression and throwing objects into the stadium, about 62% of persons belonging to this category are involved in fights occasionally, while 34% participate often), and 5% hooligans—viewers who are the most extreme and very active in all forms of aggressive behavior (1997). It is important to note that hooligans are not particularly interested in the match itself no matter how stressful it can be. Their "show" goes on regardless of the developments on the pitch: fireworks will certainly be used and a specially prepared set design as well. Importantly, both victory and defeat can be used as an excuse for street violence after the match.

According to the Serbian police estimates there are approximately 6000 extreme sports fans. For their purpose the police classified them into three categories: nonviolent—2800 (47%, 67%); potentially violent (against whom criminal or misdemeanor charges were filed, on suspicion that they committed crimes or offenses with elements of violence at sporting events)—1800 (30%); violent (convicted for violence and criminal acts)—1400 (23%, 33%).

The Ministry of the Interior estimates that there are about 40 organized fan groups and subgroups, with about 3000 members, mostly belonging to the violent and potentially violent categories. However, the fact that the members of the nonviolent category are rarely recorded may be one of the possible reasons for the existence of differences between the estimated and the registered numbers.[*]

Although it is true that hooligans are always in the minority, in Serbia they constitute a *considerable* minority that causes serious security problems even abroad. The media reported in detail that the riots in Genoa in October 2010 were caused by approximately 1600 football fans from Serbia, of which 300, split in two groups, blocked city routes, threw firecrackers on passersby, smashed shop windows, destroyed one police car, and wrote graffiti on the walls of the Ducal Palace. In the end, 50 persons were arrested, out of which 33 were released and 17 were kept in remand (Savković, 2010).

The main perpetrators of violence at sports events in Serbia are football fan groups who show a high level of organization. Each group has several hundred of the most extreme fans while there are 10 "leaders" who between themselves have established a hierarchical relationship with an undisputed leader, who in addition to the usual fan activities, starts a conflict with supporters of a rival team, the police, or other extremists. Success and prominence in fights affect the popularity of leaders who, after reaching a certain position in the hierarchy of the group, no longer take an active part, but stand on the sidelines leaving the young to prove themselves. Some of these actors reap more tangible rewards (e.g., tickets, travel to matches abroad) from organizations associated with various clubs (Misić, 2010).

Many authors agree that the visualization of a violent football fan nurtures the stereotype of a Serbian fan that resembles a warrior from the conflicts of the 1990s. The bases of this profile are nationalism, the alleged

---

[*] In public, there are estimates that there are even 15,000 extreme sports fans. However, it is very hard to determine exact numbers due to vague terms and mixing up of the terms *extreme* and *passionate* sports fans.

commitment to Christianity and Orthodoxy, the hate toward the fans of rival clubs, the police, and the government.

Occasionally, conflicts between club management and fan leaders also occurred, mostly because of the privileged position of some leaders, which resulted in the division among the fan groups. A good example is the case of the fans of FC Partizan, which are divided into two groups, the "Gravediggers" and the "Southern Front," whose members often clashed with each other, and in matches where there were no fans of visiting teams, the police had to intervene in conflicts among fans of the same club.

From a security point of view, the fans of Football Club (FC) Rad (Labor) deserve the special attention. Although small in number, with the extreme core having about 80–100 fans, they have participated in a number of riots and fights resulting in serious injuries. A small number of this informal group of supporters belong to "skinheads," with elements of Nazi and chauvinistic ideology, similar to hooligan groups in Germany, with their characteristic appearance (shaved head), dress ("Dr. Martens" boots, camouflage pants, "Spitfire" jackets), and have brutally attacked Roma people, homosexuals, and others.

Sports Fan Violence

It is almost impossible to identify the volume of sports fan violence in Serbia. Due to the lack of methodology for monitoring this phenomenon, a number of unreported cases are not in official records. In 2003 the Serbian Ministry of the Interior began monitoring and recording information about serious incidents at sporting events, which included cases of disturbing public peace and order, as well as criminal offenses with elements of violence. Most serious among those incidents were 10 murders, 5 attempted murders, 43 serious injuries, and 153 injuries. The smallest number of these incidents occurred before the event (122 or 14.69%) while the majority occurred during the events (469 or 56.51%). Based on the number of fatally injured fans in the last seven years, Serbia is in the forefront of the countries in the region and in Europe. However, based on available data it is difficult to directly compare the situation and dimensions of violence and misbehavior of fans in Serbia with Great Britain, Germany, and other European countries.

According to research conducted by the Sports Journalist Association of Serbia in cooperation with the Ministry of Youth and Sports in 2009, every 136 days in Serbia one sports fan was killed, with the attackers mostly aged between 18 and 26 years. The researchers specified numerous reasons for the brutal excesses of hooliganism in Serbia; however, one of the most important is the environment in which the Balkan people have lived during the last 20 years.

Unlike other offenders that avoid contact with the police, the violence of sports fan groups is directed at the police as one target of their aggression. Historically, typical behavior included swearing, insults, throwing objects, and breaking into the venue, and verbal and physical abuse of the match participants (players, officials, and opposing fans). However, since the 1960s more clashes with the police have been registered, as well as riots before and after matches, vandalism, and increased violence expressed toward foreign fans and police (Giulianotti, Bonney, & Hepworth, 1994).

More than one fourth of sport-related crimes are committed against police officers. The antagonism that sports fans have toward the police in other countries in the world is amplified in Serbia due to the legacy of police/citizen relations, as the police were primarily protectors of the political system and the ideology rather than citizens. But even during democratic transition and profound social changes citizens direct their anger about and their dissatisfaction with their social position at the police as the visible representative of the "system." Extreme fans extend this oppositional dichotomy of "us" and "them."*

The Triangle: Sports Fan Violence, Politics, and Crime

Extreme sports fans in Serbia are closely linked to political actors. While the violent behavior of English hooligans is related primarily to heavy drinking, events at the football match, and clashes with the fans of the rival team, in Serbia it is often a function of political aspirations of the sports fans and their leaders. Fans and supporter groups actively participate in public meetings and demonstrations organized by "right-wing" extremist organizations on different occasions including protests against war crime suspects' extradition to the Hague tribunal, gay pride events, and the proclamation of Kosovo independence. Sports fans are present at most public political gatherings in Belgrade. During those events, rivalry and animosity between the supporters of different sport clubs is put aside as they find solidarity in fighting the police, looting, and/or destructing public and private property. Participating in these events is a specific form of political engagement.

---

* For example, 275 criminal charges were filed for obstructing police officers in the performance of their official duties and only in 138 cases have they resulted in charges and passed: the 125 convictions are mostly suspended sentences—85, imprisonment—32, and fines—8. Also, there were 407 submitted criminal charges of assault on a police officer while performing official duties and only in 162 cases have there been accusations, and passed: the 154 convictions, of which the majority are of suspended sentences—90, imprisonment—58, and fines—6. (From *Judiciary statistics*, Year LIX, Report No. 137/2009. http://webrzs.stat.gov.rs/axd/dokumenti/saopstenja/SK12/sk12122008.pdf. Accessed April 30, 2010.)

Links between politics and sports began with the manipulation of sports fans by politicians at the beginning of the dissolution of Yugoslavia, when they were treated as "patriots" and sport was framed as a kind of premilitary training. Football fans had a political role in Serbian society since the early nineties as their members were recruited as volunteers to fight in Yugoslav Wars. One of the most notorious career criminals (Željko Ražnatović Arkan), who was notable for organizing and leading a paramilitary force in the Yugoslav Wars, was also the leader of Delije, the football hooligan firm of the Belgrade club Red Star. He created a paramilitary group named the *Serb Volunteer Guard*,* possibly under the auspices of the Department of State Security,† recruiting members among football fans.

Since Slobodan Milosevic's time political leaders were celebrated in stadiums and over time the chanting of sports fans also marked the beginning of their end. This shift was marked by slogans such as "Slobodan, save Serbia and kill yourself," with subsequent political leaders experiencing a similar fate. This is one, among a number of reasons why the authorities have both a certain hesitation and regard for fans of extreme behavior.

Sports fans had a historic role on October 5, 2000, participating in the Serbian "Velvet Revolution" and overthrow of the regime of Slobodan Milosevic. Extreme fans of the Belgrade clubs Crvena Zvezda, Partizan, and Rad are credited with raiding the Parliament, disarming police officers in the nearby police station, setting a fire, and engaging in acts of theft and damage to public property. For their role in these events, the fan group leaders of Delije-North were given a medal for their contribution in the revolution by B92 Radio.

It should also be noted that leaders of some fan groups have been involved in the security service of Serbian political leaders with some actually becoming politicians. As well, politicians often count on these fans as a significant source of votes and often protect them from prosecution and public condemnation as necessary to ensure their support.

Politicians also serve on the management boards of sport clubs. This intermingling of politics and sports in Serbia in the form of politicians using events as opportunities to lobby for support contributes to the violence (Savković, 2010) and the reluctance of authorities to deal with hooligans. One recent example is the cancellation of the Pride Parade in fear that the nationalist groups that opposed the event might cause incidents. The authorities are

---

* This would later grow into the Special Operations Unit, an elite special unit of the Serbian Service of State Security. Patrons and numerous members of the unit and its predecessors were sentenced, accused, or held responsible for numerous war crimes in the Yugoslav Wars, as well as political assassinations in Serbia. The unit was finally disbanded in March 2003, after the Prime Minister of Serbia, Zoran Đinđić, was assassinated as a result of a conspiracy in which some members of the unit were involved.
† See more at http://www.slobodnaevropa.org/content/article/1329127.html

responsible for creating a social environment in which they seem powerless to prevent vandalism. It might even be said that incidents of hooligan violence serve the authorities as they divert people's attention from the numerous problems that plague Serbian society.

Even in democratic Serbia, the stadiums still remain the most powerful place to instigate a change in club management, change of government, and call for lynching, expression of national identity, as well as the spread of interethnic hatred and intolerance. Thus, for example, sports events in Novi Pazar, a town with a dominant Muslim ethnic minority, are followed by chanting and the display of banners with political, nationalist, or offensive content. Every event related to sports is politicized to such an extent that it may instigate violence that is not limited to the sporting environment.

Sociologists, political scientists, and other researchers of this issue recognize the connection between violent fans and politics. Božovic points out that the problematic fan groups are often being manipulated by political parties, particularly those that have more right-wing perspectives:

> I think that the fans, those who are stressed as a problem are just contractors of those who want to use and abuse them. They originate from the dark space of social uncertainty or internal interests, which is constituted for the sake of the needs of those in power, or in order to win the power.[*]

In that context, the transformation of sports fans is not surprising. The ex-fighters for democracy against the regime of Slobodan Milosevic and active participants in the October changes now locate themselves in a more right political position. It appears that regardless of their claims to patriotism and the national interests of Serbia, these extreme fans are simply finding opportunities to engage in violence. However, it is also possible that the violence disguises real political goals of hooligan groups. Club management boards are made up of politicians, public figures, judges, as well as leaders of hooligan groups.[†]

Apart from politicians, the representatives of other state structures, the judiciary, police, and businessmen, there are also individuals from the criminal milieu involved in the management of sport clubs. In Serbia, sports are becoming a serious business with sports clubs operating as corporations who are engaged in illegal behavior as the financial stakes become higher.

There are some illustrative examples of the criminalization of sports, including the murder of the Secretary General of the Football Association

---

[*] http://www.slobodnaevropa.org/content/tema_sedmice_navijaci_nasilje/1848577.html (accessed October 12, 2009).

[†] Dragaš Drazen, one of them, was in custody for illegal possession of weapons. Red Star spokesman Marko Nikolovski said he would remain a full member of this body because he was only charged but not convicted.

of Serbia and Montenegro (March 2004), the arrest of the president of the Serbian Football Association (2010), as well as the arrest of several managers and trainers suspected of the illegal transfer of football players (Misić, 2010).

Responsibility of the Media

Newspapers, especially tabloids in the UK, have covered hooliganism as a lucrative target for their sensationalistic approach to reporting. This style of reporting often relies on strong headlines using war metaphors, all supported by photographs of riots and fights between sports fans. This style of reporting has developed over the past 50 years and is cited as causing a "moral panic" (Cohen, 1973), being associated with an increase in crime and juvenile delinquency. Some authors argue that sensational tabloid reports encourage hooligans, who then increasingly resort to violence in order to be in the spotlight. Tabloids are often accused of encouraging xenophobia, racism, and other forms of hatred and intolerance through its coverage of hooliganism. For example, before the semifinal between England and Germany during the European Championship EURO 96, in English newspaper headlines appeared "Attention Surrender" ("Achtung Surrender"—*Daily Mirror*, June 24, 1996) and "Surrender Fritz" ("Let's Blitz Fritz"—*Sun*, June 24, 1996.). Tabloids created an atmosphere characterized by language and metaphors that invoked war imagery. English footballers were presented as war heroes who would win over Germany replicating the results of World War II. After the English win, this atmosphere resulted in numerous attacks on fans, the rollover of German vehicles in the streets of London, and ultimately major clashes with police in Trafalgar Square during which about 200 fans were arrested (Gabriel, 1998).

The situation in Serbia is similar. Sports fan groups were presented as fighters for democracy when they clashed with police at the time of Slobodan Milosevic. Sensational headlines in the press were frequent and were generally followed by photographs of explicit violence. Coverage and game broadcasts highlighted scenes of violence in the stands and reflected the generally positive attitude of political leaders and institutions.

A study conducted in 2009 by the Ministry of Youth and the Sport and the Sport Journalists Association analyzed 10 categories of media content: types of violence, direction of violence, causes, actors, victims, relationship to violence, engaging of other parties, understanding, depiction of violence, and checking the facts (Samardžić-Marković, 2009). The most pervasive form of violence covered was physical violence (56.4%), followed by verbal violence (12.1%), and virtual violence through threats (28.3%). Violence was mostly directed toward law enforcement (26.5%), supporters of the rival team (18.8%), and the judiciary (13.8%). The most common cause of violence was conflict that was not connected with the match (59.8%) or even with the sport (26%), while conflict resulting from the competition was much less frequent (8%). The actors engaged in the violence were mostly sports fans (61.8%), athletes (17%), and representatives of sports clubs and associations (14.9%), with general spectators representing the smallest category (1.6%). According to the study, victims of violence were mostly law enforcement personnel (27%) and sports fans (19.1%).

Finally, when it came to the relationship between media and violence, the survey results showed that the Serbian print media* were rather reserved and reluctant to condemn violence. Only 33.1% of the analyzed sample (N500) of newspaper articles† condemned the violence while the passive attitude was present in 51.5% of the analyzed items. However, there were many in-depth articles condemning the violence (45.7%) and trying to explain the behavior (14.8%).

The treatment of this form of violence in the media in Serbia‡ creates and perpetuates a general attitude about sports fans nationally and internationally. In addition, there is the potential for this coverage to contribute to the long-term goal of eliminating this form of violence by shifting the values and attitudes of young, future spectators as well as: organizers, athletes, clubs, officials, general spectators, extreme fans, law enforcement personnel, private security agencies, and court officials.

Sensationalist media representations often provide a distorted image of the violence and misconduct thereby contributing to the popularization of hooliganism and fan groups, and crime as a kind of shortcut for achieving aims that are hard to achieve by legal means.

Investigative journalism is still rare and potentially dangerous in Serbia. In spite of this, one Serbian journalist bravely created a television documentary critical of sports fan violence called *The Impotence of the State* that launched a number of questions on the subject of fan violence. After the airing of the show, the journalist was exposed to numerous threats electronically, by phone text messages, in online forums, and at a football stadium during the match where the rubber doll that represented her was stabbed while the fans were cheering. Although the police filed a criminal complaint for the crime of endangering public safety against six persons, and a prosecutor filed an

---

* Project comprised 500 articles from the daily press and/or their supplements in range from 8% (*Danas* and *Danas Vikend*), 8.4% (*Dnevnik*), 9% (*Press*), 11.4% (*Glas javnosti*), 14.2% (*Blic*), 14.8% (*Kurir*), 15.6% (*Politika*), 17.6% (*Večernje novosti*), and 1% (other newspaper).

† Articles are classified by volume (1—short, 2—middle, and 3—long).

‡ According to the research done by CESID, every ninth article among 23,387 written in the last two years paid attention to extreme sports fans, hooligans, and the police. The majority of articles relate to football fans violence—66%, while unsportsmanlike conduct in basketball comprise 22% of the articles. Every third text referred to sport matches in purely military terms. See more: "Oštrije kazne samo jedno od rešenja nasilja u sportu," *Blic*, November 19, 2008.

indictment, the first court in Belgrade rejected the allegations in the indict-ment on the grounds that this type of case should be prosecuted through private action. The prosecution responded and announced an appeal.

The media are just one of many factors that influence the occurrence and spread of fan violence, but it can also be a very important factor in the prevention of violence and misbehavior of fans, primarily through objective reporting, critical review of incidents, promotion of positive attitudes, and attention to fair play. A positive example of the influence of the media is the reporting on the famous nonviolent Scottish fans' Tartan Army or the Danish Roligans, which stand out as positive role models for other fans. These groups have shown that supporting one's team can be fair, friendly, and free of violence.

The media in Serbia still lack an adequate response to the phenomenon of violence. The initial results of research examining violence in sports that has been undertaken by the Republic Institute for Sports and CESID show that aggressive behavior has become commonplace and that journalists are complicit due to the way they monitor and report on sporting events.[*]

The positive potential of the media lies in the possibility of exercising a kind of pressure on public authorities, government, judiciary, police, sports organizations, and teams to take these issues seriously by passing appropri-ate legislation, improving preventive and repressive activities, and encourag-ing the entire community to act more effectively in the treatment of violence and misbehavior of fans (Misić, 2010).

Social Reaction to Sports Fan Violence

Efforts to address the problem of fan violence on a normative legal level has resulted in the Law on Prevention of Violence and Misbehavior at Sports Events (adopted in 2003), which has undergone several revisions. According to this law, the organizer is the one who "supervises the work of monitors" (Article 3). However, this solution is not appropriate in situations where the by-laws regulating the work of monitors or laws which would regulate the work of the physical security staff do not exist (Savković & Dordevic, 2010). In addition, persons tasked with security and organization of sports events are rarely professionals.

The Draft Law on Sports, the consistent implementation of which should make the proprietary structure of the clubs more transparent, was

---

[*] According to the aforementioned survey 97% of articles do not have assessment of behavior in the game, 83% of articles do not comment on behavior of the public, 83% of articles do not evaluate the organization of the match, 38% of articles discuss the responsibility for the violence, and so on.

adopted in spring 2011. The norms of this piece of legislation established a wide range of both preventive and repressive measures to address violence at sporting events. However, an increasing number of incidents involving violence at sporting events, as well as the perceived vagueness of certain legal provisions, required adoption of new amendments to the Act in 2007 and then 2009.* These changes increased the responsibility of all stakeholders in sports events by introducing more restrictive penal policy. The existing responsibilities of participants in sporting events and the Ministry of the Interior are specified and expanded to be more efficient and effective in reducing the risk of violence and misbehavior of fans and enhancing the powers to address hooliganism. The most important change is the extension of the law to the events outside the sport terrain that are in connection with sports events. However, a major drawback in practice is the regulation of the powers, responsibilities, and tasks of private security agencies in the absence of specific law regulating this area.

Meanwhile, it seems that the main problem is not associated with normative regulation, but is the implementation and application of laws in penal policies and judiciary practices. The Minister of Sport in Serbia has stressed that a court ruling was made in only 2.4% of cases, which is an implicit confirmation that the suppression of hooligan violence has not been on the state priority list in recent years (Savković, 2010). The following case is, therefore, paradigmatic. In December 2007, Uroš Mišić, a fan of the soccer club Crvena Zvezda, tried to kill gendarme Nebojša Trajković, putting a lit torch in his mouth during a football match in Belgrade. The gendarme was seriously injured. This case received tremendous publicity[†] and was condemned by the general public. However, there were other reactions as well. On fan blogs one could read messages such as "He got what he was looking for," while graffiti appeared throughout Serbia demanding "Justice for Uros." Even the football players of Crvena Zvezda began wearing T-shirts with the slogan "Justice for Uros" and were fined $1500 for their behavior. On the other hand, in official reactions the Ministry of Justice, judges, and prosecutors condemned these acts as unacceptable. Various pressures on the court were recorded including banners at the stadium with threats to the judge in charge. Mišić was convicted on two charges resulting in a 10-year prison term, which is the minimum legal sentence for attempted murder. However, the Appellate Court cut his sentence in half, lessening the charge from attempted murder to assault on a police officer in performing official tasks. As a result, gendarme Trajković is planning to leave Serbia and seek political asylum in a foreign country.

* Službeni glasnik RS, br. 111/09.
† On Google there are more than 350,000 results connected with the case.

The Constitutional Court is debating banning a number of football organizations; however, as noted by Serbian Ombudsman Saša Janković, bans are not a cure for the sickness but for the pain, having in mind that fostering a culture of respect for human rights is much more important.

Concluding Remarks

The most relevant and the most frequently employed models for an understanding of fan violence and misbehavior relate to subculture norms, mass psychology, and other deviant models of behavior. In the case of Serbia, however, it seems that anomie theory and Durkheim's discussion of "social facts" in a transitional crisis provide helpful explanations for the escalation of violence and misbehavior of fans and the associated conditions and dimensions of this problem.

The context in which sports fan violence occurs is marked by the heritage of ethnic conflicts, political instability, and weak social and political institutions. This violence should be seen in the larger cultural climate in the former Yugoslavia, which is dominated by postwar trauma due to the absence of dealing with criminal responsibility, lack of reconciliation, interethnic hostility, and feelings of hopelessness due to the extremely problematic transition. For youngsters growing up in this atmosphere characterized by the isolation of the country and associated lack of opportunities to travel around the world, violence is becoming a kind of subcultural symbol: the valve for frustration and the mechanism that they use to establish their own principles of justice and system of values as opposed to officially accepted norms. The slow and inefficient transition of values and institutions in Serbian society has been accompanied by numerous problems that have impacted the real and perceived safety of citizens. The crisis of morality and social values, unemployment, increasing numbers of poor, difficulties in the functioning of state bodies, marginalized status of the youth, and especially the rise of violence continue to shape social and political responses to the more specific issues associated with fan violence.

The police are a critical institution in addressing the problem of sports fan violence, but the police alone cannot solve this complex social problem, especially given the enormity of the social conditions described above. In the situation where there is no consistent state policy and clear strategy, where different influences and interests are in place, followed by conflicting actions and rhetoric of the state (police, prosecutor, courts) and non-state (sport clubs and associations, media) actors it is almost impossible to address the problem of fan violence.

What is necessary is the holistic approach and political will. In addition to the existing strategies, the adoption of national strategies for prevention of violence and misbehavior seems the only possible and acceptable solution, which would be a competent and comprehensive way to address the problem of hooliganism. This strategy should include a wide network of actors, working together as partners and sharing the system of values in which violence is not acceptable. These efforts should be based on scientific approach, comparative research, and best practice, referring to legislative measures, organizational coordination, new role of the media, responsible politics, efficient judiciary, education and social stigmatization of violence, and promotion of tolerance.

References

Armstrong, G., & Giulianotti, R. (1999). *Football cultures and identities*. Basingstoke: Macmillan.

Cohen, S. (1973). *Folk devils and moral panics*. St. Albans: Paladin.

Gabriel, J. (1998). *Whitewash: Radicalized politics and the media*. London: Routledge.

Giulianotti, R., Bonney, N., & Hepworth, M. (1994). *Football violence and social identity*. London: Routledge.

Ignjatović, D. M. (1998). *Organizovani kriminalitet*. Beograd: Policijska Akademija.

Koković, D. (2001). Nasilje sportske publike. *Defendologija*, 4(10), 9–29.

Harnischmacher, R., & Apel, I. (1989). *Huligan i njegov svjetonazor u okviru nogometnog vandalizma*. Izbor 2.

Mihajlović, S. (1997). *Rat je počeo na maksimiru*. Belgrade: Media Center.

Misić, Z. (2010). *Nasilje i nedolično ponašanje navijača kao faktor ugrožavanja bezbednosti* (Violence and Misbehaviour of Fans as a Factor Jeopardising Security), Master's Thesis, Belgrade University, Faculty of Security, Belgrade.

Samardžić-Marković, S. (2009). Media, sport and violence—Research project. Ministry of Youth and Sport. Found at: http://www.mos.gov.rs/preuzmi/mediji_sport_nasilje_prezentacija.

Savković, M. (2010). Kontekst i implikacije huliganskog nasilja u Srbiji. *Bezbednost Zapadnog Balkana*, 5(18), 91–99.

Savkovic, M., & Dordevic, S. (2010). *Toward the prevention of violent acts at sports events: Proposal on regional cooperation framework*. Belgrade: Belgrade Centre for Security Policy.

Žugić, Z. (1996). *Uvod u sociologiju sporta*. Zagreb: Fakultet za fizičku kulturu.

About the Authors

Kesetović Želimir, Sladjana Djurić, and Vladimir Cvetković are on the Faculty of Security Studies at the University of Belgrade in Serbia.

The Planning and Execution of Security for the 2010 Winter Olympic Games in Canada

6

DARRYL PLECAS, MARTHA C. DOW,
AND JORDAN DIPLOCK

Contents

Introduction

The overwhelming success of the 2010 Winter Olympic Games, hosted by Vancouver, Canada, was noted around the world (Bellett, 2010). A contributing factor to the success of the Games was the fact that the Royal Canadian Mounted Police (RCMP)* led Vancouver 2010 International Security Unit (ISU) was successful in fulfilling its mandate to secure the Winter Games

---

* The Royal Canadian Mounted Police is Canada's national police force. It is one of many police forces in Canada, and provides police service to Canadians through federal policing, as well as provincial and municipal police contracts.

and to do it in a manner that was responsive to threat assessments, fiscal realities, and providing the least restrictive venue access possible for the public. The task of providing security operations for a major event such as the Winter Games had very clear challenges, not the least of which is the sheer magnitude of the event and the consequent complexities of the planning and execution of the associated operations. It is the focus of this chapter to document the perceptions of those most intimately involved with this undertaking as they relate to "what went right?" and "what could have gone better?" with the goal of capturing the lessons learned in a meaningful and useful manner to support the security operations associated with future major events.

Currently, the existing literature on providing security for major events on the scale of the Olympic Games is relatively scarce. In general, this lack of accessible information is not due to low levels of interest, but rather that detailed security information is often not made public (Samatas, 2007; Thompson, 2008). Further, the expertise gained through the exercise of planning and executing a major security project may be too valuable to share openly. Indeed, many host nations use the Olympic Games as an opportunity to substantially upgrade their security infrastructure and gain knowledge and technologies that can be marketed globally in the aftermath of the Games (Boyle & Haggerty, 2009). Therefore, while there is an enormous legacy value that accompanies each successive Olympic Games, there is the risk that some of the most valuable lessons learned through securing these events will be inaccessible to future planners who could potentially make costly and time-consuming mistakes that could have otherwise been avoided had information been available. It is the goal of this chapter to add legacy to a growing body of knowledge on major event security by highlighting the most impactful lessons learned during the planning and execution of the security project for the 2010 Winter Olympic Games.

The information presented in this chapter came about as a result of the ISU's interest in an independent evaluation and documentation of its work as the section responsible for the planning and execution of Games security. While there are always lessons to be learned from any security operation, in the case of an event the size of the Olympics, those lessons are magnified because of the heightened interest of the public, the enormous fiscal commitments, and the international nature of the event. In some cases, the lessons learned discussed in this chapter simply reflect processes and structural responses that worked well and should be integrated into the planning of future major events. In other cases, the lessons learned capture suggestions for how the planning and execution of security operations could have been improved.

Methodology

The study incorporated multiple data collection strategies, both quantitative and qualitative; to examine the perceived successes and challenges associated with the security operations of the ISU. The methodology employed to carry out the original evaluation included in-person interviews of key stakeholders; a survey of security personnel; a content analysis of media coverage; statistical analysis of crime and security data; and a clipboard survey of visitors to the Games. Given the focus of this chapter, the methodologies that informed the main findings presented here were the in-person interviews and security personnel surveys.

The in-person interviews were conducted with 100 lead planners, commanders, and other individuals having a key role in the planning and/or the execution of Games security. These interviews were guided by a series of questions focusing on how interviewees felt about their readiness to take on their respective roles, what they saw as their most significant challenges, what went especially right, what went wrong, what they would do differently if starting over, what did they see as lessons learned, and what they saw as legacies (if any) for the planning and execution of future major events. A purposive sampling technique was used in an effort to identify a pool of participants that reflected the complexities of the functions of the security operations for the Games. All of the selected participants contacted agreed to be interviewed.

A survey of security personnel was conducted of the 4000 police officers deployed to the Games, 3500 of whom were housed on accommodation vessels docked in Vancouver and 500 of whom were housed in rented private accommodation and hotels in Whistler. Each of these officers received a questionnaire asking them to assess their work assignment, their food and lodging, the impact of their deployment on family and home detachment work demands, and their experiences in general. Overall, 38% (1514) of the officers responded and an analysis of the response rate confirmed that those responding are generally representative of police deployed from across Canada and across police agencies. Additionally, it would appear that respondents were representative in terms of gender (20% were female), RCMP/Municipal members (25% were Municipal officers), and area deployment (12% were based in Whistler).

This chapter will highlight seven key themes that surfaced in our analysis of the data: organizational structure, finances, intelligence, exercises, community relations, staffing, and the impact of major event deployment on security personnel. These themes were viewed as the most significant components of the planning and securing of a major event such as the Olympic Games.

Organizational Structure

Leading a major event security project involves taking responsibility for both the planning and the execution of the many aspects of security for the event. This requires an organizational structure for both major phases; one that is capable of coordinating with a wide range of government and nongovernment partners. While accessing information on governmental organizations established to coordinate Olympic security can be a challenge (Thompson, 2008), this section provides a brief background on the organization structure of ISU and the importance of its legacy.

Planning Stage

In response to its lead role, the RCMP, through a combined effort of both the national major events unit and the division responsible for policing in the province of British Columbia, established the Integrated Security Unit (ISU), the umbrella organization responsible for securing the Games. The ISU, which was established in 2003, was eventually structured with an assistant commissioner at its helm and was focused on the monumental task of planning for the Games. Accordingly, the organization was initially staffed by a collection of planners. This first wave of planners was responsible for developing the plans needed to execute security leading up to and during the Games including the establishment of the requirements associated with intelligence, mobilization, accreditation, transportation, accommodation, logistics, and informatics. Overall, by the time the Games started, the planning contingent of staff had grown to more than 500 police officers, civilian members, government personnel, and contracted employees.

While the internal command structure and its associated authority lines were clearly delineated and generally understood, the same was not entirely true for reporting lines and mandates external to the ISU. This was made particularly challenging due to the nature of policing within the RCMP, as it is the accepted practice that operations are almost always the domain of the particular division and in many cases the particular detachment involved, and that the national headquarters' role is to serve as a policy center. There was a persistent theme in many of our interviews that described concerns about the national unit overstepping in its involvement with the operations of the ISU. Ironically, the mandate of the national unit clearly articulates its primary and significant role in the planning, budgeting, and oversight of any major events.

As outlined in the conclusion of this chapter, it is our view that the challenge of clearly determining and communicating the roles and responsibilities of the national and division command structures need to be addressed. We highlight the need for a national enhanced project management office that houses expertise and resources capable of fulfilling the range of support functions that would play a major role in all future major event planning.

Operations Stage—Command and Control Model

Central to the organizational structure of the ISU was the command model for the execution of security. The command model integrated the primacy of localized (ground level) decision making, a tiered authority and resource structure to respond to any escalation of circumstances, and clear lines of responsibility. Given the other policing and security partners, the command structure emphasized respectful and collaborative relations with the police of jurisdiction.

More specifically, the command model consisted of what were called *Gold*, *Silver*, and *Bronze* command levels. These levels were not related to a hierarchy as the name and Olympic symbolism may suggest. The venue level command, led by Bronze Commanders, was responsible for security operations at the venues within the theater of operations. In the event that additional resources were needed to respond to situations in one of the two Olympic areas (Whistler or Metro Vancouver), the area command level, headed up by Silver Commanders, was responsible for ensuring that the appropriate resources were deployed (i.e., emergency response teams). The Gold command, through its Gold Commanders, was responsible for having a readiness to respond to a catastrophic event and/or the need to employ air defense resources and respond to government queries, generally originating in the Prime Minister's Office (PMO), regarding security issues during the Games. During the Games, the Silver and Gold Commanders worked inside their respective command centers, while Bronze Commanders worked on site at their respective venues.

Overall, the command model received very favorable reviews and seemed to work effectively in terms of organizational expectations, lines of authority, and responsiveness to security-related concerns. However, individuals at both Gold and Silver command levels reported feeling and sometimes succumbing to the temptation, that is so characteristic of the task-oriented culture of policing, to lean into a different lane. The challenges with respect to "staying in your lane" were exacerbated by the relative quiet, from a security point of view that characterized the Games. Without exception, the Silver and Gold Commanders expressed a need to do more and a concomitant concern that they were not doing enough.

A final theme that arose in many of our interviews with commanders was that there were possible redundancies in the operationalization of the model. This sense of redundancy arose as a direct result of the high level of activity in the command center during the three major exercises prior to the Games juxtaposed to the actual low incidence of security issues during the Games period. In fact, this relative quiet in the command centers should not be expected for other major events and thus, what appeared to be a redundancy in the command and control model should not be concluded as such.

Overall, it would appear that the command structure provided a model that has tremendous legacy value as it embodied a successful organizational structure, which is operationally responsive to the key parameters associated with the planning and execution of security for major events.

Finances

When the city of Vancouver submitted its bid to host the 2010 Winter Olympic Games, the cost of providing security for the event was estimated at approximately $175,000,000—one-third of the final actual budget of $558,000,000. Given this difference, it is easy to understand the questions that arose with respect to the process undertaken to reach that initial estimate. However, even with the additional costs related to the involvement of the Canadian Forces, in comparison to other recent, post-9/11 Olympic security expenditures,* the 2010 Olympic Security Project was modest.

In the preplanning process or the initiation phase of a project of this magnitude, planners would normally have referred to the $175,000,000 as "indicative funding." That is, funding that is knowingly based on cost estimates which are bald of detail and options analysis, but which is expected to grow upward as the planning process facilitates the ability to review options and provide detailed information.

One of the most important lessons to be learned from the security planning experience for the 2010 Winter Games is that prior to the initiation phase a clearly understood financial responsibility matrix must be developed to give clarity on the matter of who is ultimately paying for what. Further, no discussion about finances associated to the planning and execution of major events would be complete without calling attention to the matter of threat level determination and what it means in terms of security costs. The cost of providing security for any major event is driven largely by a threat level established by organizers of the event. In the case of the 2010 Winter Games, a threat level was established very early in the process and planning was conducted based on that level and with a view to providing some readiness to move to a higher level if needed or to scale back in some respects to a lower level if possible.

---

* 2002 Salt Lake City: US$310 Million; 2004 Athens: US$1.5 Billion; 2006 Turin: US$1.4 Billion; 2008 Beijing: US$6.5 Billion; and 2012 London: estimated and likely to escalate from US$2.2 Billion (Decker, Varano, & Greene, 2007; Giulianotti & Klauser, 2010; Johnson, 2006).

Intelligence

Intelligence is the single most important component in preparing for and responding to security-related threats for any given major event. More specifically, it is this intelligence and the subsequent threat assessments that drive both the level and the nature of security required to provide a safe and secure event.

There are multiple agencies sharing responsibility in assessing threat to public safety. While major events such as the Olympics may in themselves generate an increased level of threat, the reality is that threats to national security exist and are monitored on an ongoing basis. For the 2010 Games and previous Olympics, intelligence to secure the Games involved input from a number of international agencies (Migdalovitz, 2004; Samatas, 2007; Thompson, 2008; Yu, Klauser, & Chan, 2009). The cornerstone of the intelligence function for the Winter Games was forming an intelligence group that drew upon existing expertise and resources in a manner which would facilitate a responsive, effective intelligence infrastructure. For the ISU, this model was known as the Joint Intelligence Group (JIG). The JIG processes and functions were in place prior to Canada's hosting the G8 Summit in 2002 and were further refined for that event, and then became the basis for the model employed at the Winter Games. It is important to emphasize that, due to the nature of intelligence, the group responsible for this function for any major event must build upon existing intelligence business lines and be established well in advance of the planning stages of the major event. In the case of the JIG, intelligence gathering started as early as six years prior to the Games.

While one of the challenges the JIG faced was the apparent need for better communication, communicating threat levels is not a simple matter. While on the surface it may seem to be a straightforward function of classifying information into a low, medium, or high threat level, a combination of the physical event area, the changing situation around the world, and the level of internationally protected persons (IPP) attending, all need to be individually and then collectively considered. Not only do venue resources need to be scalable to possible shifts in threat requirements, command resources need to be scalable according to which IPP attends which venues. Communicating this in a briefing to event planners is a fundamentally important yet incredibly complex task, particularly given some of the sensitivities associated with the dissemination of intelligence information. One of the most significant challenges facing any intelligence-centered agency or group is the tendency to be overly concerned with "the need to know" sometimes to the detriment of effectively sharing intelligence information.

While it is fair to say that in the future the JIG needs to be more attentive to communicating threat levels, ultimately, those providing intelligence are not the ones deciding how to use the information. There is a natural inclination of people to think in terms of higher, rather than lower levels of risk. This is especially the case in the years following 9/11 and given the previous attacks that have occurred against the Olympics (Bolye & Haggerty, 2009; Johnson, 2006). Therefore, it is critical that those responsible for acting on the intelligence information provided must be positioned in terms of experience, expertise, and leadership style to make intelligence-based decisions.

Exercises

Exercises, in the context of major events, involve practicing both the planned procedures and the execution of the plan prior to the actual event. Establishing exercises to test operational plans is essential in highlighting the aspects of the plan that are working effectively as well as those components that need to be modified. It follows that exercising a plan or model of response as early as possible in the planning process is critical to the ability of planners to use the information accrued through the exercise. The results generated from exercises not only help to modify potential shortcomings of security measures, but extend to possibly influencing everything from identified resource requirements to financial costs. In short, exercises should be considered one of the most important components in planning a major event.

The ISU had a team dedicated to the planning of several large exercises. Ultimately, the goal of the Exercise team was to exercise the 48 plans and 110 standard operating procedures (SOPs) that had been produced within the ISU as well as the plans of integrated external partners as they related to the possible threat to security being considered in planning. While it would seem that the plans produced internally were not as timely as they needed to be, it is not an exaggeration to say that the external agencies were not able to bring any meaningful plans to the table.

While the objective of the Exercise team was to plan overarching ISU exercises to integrate the various plans of action, exercising specific plans of action was the responsibility of the respective planning units. It was evident that there was inadequate attention paid to the need to exercise plans specific to particular functional areas. It would seem reasonable that a greater emphasis on more micro level exercises might have highlighted the need for the more timely completion of plans.

It seems very clear that the Exercise team should have reduced the emphasis placed on exercising major catastrophes and increased its attention to more likely events such as the late arrival of a motorcade or a lost child. It seemed that there were few (if any) exercises executed to cover the mundane events. This being said, this concern could be partially addressed by ensuring individual units understand that their role includes relevant exercises as it is arguable that practicing routine events in a venue could be the responsibility of a Venue Commander. Of course there is a need to have a clear understanding of what to do should a catastrophic event take place, but attention to this should be guided by existing intelligence.

Community Relations

The primary responsibility of the Community Relations Group (CRG) was to engage with key community stakeholders regarding security-related concerns for the Games. The obvious goal of this work was to minimize the number and nature of contentious issues and situations that would inevitably arise given the magnitude of the Games. This chapter highlights three key themes that consistently arose in conversations about the role of community relations: integrating the CRG within the command structure; maintaining the distinction between the goals and functions of Community Relations and that of Public Affairs; and developing more effective mechanisms to share timely and accurate information with key stakeholders.

An overarching philosophical and operational approach to all areas of the ISU was the differentiation and ultimately transition from the planning phase to the execution phase. However, unlike so many other areas, CRG required an uninterrupted flow of information and continuity of messaging and personnel that was outside this more dichotomous model of before and during the Games. While there did not appear to be any disagreement about the need for continuity as the CRG worked with key stakeholder groups before and during the Games, a key practical challenge quickly surfaced as the command structure was installed and became operational. While the Command and Control plan had the CRG reporting to the Gold command, it appeared that operationally the CRG needed to have a mechanism or position that could liaise more directly with the Venue Commanders as they responded to what were more venue-specific community relations issues. There were a number of comments that pointed to a persistent frustration that so much of the ground work completed in advance of the Games with business and community groups was threatened and sometimes undone by Venue Commanders not accessing the CRG as a resource as situations arose in and around the venues.

A second major theme revolved around the challenges associated with maintaining the community relations mandate in the face of pressure to engage in more public relations type activities (e.g., acting as media contacts). Clearly, community relations activities are not organized around message management, but rather they are based on relationship development achieved primarily through the sharing of meaningful, accurate, and timely information. It was the impression of members of the CRG that this critical differentiation in role and responsibilities was at risk of being collapsed under the umbrella of Public Affairs for future major events. All evidence from this evaluation would suggest that abandoning the model of a separate and responsive CRG would immediately and negatively impact the ability of members to function effectively to minimize community-based tensions that may impact the security of any major event.

Finally, while the Command and Control plan articulated strategies to share information with key stakeholders there was a clear and consistent message from interviewees that in practical terms, this was a major source of frustration for both the CRG and for those community members and groups seeking clarity on everything from road closures to fence lines. It is this latter example that most clearly exemplifies the challenges faced by the CRG and indeed the ISU as it tried to keep the public generally and key stakeholders more specifically informed.

In some cases, the CRG was actively trying to attain the information regarding the security footprint and it was simply not finalized for public consumption. In other cases the CRG found itself having to aggressively present the case for disseminating information that community members needed, but that security stakeholders, internal and external to the ISU, were resisting the release because of perceived sensitivities with respect to security information.

Staffing

In the years leading up to the 2010 Winter Games, the task of hiring the workforce needed to plan the event resided with the Human Resources and Career Development team. The lengthy lead up to the Games and the magnitude of the planning workforce presented this team with an enormous challenge. Those responsible for staffing the ISU started with no job descriptions and no template from which to work. Essentially, people were brought into the organization knowing the general direction and goal of the ISU, but without details on their roles and responsibilities.

The job classifications were not based on rank, but were intended to be based on skills and experience. The expectation that rank would not factor into working relationships between job functions in an integrated unit posed considerable challenges, many of which may have been overcome by better incorporating rank and promotions into important planning positions in the organization. Admittedly, incorporating rank or promotions into the process may have added to the difficulty already inherent in competing with other policing units and functions for qualified personnel in the years prior to the Olympics.

The Human Resources and Career Development team hired more than 600 people for jobs within the ISU and had to plan for both the intake of the planning workforce and the exit strategy to decommission the organization at the conclusion of the Olympics. These tasks were largely successful, and the human resourcing plan will most certainly be used for future major events in Canada. In the end, after starting without job descriptions, 300 were developed to better articulate the roles and responsibilities associated with major events planning.

Mobilizing the Security Workforce and Command Center Staff

To police the 2010 Olympic Winter Games, the ISU mobilized a total workforce of more than 5600 police officers from across Canada in addition to a private security force of 6000 employees. These numbers are on par with those from Sydney (5000 police and 7000 contract employees; Giulianotti & Klauser, 2010), Salt Lake City (12,000 total police, military, federal, and volunteer security personnel; Decker et al., 2007), and Turin (15,000 law enforcement and military personnel; Johnson, 2006), but are dwarfed by those from Beijing (approximately 110,000 security personnel; Giulianotti & Klauser, 2010) and the FIFA World Cup in South Africa (40,000 police, 50,000 reservists, and thousands of additional security agents; Giulianotti & Klauser, 2010). These police officers from across Canada were meant to fill positions as outlined in the Olympic security plans for the multiple venues, command centers, and specialized support units. The responsibility for filling these positions, mobilizing all of the necessary policing resources from across the country, scheduling their travel, and planning their shifts resided in the Mobilization unit of the ISU. An additional force of 950 police officers had to be arranged as a contingency force that could be deployed to the Games within 72 hours if they were needed.

By any measure the task was incredibly complicated. Therefore, in the future, ensuring that enough resources are dedicated to the task of mobilizing the workforce is critical to reducing the impact of some of these challenges. Importantly, mobilization represents an excellent example of the need for a detailed options analysis to explore "build" options as well as "buy" options.*

Although the security workforce was comprised of police personnel running the spectrum of ranks, the majority of security positions were not filled based on the person's specific skill sets. Due to the importance of securing a major event, there can be a tendency to want to fill all of the important positions with senior personnel who bring with them the previous experience that is critical to performing key roles. These people are invaluable to and often hold high ranks within their respective organizations. However, in order to maintain a high level of major event experience

---

* With "build" referring to fulfilling the role in-house and "buy" referring to entering into a service contract.

within policing organizations, the task of staffing important positions in both planning and operations requires balancing the present and future needs of policing organizations. Therefore, incorporating personnel with less experience into learning and developmental roles allows for the transmission of vital knowledge and experience from those in key leadership positions in the hope of developing future leaders. This was one of the key considerations when filling positions in the ISU for the 2010 Olympics. The importance of cultivating tacit knowledge within the organization in addition to documenting formal knowledge was also emphasized by Boyle and Haggerty (2009) in their discussion of legacy value of major security events in Canada and the United States.

Impact of Major Event Deployment on Police Personnel

Staffing the security component of a major event on the scale of the Olympic Games is an undertaking rife with challenges. In addition to enlisting enough police and other security personal and mobilizing that security workforce from all across Canada, there were many other concerns that naturally accompanied such a large-scale, long-term deployment. Those planning for this event were aware that there would be difficulties facing a workforce that was living and working away from their families and their home detachments for several weeks; however, the impact of this type of deployment on a police workforce had not been previously documented.

The primary source of information used to explore these issues was a survey of police personnel who participated in the security workforce for the 2010 Olympic Winter Games. The survey asked respondents to provide feedback about their opinions and experiences with regard to their work assignments, living accommodations, and the impact of the deployment on their home lives. Given the legacy value of maintaining tacit knowledge, the focus will be placed on those factors that were associated with responses that indicated a person would volunteer to participate again in a major security event.

In order to provide security for the Olympics, police officers from all across Canada had to leave their home lives and put their work at their home police departments on hold. When assembling such a large security workforce, it is inevitable that important policing resources are going to be drawn from their respective departments, leaving those police forces under increased strain throughout the deployment. In general, the police personnel deployed for the 2010 Games were very experienced, with 61% of the workforce sample having more than 10 years police service. Therefore, not only were a large number of policing resources temporarily removed from police work across Canada, but also, many were taken from leadership or specialized roles.

In addition to being police personnel, the security workforce was naturally made up of people with families and social responsibilities. More than 90% of the responding security workforce indicated that they were involved in a committed relationship, and the majority (67%) of respondents indicated that they had at least one dependent. It is important to recognize that a large-scale and long-term security deployment for a major event like the Olympics will affect a large number of police personnel and their families, potentially in a negative way.

The majority of respondents found the deployment disruptive to their home life responsibilities (71%), their social lives (60%), and their ongoing workload (51%). Fewer respondents (18%) reported that the deployment would impact their relationships with coworkers in their home departments. Those who found the deployment disruptive to their home, social, and work lives were less likely to agree that they would volunteer to work a major event again. However, 60% of those who found the deployment disruptive still indicated that they would volunteer for a future major event. This finding demonstrates that even though a major event deployment can be disruptive to the majority of the workforce, there may be benefits to the deployment that can compensate for that disruption.

Predictably, there was a relationship between a respondent's level of agreement that the work assignment was enjoyable and the likelihood that the respondent would agree to volunteer again.[*] Of course, it may be impractical to assume that, amid all of the competing challenges of policing a major event, measures can be taken to increase the level of enjoyment related to their work assignments felt by police personnel working as part of the security workforce. However, it may be possible to offset some of the more negative aspects of some work assignments by ensuring that other factors related to the deployment are more positive. For example, respondents' overall satisfaction with their accommodation was related to whether or not they would volunteer for a future major event. Those who were satisfied or very satisfied with their accommodations were much more likely to agree that they would volunteer for a future major event than those who were dissatisfied.[†] Satisfaction with many other factors contributed to the overall satisfaction with the accommodations including the comfort,[‡] privacy,[§] level of noise,[¶] roommates,[**] cleanliness,[††] security of belongings,[‡‡] and the quality of

---

[*] (Gamma = .515, approx. Sig: 0.000).
[†] (Gamma = 0.454, approx. Sig: 0.000).
[‡] (Gamma = 0.849, approx. Sig: 0.000).
[§] (Gamma = 0.841, approx. Sig: 0.000).
[¶] (Gamma = 0.626, approx. Sig: 0.000).
[**] (Gamma = 0.593, approx. Sig: 0.000).
[††] (Gamma = 0.538, approx. Sig: 0.000).
[‡‡] (Gamma = 0.537, approx. Sig: 0.000).

the food.[*] Although accommodating such a large workforce can pose major challenges during an event like the Olympic Games, it appears that paying attention to the quality of accommodations may greatly affect the likelihood of encouraging personnel to volunteer for future events.

In summary, it was evident that there is a certain appeal to participating in a major event that exists despite any negatives with respect to work assignments and disruption to home life. One of the main findings of the survey clearly indicated that those who joined the security workforce believing that there would be benefits generally had those expectations fulfilled. There was a strong relationship between a respondent's level of agreement that they had volunteered to participate and their level of agreement that they would volunteer to participate in a future major event.[†] Of the 988 respondents who agreed or strongly agreed that they volunteered to participate, 758 (77%) agreed or strongly agreed that they would volunteer for a future major event. This relationship remains strong even for those respondents who indicated that the deployment was disruptive to their home life responsibilities.[‡] This finding further emphasizes the importance of volunteering and properly managing those who willingly attend special events to the overall success of a major event deployment that has been discussed in previous special event literature (Nichols & Ojala, 2009). For future major events, emphasis should be placed on ensuring the workforce consists of as many genuine volunteers as possible. This strategy would alleviate some of the challenges involved in mobilization and help to ensure overall satisfaction with the deployment. Finally, this emphasis on volunteerism will build a contingent of police personnel across the country with major event experience that have a willingness to participate in future major events.

Conclusion

The purpose of this chapter was to share some of the lessons learned through the planning and execution of the security project for the Vancouver Olympic Winter Games. The methodology employed in this study has provided a comprehensive examination of the operations associated with the Integrated Security Unit in the planning and execution of security for the Games. It is clear that the most critical elements of major event planning revolve around organizational structure, financial accountability, threat assessment, communication, and human resources.

There are several important lessons that can be gleaned from the findings of the work presented here. Importantly, roles, responsibilities, and

---

[*] (Gamma = 0.479, approx. Sig: 0.000).
[†] (Gamma = 0.627, approx. Sig: 0.000).
[‡] (Gamma = 0.605, approx. Sig: 0.000).

reporting lines need to be clearly articulated throughout the security organization to avoid confusion and the perception of multiple and competing authorities. Ensuring there is a clearly defined responsibility for funding is also essential, as security expenditures run the risk of "ballooning" quickly if planners are not controlled by checks and balances that emphasize the importance of both intelligence-based threat levels and fiscal responsibility. This is just one aspect of why intelligence is of vital importance to the success of a major event security operation. However, in order to ensure that the necessary precautions are taken and security is optimized to the appropriate threat level, clear communication of threat is critical, as is an organization-wide understanding of the meaning of the various threat levels. The importance of intelligence is further emphasized by the necessity to have well-prepared exercises that are built around timely plans and appropriate scenarios. It is also important to maintain a well-informed community relations group throughout both the planning and operational phases of the project; one that is distinctly positioned apart from the role of public relations. Finally, it is critical to promote the retention of knowledge and expertise through staffing practices that emphasize mentorship and a reliance on willing volunteers.

Our examination of all of the "lessons learned" highlights a central finding that underpins all of the issues identified and provides a framework for change that would ensure that the legacy of the Games is not lost as individuals and groups try to reinvent the wheel. The overarching recommendation is that a central unit or organization dedicated to major event planning should exist in order to perform the functions of a support and resource center that would aid in the planning for and execution of security for future major events. This unit would be positioned to be more heavily involved in the initiation stages of the planning for any major event and then transition to assume a support and resource function as the local authorities move forward operationally. A project management orientation would emphasize options analysis within a context that situates risk at its foundation with attentiveness to rigorous and timely definitions of project scope, timelines, financial parameters as well as human resource considerations, communication strategies, and procurement policies. Perhaps most importantly, this model would ensure that the legacy value of major security events will not be lost and will instead be the foundation for the planning and operations for all future major events.

References

Bellett, G. (March 1, 2010). Early critics among world media change their tune. *Vancouver Sun*. Retrieved October 1, 2010 from: http://www.vancouversun.com/sports/Early +critics+among+world+media+change+their+ tune/2626815/story.html

Boyle, P., & Haggerty, K. D. (2009). Spectacular security: Mega-events and the security complex. *International Political Sociology, 3*, 257–274.

Decker, S. H., Varano, S. P., & Greene, J. R. (2007). Routine crime in exceptional times: The impact of the 2002 Winter Olympics on citizens demand for police services. *Journal of Criminal Justice, 35*(1), 89–101.

Guilianotti, R., & Klauser, F. (2010). Security governance and sport mega-events: Toward an interdisciplinary research agenda. *Journal of Sport and Social Issues, 34*(1), 49–61.

Johnson, C. W. (2006). A Brief Overview of Technical and Organisational Security at Olympic Events. Retrieved September 8, 2009 from: http://www.dcs.gla.ac.uk/~johnson/papers/CW_Johnson_Olympics.pdf

Migdalovitz, C. (2004). Greece: Threat of Terrorism and Security at the Olympics. *CRS Report for Congress.* Retrieved September 8, 2009 from: http://www.dtic.mil/cgi-bin/GetTRDoc?Location=U2&doc=GetTRDoc.pdf&AD=ADA444831

Nichols, G., & Ojala, E. (2009). Understanding the management of sports events volunteers through psychological contract theory. *Voluntas: International Journal of Voluntary and Nonprofit Organizations, 20*(4), 369–387.

Samatas, M. (2007). Security and surveillance in the Athens 2004 Olympics: Some lessons from a troubled story. *International Criminal Justice Review, 17*(3), 220–238.

Thompson, D. (2008). Olympic security collaboration. *China Security, 4*(2), 46–58.

Yu, Y., Klauser, F., & Chan, G. (2009). Governing security at the 2008 Beijing Olympics. *The International Journal of the History of Sport, 26*(3), 390–405.

About the Authors

Darryl Plecas, Martha C. Dow, and Jordan Diplock are researchers at the Centre for Public Safety and Criminal Justice Research at the University of the Fraser Valley in British Columbia, Canada.

Policing Major Events in Australia

7

A Private Security Model of Police Cooperation

RICK SARRE

Contents

Introduction

Can police alone solve the problem of violence and disorder? The simple answer is no. Indeed, governments and private citizens are now relying more and more upon private security personnel for their protection and crime prevention. But risks to policing "legitimacy" arise when private agents assume general policing tasks, especially given the scandals over security officer conduct in recent years in Australia. There has been, for example, the infiltration of nightclub security by organized crime figures trading in illicit drugs. There have been widespread problems with serious assaults by crowd controllers. There remains a suspicion among many senior police that private operators are simply "cowboys." As a result of these scandals (and the perceptions that arise therefrom), major reforms have been introduced in Australia to strengthen private security licensing regimes and increase training requirements. These reforms have been crucial to building public confidence in security industry personnel with whom police now interact on a daily basis. In order to ensure that these cooperative endeavors work successfully, there is a growing need for the law to accommodate better the public/private policing landscape. The issues arising from these concerns are dealt with in the pages that follow.

Police and Security Cooperation: A Short History

Owing to the rise in the number of public/private policing partnerships over the last three decades, private sector security personnel are now involved in a vast array of "policing" responsibilities on a daily basis, and are regularly engaged in tasks (in a partnership capacity) that have traditionally been seen as solely police responsibilities. The roles shared today include not only more traditional police roles, namely surveillance, investigation, crowd control, prison escorts, court security, guarding, and patrolling, but also proactive crime prevention, risk management and assessment, weapons training, crime scene examination, assistance with forensic evidence gathering, information technology advice, hi-tech systems development, and communications support. In summary, the private sector continues to expand significantly (Sarre & Prenzler, 2009). The trend toward partnership models of public/private policing shows no signs of abating (Sarre & Prenzler, 2011).

Throughout the 1970s and 1980s, police had a patronizing, if not suspicious and antagonistic, attitude toward their private counterparts (Shearing, Stenning, & Addario, 1985). This attitude was premised upon the view that private security personnel are, by legal contract, required to act in an exclusionary manner, and will protect only those who can afford them, to the detriment of others. Put differently, the availability of policing and security services in an open marketplace allows wealthy individuals and organizations to buy more protection than their less-privileged counterparts. Private guards, in this view, act in favor of their contractors' interests rather than the best interests of the community as a whole (Zedner, 2006). Indeed, one can readily identify opposing historical principles, roles, authority, and status ascribed to the two sectors (Prenzler & Sarre, 2006). Key features include the different obligations owed: one to egalitarian public service and the other to a contractual client. Moreover, police have a core responsibility to the public, whereas private security personnel are obliged to focus on prevention of crime.

In theory, if not in practice, police have a democratic duty to provide protection and law enforcement universally, or at least on the basis of the greatest need. Private security, on the other hand, focuses on supplying risk protection based on a client's financial choices and budgetary imperatives. In addition, there continue to be training and qualification disparities between public and private policing personnel, differing abilities to assist victims, confusion over jurisdictional boundaries, and imbalances in information sharing (Prenzler & Sarre, 2007).

Be that as it may, what has emerged is a new "public-private security constellation" which transcends "the established conceptual boundaries drawn between 'public' versus 'private' agencies, places, and functions"

(Loader, 2000, p. 333; Kempa, Carrier, Wood, & Shearing, as cited in Williams, 2005, p. 318). As policing expert Philip Stenning has said more recently,

> "[t]he police", as commonly thought of, are now but one member—albeit still a very significant and influential one—of an ever extended "policing family." (Stenning, 2009, p. 23)

Nevertheless, the change came about slowly but gathered momentum through the 1990s (Wakefield, 2003). The great impetus for a growing confidence in private operators came from the local government sector and private sector (Sarre, 2005). Increasing disillusionment with state police services initiated a trend toward councils hiring private security firms, for example, to maintain a presence at sports venues (Prenzler & Sarre, 2012). These large areas, mixing public and private space, are often prone to problems of public disorder. Thus, local governments embraced the opportunity for private services with enthusiasm and have consequently been in the forefront of endeavors toward complementarity (Sarre & Prenzler, 2000).

Recently, several factors have given considerable impetus to the growth in public-private security arrangements (Van Steden & Sarre, 2007). These include greater demand from consumers for effective security in their neighborhoods, an increasing cost differential between private security options and police, and improvements in the ability of security services to provide technological solutions to security problems (Prenzler, Sarre, & Earle, 2008). Moreover, there has been an ongoing shift in public consciousness away from reliance on police and toward *self*-protection or, as it has been referred to by Jan van Dijk (2008), "responsive securitization."

Two Case Studies in Policing Major Events: Sporting Venue Cooperation

On November 29, 2008, researchers attended the Adelaide (South Australia) Oval security coordination box to watch the interaction between South Australia Police (SAPOL) and Weslo, the largest security firm in South Australia, during a cricket "test match" between New Zealand and Australia.

Weslo staff at the ground were principally engaged in perimeter security and bag checking with 40 SAPOL officers at the ground also. The ratio of public police to private security (approximately 1:2.3) was maintained throughout the match. The SAPOL numbers are inclusive of operational and support members on duty at the ground (that is, including those who worked in the police office and police command center on each day). The figures also include the plainclothes "spotters" who stand in the crowd and direct (by microphone) police to the troublemakers ahead of any apprehension by SAPOL officers.

In the Adelaide Oval precinct, then, Weslo staff more than doubled police, but police took the lead role in dispatching officers to deal with unruly patrons. Not one Weslo staffer was seen to confront or physically engage with anyone. While there were some 20 arrests, all were effected by SAPOL. Two SAPOL officers were in charge of the control room and the discussions with the two Weslo staff who were also present were more to do with seeking information about exits and gate control than anything else. Weslo had no access to the SAPOL electronic database. Details of any escort from the sports grounds were fed into the database such that if that person were detained again, the police would be in a position to arrest him or her for failing to comply with a police order. It appeared that, at all times in the operation, power remained with SAPOL.

On July 3, 2009, researchers observed the interactions between VicPol (Victoria Police) and MSS Security during an Australian Football League (AFL) game between two Melbourne-based teams, Essendon and Collingwood. The security cooperation was organized through a partnership arrangement with the Melbourne Cricket Club (MCC), the private security firm MSS, and VicPol.

The different demographics between cricket, football, and soccer crowds mean that different security arrangements are required for each sporting event. Determining the ratio of security to police for any event is established by a "risk level matrix." On the night in question, 125 MSS staff and 20 VicPol officers were deployed, a ratio of around one VicPol officer for every six MSS personnel.

The number of police needed for most events is declining, as risks at most events are becoming fewer and fewer, especially with bag searches that eliminate bottles and alcoholic beverages. In the MCG stadium, MSS staff outnumbered police but the police took the lead role in dispatching officers to deal with unruly patrons. MSS staff were the first responders (in charge of breaches of conditions of entry such as being in possession of contraband) while police were responsible for breaches of the criminal law. Police are empowered by legislation to apply "on the spot" penalty notices and 24-hour banning notices, and to take photos of offenders. Police are specifically directed to back up the decisions made by security personnel. Indeed, VicPol management encourage security personnel to report any police officer who does not support the decisions of security personnel.

The advantage of outsourcing the lion's share of the security tasks to MSS is primarily the cost. Police will charge organizers approximately twice the cost that private security will charge, although this advantage may be under threat as more training is undertaken (at the demand of the licensing authorities) and consequently the charges levied by private operators may increase.

Caution: Is Regulation Keeping Up?

The early cooperative endeavors involving public/private policing arrangements in Australia were ad hoc and somewhat risky. What the above case studies reveal is that cooperation between police and private security is now commonplace and need not be a risky operation. Partnerships can be effective in bringing about desired crime reductive results in and around major events.

Such success stories are causing some authors to predict the end of public policing, as we know it (McLaughlin & Murji, 1995). While that claim is clearly overstated, there is little doubt that the pluralization of policing is another example where social policy and criminal justice are converging. According to Dutch security expert Ronald van Steden:

> private security companies increasingly work with police forces and public prosecution agencies, as well as with normative institutions (e.g., schools, welfare services, housing corporations), to tackle crime and disorder problems. In this way they form defense lines around state authorities, uniting penalty and prevention strategies that should not be merely explained in negative terms of power and repression. (2007, p. 34)

Some caution needs to be exercised, however. The existence and adequacy of accountability mechanisms are still being hotly debated (Prenzler & Sarre, 2008a). There persist perceptions that private operators are far less accountable than their public police counterparts (Stenning, 2009). Research reveals, however, that there is a high degree of regulation of the security industry in Australia, although it is inconsistent across the nation and, in some respects, still open to exploitative activities and unscrupulous characters and behaviors (Prenzler & Sarre, 2008b). In order for the public to maintain (or gain) confidence in the private security industry, the industry itself must present as skilled personnel with high integrity, who have been well trained.*

> Philip Stenning, indeed, remains upbeat about the changing perceptions of accountability: those who are tempted to pessimism about this might do well to remember that it took over 50 years to persuade Parliament to establish the "new police" in the 19th Century. Patience and perseverance may yet eventually be rewarded. (Stenning, 2009, pp. 31–32).

---

* In March 2007, the Australian Crime Commission (ACC) conducted a strategic intelligence assessment of the private security industry. The Commission found instances of criminal infiltration in the industry but it also found that the vast majority of security providers did act appropriately.

Legal Frameworks

Given the rapid expansion of the tasks now being carried out on a daily basis by private security personnel in policing partnerships, one might assume that careful attention would have been paid to the legal framework within which these cooperative activities take place. Regrettably, this has not been the case. One can sympathize with lawmakers. It would be a very difficult task for parliaments to specify private security powers across the board, given the many forms and varieties of private operatives and the multitude of activities in which they may be engaged. In addition, many private security firms are national corporations, and any general attempt to set legislated rules which transcend state and territory boundaries would be difficult to do, let alone to implement and enforce.

However, this lack of legislative direction is potentially confusing for security personnel and the public alike. There is some evidence that as many as 10% of security guards in the United Kingdom believe that they possess the same powers as police officers (Button, 2007). Moreover, there are few legal decisions and precedents emerging from the courts, essentially because so many of these matters (if they do get as far as court) are settled before trial. Hence, it is difficult for anyone to find a satisfactory body of law on the subject.

Public police have coercive powers that are delineated in legislation. These delineations reveal distinct differences between the powers of public and private officers in and around public events. For example, public police are given statutory immunity from legal suit in circumstances where their beliefs and acts are "reasonable." Private personnel are afforded no such luxury. Indeed, private security, in carrying out their duties, constantly run the risk of being sued in the torts of assault, false imprisonment, intentional infliction of mental distress, defamation, nuisance, and trespass. This is not to say that police do not run these risks, but because they have immunities in place, the police are far less likely to find themselves on the losing end of a lawsuit brought by an aggrieved person.

Moreover, public police may act to prevent the commission of an offense before it actually happens (acting upon a suspicion). This concession is not granted to private security personnel. Police powers, duties, rights, responsibilities, and immunities have been so often debated in the courts that there is now a large and continually expanding body of law on these issues. The same cannot be said for private security law.

From where do private security personnel source their power? Starting from first principles, and speaking generally, unless there is specific legislation that empowers specialized security staff to undertake certain tasks for some particular event, the law confers no powers upon security personnel beyond the powers given to the ordinary citizen (Sarre, 2010). That having been said, the powers of the private citizen are considerable. The law of property, for example, grants to an owner of private property the power to require visitors to leave the premises (using reasonable force if necessary), or to subject visitors to stipulations (such as a search of their bags) prescribed and advertised by the property owner. Each of these powers can be delegated to agents (private security) who are entitled to wear uniforms, and even to carry a firearm if they have the correct training and carry the appropriate license.

Where should we proceed from here? What legislative guidance should be afforded the thousands of security personnel who are not specifically directed and guided by specific legislation? There is one view that argues that leaving the law ambiguous encourages fewer lawsuits against private security, forcing those aggrieved to negotiate more and litigate less. What this means for the general law, however, is that there is no guidance concerning when security personnel can safely rely upon legal immunity from a lawsuit. There is a strong view that parliaments could and should legislate to protect security personnel who can demonstrate that they were engaging in a bona fide act of crime prevention when a claimed injury occurred, especially when police and security are both at the same major event doing the same tasks. For example, consider a case where a person attending a sports fixture was attacked by another patron. Assume the attack could have been prevented if a police officer had intervened to restrain the aggressor. If a security officer were not permitted to intervene before the commission of the offense it would leave patrons at greater risk.

The idea of a person being protected from legal suit when exercising good faith is not novel. For example, s 74(2) of the *Civil Liability Act 1936* (South Australia) states that "[a] good Samaritan incurs no personal civil liability for an act or omission done or made in good faith and without recklessness in assisting a person in apparent need of emergency assistance."* There is similar legislation in all Australian States and Territories (Sarre, 2011). A "reasonable suspicion and good faith immunity" could easily be installed by legislation for all people who engage in security functions, especially those who have satisfied a certain level of training.

---

* A "good Samaritan" is defined in the Act as "a person who, acting without expectation of payment or other consideration, comes to the aid of a person who is apparently in need of emergency assistance." The problem for security personnel with this definition is that they cannot access immunity if they are taking payment for their duties, which is usually the case.

Conclusion

As illustrated by the evidence provided above, there has been an undeniable shift in confidence in Australia regarding privatized forms of policing. In the past, it was nearly impossible to conceive of private security personnel operating entirely in the public interest. That notion has been consistently challenged in the last three decades, as public expectations of security have shifted and as policy makers and the public alike have witnessed successful partnerships. Complementary public and private partnerships have been put in place to control violence and disorder in and around major events. This is now a common phenomenon worldwide.

Indeed, the private sector has shown itself capable of filling a need to assist the public police to perform its roles. In response to scandals regarding the private sector delivery of security services, there have been policy shifts in Australia to lift the standards of regulation so that private sector personnel can be trusted to perform general policing roles, especially around securing and managing major events. The short case studies presented above show that it is possible for communities to experience diversified public/private policing partnerships that are successful. One anticipates that they are the forerunners of many cooperative endeavors to come.

References

Button, M. (2007). Assessing the regulation of private security across Europe. *European Journal of Criminology, 4*, 109–128.

Loader, I. (2000). Plural policing and democratic governance. *Social and Legal Studies, 9*, 323–345.

McLaughlin, E., & Murji, K. (1995). The end of public policing? Police reform and "the new managerialism." In L. Noaks, M. Levi, & M. Maguire (Eds.), *Contemporary issues in criminology* (110–127). Cardiff: University of Wales Press.

Prenzler, T., & Sarre, R. (2006). Australia. In T. Jones & T. Newburn (Eds.), *Plural policing: A comparative perspective* (169–189). London: Routledge.

Prenzler, T., & Sarre, R. (2007). Private police: Partners or rivals? In M. Mitchell & J. Casey (Eds.), *Police leadership and management in Australia* (50–60). Sydney: Federation Press.

Prenzler, T., & Sarre, R. (2008a). Developing a risk profile and model regulatory system for the security industry. *Security Journal, 21*(4), 264–277.

Prenzler, T., & Sarre, R. (2008b). Protective security in Australia: Scandal, media images and reform. *Journal of Policing, Intelligence and Counter Terrorism, 3*(2), 23–37.

Prenzler, T., & Sarre, R. (2012). Public-private crime prevention partnerships. In T. Prenzler (Ed.), *Policing and Security in Practice* (149–167). Houndmills, UK: Palgrave Macmillan.

Prenzler, T., Sarre, R., & Earle, K. (2008). Developments in the Australian security industry. *Flinders Journal of Law Reform, 10*(3), 403–417.

Sarre, R. (2005). Researching private policing: Challenges and agendas for researchers. *Security Journal, 18*(3), 57–70.

Sarre, R. (2010). Private security in Australia: Some legal musings. *Journal of the Australasian Law Teachers Association, 3*(1/2), 45–54.

Sarre, R. (December 2011). Private security powers and immunities: Is it time for legislative action? *Australian Security Magazine,* 37–38.

Sarre, R., & Prenzler, T. (2000). The relationship between police and private security: Models and future directions. *International Journal of Comparative and Applied Criminal Justice, 24*(1) 91–113.

Sarre, R., & Prenzler T. (2009). *The law of private security in Australia* (2nd ed.). Sydney, Australia: Thomson Reuters.

Sarre, R., & Prenzler, T. (2011). Public/private security partnerships in Australia. *Proceedings of the Korean Police Forum Conference, Korean National Police Agency and Soon Chun Hyang University* (309–319). Daejoen, Republic of South Korea.

Shearing, C., Stenning, P., & Addario, S. (1985). Police perceptions of private security. *Canadian Police College Journal, 9*(2), 127–154.

Stenning, P. (2009). Governance and accountability in a plural policing environment—The story so far. *Policing: A Journal of Policy and Practice, 3*(1), 22–33.

Van Dijk, J. (2008). *The world of crime.* Los Angeles: Sage.

Van Steden, R. (2007). *Privatizing policing: Describing and explaining the growth of private security.* Amsterdam: BJU Publishers.

Van Steden, R., & Sarre, R. (2007). The growth of privatized policing: Some cross-national data and comparisons. *International Journal of Comparative and Applied Criminal Justice, 31*(1), 51–71.

Wakefield, A. (2003). *Selling security: The private policing of public space.* Devon: Willan Publishing.

Williams, J. (2005). Reflections on the private versus public policing of economic crime. *British Journal of Criminology, 45,* 316–339.

Zedner, L. (2006). Liquid security: Managing the market for crime control. *Criminology and Criminal Justice, 6*(3), 267–288.

About the Author

Rick Sarre is a professor at the School of Law and Associate Head (Research) at the School of Commerce at the University of South Australia.

Police Planning to Curb Insurgency in Nigeria
The Need for a Strong and Effective Police–Public Partnership

8

A. OYESOJI AREMU

Contents

Introduction

The greatest contemporary challenge to national security in Nigeria is the insurgency orchestrated by the sect called *Boko Haram*. Not until 2009, insurgency and its concomitant effects (both emotional and physical) were alien to Nigeria. Nigeria, most especially, the northeastern regions of the country, through ceaseless terrorist attacks, has become unsafe for socioeconomic, political, and educational activities. The current spate of bomb blasts and kidnappings have made human life unsafe and unpredictable. While terrorism and insurgency have been a common occurrence in other parts of the world like America, Europe, Asia, and some parts of Africa, little or nothing had been heard of terrorism in Nigeria until the sudden appearance of the Boko Haram sect.

Scholars have approached the definition of terrorism or insurgency from different viewpoints depending on their academic or professional biases. It would suffice to look at a number of perspectives. Terrorism is defined by Kydd and Walter (2006) as actions focusing on harming some people in order to create fears in others by targeting civilians and facilities or systems on which civilians rely. Relying on the definition of Kydd and Walter may not seriously hold operationally as to what terrorism constitutes in Nigeria. Nevertheless, terrorism is seen as any form of unwarranted attack that is ideologically provoked. According to Aremu (2014), the word *terrorism* is from the French word *terrorisme*, with the Latin derivative in the verb *terro*, which means to frighten or coerce. The concept is therefore a way of "legitimizing" a position, ideology, or philosophy by creating fear or using force. More often, therefore, it is followed by casualties of huge dimensions, either in substantial property damage or in death and serious injury.

Terrorism as unleashed by Boko Haram has primarily targeted government security agencies, most especially the police. Although there have been more civilian casualties than government representatives, the target of Boko Haram at inception was on law enforcement officials in order to avenge the death of the sect's leader, Mohammed Yussuf, who was reported to have been killed extrajudicially. This perspective has been affirmed by Alao, Atere, and Alao (2012), when they posited that the scope of the Boko Haram sect has moved beyond civilian targets to include police and military establishments. This notwithstanding, terrorism has become a deadly weapon resulting in numerous attacks on ordinary civilians.

Evolution of the Insurgency in Nigeria

With over five decades of nationhood, Nigeria has never witnessed the kind of insurgency that has engulfed the country in the last five years. The post-presidential election of 2011 and the concomitant uproar it generated most especially in the northern part of the country fueled the upsurge of insurgency, most apparent in the northeastern region of the nation. Prior to the 2011 election year, there had been pockets of insurgency in some parts of the country. In 1980, the country was engulfed in what was popularly referred to as the Maitatsine riot. The word *Maitatsine* is a Hausa word meaning "the one who dams." The leader of the group was Mohammed Marwa. The Maitatsine insurgency claimed over 3000 lives in the northern part of the country.

In 2001, an Islamic sect, Boko Haram, was formed by Mohammed Yusuf. Boko Haram, according to Aremu (2013) is an Islamic group based in Maiduguri, Borno State. Aremu further noted that Boko Haram, which translates into English as "western education is evil," is a *Salafist jihadist* terrorist organization based in the northeastern corner of Nigeria, in the area predominated by the Kanuri people. The group was founded by a civil servant, Mohammed Yusuf, who, ironically, was well educated. The group's activities initially were "peaceful" and minimally uneventful until 2009, when the founder was reportedly extrajudicially killed by the police. This event marked the beginning of hostility between the group and the police up to current times. The first recorded terrorist attack on four people was in January 2010. From then, and under the new leadership of Abubakar Shekau, terrorism has become an almost daily occurrence predominantly in the northeastern region; and the group has killed over 3500 people including many police officers. Stressing the menace of the sect, Opeloye (2012) asserted that the group in pursuit of its ideology has engaged in arson, bombing, shooting, and stabbing with disdain and impunity.

The Federal Government of Nigeria did not take interest in the activities of the sect until 2009 when intelligence reports showed that the group had the potential of being dangerous to the general safety and welfare of Nigerian citizens. Although the group was labeled as a terrorist organization in 2011 after the bombing of the United Nations headquarters in Abuja, the actual classification of the group as a terrorist group associated with Al-Qaida did not occur until November 2013 by the United States government. Aremu (2014) notes that this did not go down well with the Federal Government of Nigeria in spite of the fact the country continues to be mentioned on the "terrorist radar" in the United States of America and Europe. Prior to this period, the administration of President Goodluck Jonathan had made efforts to curb the group's insurgency by declaring a six-month state of emergency in May 2013 in three states (Adamawa, Borno, and Yobe) where activities of the group were pronounced and obviously ferocious. This was extended in November 2013 for another six-month period.

The Profile of Boko Haram's Insurgency

The operations of Boko Haram at inception were not overwhelmingly deadly. While a good number of the sect's activities were officially reported, there were many terrorist incidents that were not documented or had been underreported. This notwithstanding, Boko Haram's profile of insurgency, whose numbers continue to increase, includes: September 7, 2010 jailbreak; December 31, 2010 bomb blasts; April 8, 2011 bombing of United Nations Headquarters in Abuja; April 22, 2011 jailbreak at Yola, Adamawa (14 prisoners escaped); May 29, 2011 bombing near Abuja (15 lives lost); June 16, 2011 bombing of police headquarters in Abuja (scores of people were killed and wounded); June 26, 2011 bombing of a garden in Maiduguri; July 3, 2011 bombing of a clubhouse in Maiduguri (20 lives lost); July 10, 2011 bombing of a church in Suleja, Niger State (scores of worshipers were murdered); August 12, 2011 killing of a prominent Muslim cleric; August 26, 2011 bombing of a United Nations building (over 40 people killed and 80 injured); September 22, 2011 killing of five Christians who could not recite the Q'uran in Niger State; November 4, 2011 a string of bombings at Damaturu and Potiskum (over 100 lives were lost); November 23, 2011 bomb raids at Yobe (five people killed); November 25, 2011 bombing of Geidam, Yobe State (more than 20 people killed); and December 25, 2011 Christmas evening bombing of St. Theresa's Catholic Church at Abuja when over 45 worshippers were killed (Anonymous, 2012).

The spate of insurgency continued early in 2012 with the following time-lines: January 20, 2012 bombing in Kano metropolis (over 200 people were killed); January 21, 2012 sporadic attacks of police stations and military check-points in Bauchi State (more than 30 security personnel killed); January 24, 2012 attack in Kano State where over 35 people died; January 25, 2012 bomb explosives in Zamfara State (20 people were killed); January 28, 2012 coordinated invasions of police and immigration formations and State Security Service office (over 128 lives were lost); and March 11, 2012 bombing of St. Finbar's Catholic Church where more than seven worshippers were killed.

The sect's activities are also well pronounced in 2013 and started with the bombing of a popular luxurious bus park in Kano where more than 60 people were killed on March 18. Other incidents include: April 29, 2013 bombing of a Catholic church in Kano State where over 20 worshippers including a university professor were killed; June 18, 2013 gruesome killing of 16 secondary school students in their dormitories in Maiduguri; July 6, 2013 another gruesome cold murder of 46 secondary school students in Maiduguri; July 11, 2013 killing of 11 people in Maiduguri; July 13, 2013 bombing of a mosque at the palace of Sheu of Borno where five people were reportedly killed; July 29, 2013 twin and simultaneous bomb attacks at Kano and Borno States where more than 45 people were killed including 25 members of the Joint Police and Military Task Force; August 2, 2013 over 40 people killed in Borno State; August 3, 2013 killing of 20 residents of Dawashe village in Kukawa Council, Borno State; August 5, 2013 two separate bomb attacks on the police in Borno State; August 11, 2013 killing of 63 people in Borno State; August 15, 2013 killing of 11 people at Damboa town, Borno State; August 20, 2013 killing of 44 people at Dumba village, Borno State; August 29, 2013 killing of 14 people in Borno State; August 31, 2013 killing of 24 people at Monguo town, Borno State; September 5, 2013 twin and coordinated attacks of Gajiram and Bulabulin villages, Borno State (20 people killed); September 8, 2013 killing of 11 vigilance group members at Benishiek, Borno State; September 18, 2013 killing of 150 people in Borno State; September 22, 2013 killing of three police-men in Kano; September 25 and 26, 2013, 27 people killed in two different attacks at Fulatari and Kanumburi communities in Borno State; and between September 28 and November 21, 2013, 175 people including 23 soldiers were brutally killed by Boko Haram in Adamawa, Borno, and Yobe States. Similarly, the insurgents killed 24 people on December 2, 2013 at Madayi village and Sabon Gari town in Borno State. While the country and the military (JTF) were still grappling with the latest attack, another fatal damage was unleashed by the sect on military locations in Maiduguri on December 2, 2013. The attack was the heaviest so far on the military in which two Air Force personnel were wounded and three decommissioned military aircrafts and two helicopters were incapacitated. The sect also lost 24 lives in that encounter.

The Nigerian Police and the Boko Haram Insurgency

The history and philosophy of the Nigerian Police are tied to the legacy of the British colonial government. Right from the post-independent year, the Nigerian Police has been organized to quell internal rifts and made to uphold law and order most especially in the north and southwest, where the indirect rule of the British colonial government had been viewed as a huge success. From the period of Louis Edet (the first indigenous Inspector General of Police) in 1964 to date, the Nigerian Police agency has gone through various reforms. However, through all of these reforms, little or no emphasis had been placed on dealing with terrorism and counterinsurgency (COIN). No training for the police was provided until the period of Hafiz Ringim (2010–2012), the 14th Inspector General of Police. Hafiz Ringim himself has become a "victim" as the police have lacked the ability to curtail Boko Haram's insurgent activities. It is during the tenure of the current police chief, Mohammed Abubakar, that the national police agency has exhibited a degree of commitment to COIN. However, this in itself has not yielded the expected results.

As previously asserted, the police have become the chief target of the Boko Haram sect. And from 2009 through the end of 2013, the Nigerian Police Force has lost approximately 96 police personnel in different coordinated operations carried out in the North Eastern States. Although there had been a swift tactical response to Boko Haram's insurgency through the establishment of a Joint Military Task Force (JTF), this has not seriously curbed the growing menace of the sect. The JTF, created in July 2011, has police personnel in significant members. This in itself was the result of the apparent operational failure of the Nigerian Police to curtail the homegrown insurgency. It is clearly worrisome, however, when the police are found to be incapable of providing this primary service, that is, the safety of ordinary citizens engaged in daily activities. On the other hand, the responsibility and fault are not solely that of the police. It is part of what has been referred to as "systemic crises" in which the agency has been purportedly engulfed. In Nigeria, police and law enforcement activities are the exclusive jurisdiction of the federal government. Activities of the national police are centrally controlled, and the agency police chief is answerable only to the President. This is operationally deficient in a country of over 165 million people with about 365,000 police officials. This could be one of the reasons why insurgency thrives. In many other countries, there are state or provincial police that work in specific regions in which familiarity in citizen concerns is often abundant.

Policing Insurgency: Lessons from Other Countries

Arising from the challenges confronting the police agency and its limitations within the context of its activities, and the concomitant homegrown insurgency of Boko Haram, the Nigerian Police can be said to be facing a very serious operational dilemma. Certainly, this is not the best of times for the Nigerian Police. Terrorism and insurgency have been successfully tackled in other climates through effective counterinsurgency and significant intelligence collection. It is therefore relevant to examine the lessons drawn from other countries.

Some countries in Europe, the Americas, Asia, and Africa have successfully curtailed terrorism and insurgency using a number of human and military tactics. Specifically, counterinsurgency (COIN) and counterterrorism in such countries have more often than not been tailored to specific ideological beliefs, with emphasis on intelligence gathering and information exchange. Beyond these, many countries invest heavily in their police agencies not only to detect insurgency, but also to effectively curtail it. In Pakistan, the police successfully overwhelmed militant groups in Punjab and also defeated the insurgency in Karachi in the 1990s. According to Rohde (2002), a timely police action could be more effective in counterterrorism. Generally, the relative success in counterinsurgency in Pakistan has been hinged on police and military collaboration. One interesting point arising from Pakistan's experience with COIN is that the country continues to practice a dual level system of policing: federal and provincial. The two police agencies act independently of each other, but reportedly share intelligence.

In all COIN operations, the collaboration between the police and the military cannot be overemphasized. Due to the firepower of insurgents and terrorists, police are ill-equipped tactically to match them. Although joint COIN of the police and the military appear not well defined, these exercises have often brought success.

The post "9/11" experiences have shaped and influenced many countries' strategies on counterterrorism and counterinsurgency. More often, the experiences of countries like Afghanistan, Algeria, and India have revealed that it was the culture and complexities of the environment that determined where insurgencies had erupted. Musa, Morgan, and Keegan (2011) argued that COIN is a grassroots battle that not only requires military force, but the establishment of security at the local level through everyday police presence that ensures the rule of law and responsible governance. In the opinion of Musa et al. (2011), COIN requires a thorough and clear understanding of the culture of the land. This can only be achieved through indigenous policing, which would involve close contact with all members of the community.

In some countries where insurgency of terrorists has been checked, the police had been deployed to areas in which they have had vast knowledge and exposure. This has often been referred to as neighborhood or community policing. This tactical approach is premised on the fact that terrorists and insurgents routinely use the public as a "war buffer." Supporting this, Jackson (2007) is of the view that it is difficult to win the war over insurgents. According to him, insurgents blend with the public and are therefore very difficult to identify. To identify them therefore, requires the use of intelligence collection.

A Police–Community Intelligence Partnership

Intelligence collection within the security circle is therefore very crucial to effective counterinsurgency. Stressing the importance of intelligence gathering, Hoffman (2004) has submitted that one indispensable component of counterinsurgency warfare, which cuts across the entire spectrum of operations, is the requirement for actionable intelligence. Similarly, Jackson (2007) has proposed that intelligence must deliver the strategic insight needed to know what actions will be effective and what levels of commitment are required, the tactical insight to hit the insurgent target when military action is taken, and the context needed to understand the broader political and other effects of potential security activities. This indicates that through effectual intelligence analysis, COIN could be effectively implemented. The essence of intelligence in COIN is to ensure a proactive approach to public safety and security.

Boko Haram's insurgency in Nigeria has forced the federal government through the Office of the National Security Adviser to be more tactical and intelligence-driven. The coordination is mutually inclusive of all security agencies in Nigeria. This notwithstanding, the primary responsibility of the police in ensuring peace and order cannot be downplayed. Another stratagem would include intelligence-led policing (ILP). Although ILP as a concept has gained currency in academic literature in recent times, its acceptance among police scholars and practitioners is laudable and of tremendous importance as an intervention tool for security enhancement. Peterson (2005) has described ILP as a collaborative enterprise based on improved intelligence operations combined with community-oriented policing and problem solving. In effect, ILP can be explained as police and community collaboration for effective security interventions. The new paradigm in public safety is to enable the police to make good use of the community for intelligence gathering and exchange. This becomes imperative given the fact that COIN cannot be effective without direct community involvement. Aremu (2014) has noted that many of the crimes, including terrorism, are asymmetric and therefore require a strong police–public synergy. Specifically, Aremu posits that the police need intelligence that is community-driven.

Police–community intelligence, if effectively analyzed and strategically utilized, should drive COIN activities. It is critical to note that in Nigeria and in many other countries where militancy and terrorism are rife, security personnel, most especially the police, are routinely targeted by the militants. This places more challenges and strain on the police. As such, it is vital that the respective police agency implement an ILP model and create strong synergy with all members of the community.

Conclusion

As it is now in Nigeria, terrorism and insurgency have unfortunately become international phenomena. The implications and repercussions of this are placed not only on the citizenry, but also on the image and the psychology of the country involved and her neighbors. Through May 2013, the efforts to curb Boko Haram's homegrown insurgency across Nigeria could be labeled as being political and naïve. The presidency and federal government have not been effectively proactive. And when tactical and operational solutions were engineered through the many declarations of a state of emergency in three states (i.e., Adamawa, Borno, and Yobe), political and ethnic meaning were inferred. This has caused the insurgency to be well rooted in the northeastern regions of Nigeria with gradual spread to other parts in the north.

As it is presently, the Nigerian Police can be said to be ineffective and public trust in the agency has waned. Without public confidence, it has been difficult for the police to engage in ILP. The war against terrorism is also not achieving the desired result because the approach is not intelligence and information based, but rather, it can be said to be driven by emotions and political sentiment. Even with the enactment of the Terrorism Prevention Act of 2011 (amended in 2013), which stipulated the death penalty for terrorists and their accomplices, the rate of terrorist events has been on the increase. It is therefore recommended that the approach to addressing and curbing insurgency should be multidimensional and eclectic. Although the joint interventions of the police and military appear to be going in the right direction, this should be strategically driven and coordinated, and supported by the unmitigated cooperation of the public. The war on terrorism across the globe has been shown to be difficult to win. However, with adequate training, funding, motivation, and public support and confidence, this challenge could be mitigated. And public cooperation is clearly the key to successful counterinsurgent planning and crime control and terrorism eradication initiatives.

References

Alao, D. O., Atere, C. O., & Alao, O. (2012). Boko-Haram insurgency in Nigeria: The challenges and lessons. *Singaporean Journal of Business Economy and Management Studies, 1,* 4.

Anonymous. (2012). History of Boko Haram in Nigeria: Sponsors and leaders of the Jama' atul Ahlus Sunna Lid. *NaijaGists.* Retrieved November 30, 2013 from: http://naijagists.com/how_boko_haram_strated-sponsors

Aremu, A. O. (2013). The impact of emotional intelligence on community policing in democratic Nigeria: Agenda setting for national development. In A. Verma, D. K. Das, & M. Abraham (Eds.), *Global community policing: Problems and challenges.* Boca Raton, FL: Taylor & Francis Group.

Aremu, A. O. (2014). Policing and Terrorism: Challenges and Issues in Intelligence. Unpublished book manuscript. Department of Guidance & Counselling, University of Ibadan, Nigeria.

Hoffman, B. (2004). Insurgency and Counterinsurgency in Iraq. National Security Research Division. Retrieved December 1, 2013 from: http://www.rand.org/content/dam/rand/pubs/occasional_papers/2005/RAND_OP127.pdf

Jackson, B. A. (January/February 2007). Counterinsurgency intelligence in a long war: The British experience in Northern Ireland. *Military Review,* 74–85.

Kydd, A. H., & Walter, B. F. (2006). The strategies of terrorism. *International Security, 31,* 1, 49–80.

Musa, S., Morgan, J., & Keegan, M. (2011). *Policing and COIN operations: Lessons learned, strategies and future directions.* Washington, DC: National Defense University Center for Technology and National Security Policy.

Opeloye, M. O. (2012). The Boko Haram Insurgency in Nigeria: A Critical Study of the Movement's Ideological Posture and Implications. doi: 10.7763/IPEDR. 2012. V51. 38.

Peterson, M. (2005). Intelligence-Led Policing: The New Intelligence Architecture. *Bureau of Justice Assistance,* NJC 210681. Washington, DC: U.S. Department of Justice.

Rohde, D. (2002). Threats and responses: Law enforcement and Pakistan police force struggle to find the resources it needs to combat terrorism. *New York Times,* September 30.

About the Author

Dr. A. Oyesoji Aremu is a professor in the Department of Guidance & Counseling at the University of Ibadan in Nigeria and a respected expert on criminal justice matters in Nigeria. He can be reached at e-mail: sojiaremu@yahoo.co.uk.

Law Enforcement Response to Hurricane Katrina

A Multisystem Examination of Response Impact in Louisiana and Texas

9

ROBERT D. HANSER, NATHAN MORAN,
AND ANISSA HORNE

Contents

Introduction

The events that occurred in New Orleans in August of 2005 made worldwide news—the *Big Easy*, as New Orleans is affectionately called, was flooded—and media from around the world reported on the tragic events during the days, weeks, months, and even years that followed. While it is understandable why these events were newsworthy, the completely disastrous outcome that followed was not just sensational, but rather it was shocking, embarrassing, and humiliating to the citizens of Louisiana as well as other concerned persons throughout the United States and the world. In essence, transparency and exposure of a system that was ill-prepared for these events, along with the existence of negative police–community relations, coalesced into, quite literally, the "perfect storm," leaving persons throughout the United States and the global community stunned by what they observed and heard. There were clearly many unexpected turns and events that were experienced by first responders prior to, during, and after Hurricane Katrina.

In addition, a discussion of how the events of Hurricane Katrina also impacted the neighboring state of Texas and how law enforcement in that state responded to these events will be included since this perspective is often not brought to light. Attention to how law enforcement officials in Texas responded to the influx of refugee immigrants from New Orleans and how law enforcement from that state also aided police responders in New Orleans will be provided. Last, we provide a multifaceted overview of how other responders, including mental health workers, correctional staff, medical staff, and volunteers from the Red Cross were also utilized to address the crises related to Hurricane Katrina. Overall, one will gain a clearer perspective that will demonstrate how response to this disaster was a collaborative effort between police agencies throughout Louisiana, Texas, and numerous other states, and also between police and other first-responder agencies.

The Police Response: The New Orleans Police Department and Other Law Enforcement Involvement

The response of the New Orleans Police Department (NOPD) as well as other law enforcement agencies that rendered assistance before, during, and after the landing of Hurricane Katrina must be comprehensively analyzed. It is therefore important to understand the general police–community climate that existed in New Orleans prior to the occurrence of this major natural disaster. To explain further, the New Orleans Police Department did not operate in a social vacuum but was, instead, part of a broader criminal justice system in Louisiana that must also be closely examined.

The Days Prior to Striking Land

Prior to making landfall, numerous agencies throughout the city had made attempts to prepare for the hurricane. In addition, it is reported that perhaps 90% of the city's inhabitants did actually evacuate on time. This attests to the fact that, in reality, much of the disaster that followed actually had been averted for the majority of the New Orleans residents. Those who remained were mostly those who were incapacitated, did not have the economic means to leave and/or transport loved ones, or those who for various personal reasons chose to stay behind. On August 27, 2005, as the likelihood of the hurricane's strike on the city of New Orleans became increasingly more likely, the Louisiana State Police activated the Emergency Operations Center in Baton Rouge. Protocol with the operation of this center included a toll-free hotline so that persons could request assistance prior to the full wrath of the storm making landfall and could also gain valuable information as the hurricane neared. This center monitored the path of the hurricane and additional state troopers were made available to assist with the telephone service and to also assist with the continued and increased flow of traffic from evacuees who were leaving New Orleans as well as other coastal areas of Louisiana.

On August 28, 2005, the Federal Emergency Management Agency (FEMA) made public note of the potentially severe and disastrous outcomes if Katrina were to directly hit New Orleans because the city sat well below sea level and depended on a system of levees and pumps to keep ocean water out of the city and to remove standing water from rainfall out of key areas of the city. It was announced that a direct hit could submerge the city in several feet of water, depending on the area of the city. What was truly of concern was the lack of transportation for many of the residents from lower socioeconomic backgrounds, with an estimated 100,000 people still residing in the city with no means of leaving. To help facilitate recovery of these persons, in the event that the hurricane was to strike New Orleans, FEMA activated its National Response Coordination Center and the National Emergency Response Team.

Day One: Hurricane Katrina Makes Landfall

On August 29, 2005, Hurricane Katrina struck the city of New Orleans as a Category 3 storm with winds that reached 120 miles per hour in strength. The storm brought 28-foot high tidal surges that breached several areas of a complicated and somewhat dated levee system. At 6:00 a.m. on this date, the very eye of the hurricane landed over the city, making it a direct and center strike upon the city. This resulted in the flooding of nearly 80% of the city. In the process, those remaining residents who had not evacuated were forced to contend with circumstances where basic necessities became rare commodities. In addition, the police, judicial, and correctional systems in and around New Orleans were greatly debilitated; their functioning was, for a time, all but paralyzed.

It is also important to understand that, almost immediately after Hurricane Katrina struck New Orleans, agencies like the Louisiana National Guard lost all forms of communication, both in terms of intra- and inter-agency communication. Therefore, coordination of National Guard assets had become impaired and the ability for the Louisiana National Guard to work in partnership with the New Orleans Police Department (NOPD) was likewise hampered. This loss of communication also impacted the Louisiana State Police throughout much of southern Louisiana, including the Baton Rouge area. Thus, the NOPD, during the initial hours of the disaster, was literally working independently with little or no assistance and, being caught in the midst of the hurricane, had no communications or methods of coordination other than what could be engineered through face-to-face contact. In addition, movement and transportation had come to a complete halt.

During this time, the NOPD numbered around 1660 sworn police officers, which did not count other auxiliary and/or administrative personnel (Riley, 2007). All officers were notified that they should be at-the-ready during this emergency. The first breach of one of the city's levees occurred between 6:00 A.M. and 6:45 A.M. and by 7:00 A.M. that morning, the NOPD had received over 600 emergency 911 calls (Roman, Irazola, & Osborne, 2007). Naturally, officer response to these calls occurred amid forceful winds and excessive rainfall, as well as flooding in many streets. These conditions not only impaired the ability of officers to respond but, it is also important to understand that the city's levee and pump system was not designed to withstand a direct hit from a major hurricane that would hover over the city for a prolonged period of time. Further, this system was designed and built by the United States Army Corps of Engineers, so it was thought that the structures were generally sufficient to meet any weather challenges that could likely face the city. In fact, most systems of these types are not necessarily designed to withstand such impact, particularly those with systems that have dated technology and/or a prolonged history of operation. Thus, the entire situation was well in excess of what had been intended for the city to endure by engineers and other officials tasked with maintaining the city's weather-tight protection system.

From a policy perspective, other issues also impacted and impaired the ability for NOPD officers to respond effectively, if at all. These policy issues were little known by the public or the media at the time and during the days and weeks that followed the storm. For instance, the Louisiana State Emergency Preparedness plan stipulated that officers were *not* to respond to calls if winds ever exceeded 55 M.P.H. due to personal safety concerns for the officers whom, if injured or killed due to such extreme inclement weather, would no longer be of constructive service to the public. This was actually a prudent policy because, in reality, rescue attempts in such extreme conditions are more likely to simply put the citizens needing assistance in even greater danger, presuming that they are even able to make known their circumstances of distress during these conditions.

Going further, the waters that flooded New Orleans rose quickly and, within the first few hours, isolated approximately 300 New Orleans police officers from reaching others, thereby being unable to assist citizens or personnel within their department. In addition, another dozen or so officers were stranded in their homes, meaning that hundreds of NOPD officers were essentially unable to aid persons in distress, due to no fault of their own. Naturally, since all communications were impaired, during the initial hours of hurricane landfall, these officers could not inform others in the agency and their whereabouts were essentially unknown.

Amid this confusion, there were roughly 150 officers who had abandoned their positions (Riley, 2007). As with those who had been legitimately cut off from the remainder of the agency, their whereabouts and the reason for their absence were completely and officially unknown by the department. Thus, during the first day of the hurricane's landfall, approximately 25% of the sworn officers of NOPD were unaccounted for. While the magnitude of this problem was not immediately recognizable, it became increasingly apparent that police service was impaired during the days that would follow. Further compounding the issues related to missing human resources was the fact that rescue equipment was inadequately available, meaning that officers often could do little but stand by and wait until equipment was obtained, or were forced to use makeshift tools to address some of the specific emergency situations.

In addition, the district level NOPD stations were not necessarily safe from flooding problems either, meaning that these stations often had to fend for themselves while simultaneously being of service to the flooding community around them. Even the main station where headquarters was located was flooded and, as a result, hundreds of police cars were damaged and rendered unserviceable (Roman et al., 2007). Further, communication with surrounding agencies in the area was all but nonexistent due to damage to radio towers and communication equipment. Buildings typically manned by fire and sheriff's agency employees had been evacuated, so this eliminated the ability of NOPD to collaborate with other partner agencies during the initial hours of the storm. In one surrounding jurisdiction (i.e., Plaquemines Parish), the communications center was destroyed and 911 emergency calls were unavailable for over three weeks (Dowden, 2006). Jefferson Parish, the jurisdiction that includes the city of New Orleans, suffered similar damage to its communications equipment.

The use of boats and watercraft was not commonplace for the NOPD because most of the waterways were associated with the port district, which was governed by the Port Authority. Most of these vessels were completely damaged beyond use, left with no watertight integrity, and thus had become as unserviceable as many of the NOPD squad cars that had been damaged. It has been reported that less than a dozen watercraft were initially available to officers of NOPD as rescue vehicles (Riley, 2006). Though these vehicles proved to be invaluable, there were too few of them to provide an adequate response to the calls for service that existed. Also, debris and clutter from the wind strike minimized the effectiveness of these vehicles; their operation usually occurred in open waterways during prior events. The need to clear waterways and reroute one's approach due to obstructions limited the usefulness of these craft in most cases.

Communications Available

During the days after the hurricane's landfall, NOPD was forced to rely on voice radio systems using a limited number of mutual aid channels. Indeed, the entire system of communications throughout the four parish region (note that the term *parish* in Louisiana is synonymous with *county* in other areas of the United States) that was available for state and federal agencies had been damaged beyond use, leaving no form of regional communication for many weeks (even months) that followed (Dowden, 2006). Instead, public safety workers were forced to use single-band walkie-talkies and the primitive channels used with these radios became known and crowded among subscribers, rendering them useless to those who needed the lines open for official business.

To provide a clear idea of how chaotic response conditions had become, consider the fact that after landfall of the storm, several of the NOPD supervisory staff organized a crude rescue operation from the driveway of Harrah's Casino, doing so without consistent radio communications or contact with others on the ground or in the air. This and other actions similar to this led to the duplication of response efforts between NOPD and FEMA. This duplication of efforts also, by proxy, left other areas of the city unattended for longer periods of time, potentially costing lives unnecessarily (Baum, 2006). The void in effective communication also resulted in exaggerated reports of criminal activity and other activities that later turned out to be largely false or, at the very least, extreme.

Violence in the Streets?

During the early days after Katrina's landfall and when the flooding resulted in standing water throughout the city, the Louisiana Superdome was used to provide shelter for many citizens who had been unable to evacuate.

During this time, television portrayals of the disaster often focused on the Superdome as an iconic symbol of the circumstances that faced the city. Amid this period, various reports of criminal activity circulated widely throughout Louisiana by word-of-mouth and on public television. These reports included incidents of mass looting, gang rapes, and widespread murder. During this time, the Superintendent of Police in New Orleans, Edwin Compass, as well as Mayor Ray Nagin, made note of incidents of violence in the Superdome that were later proven to be false (Roberts, 2005). Unfortunately, the proof that these incidents were false did not make the headline news, though some exceptional reports of the truth to the alleged crime wave did make the press (Roberts, 2005).

While many of these reported incidents were overdramatized, there were some criminal events that did, of course, occur. In one instance, a large group of looters emptied an entire Walmart store of most of its contents. The looting, sometimes to secure items for livelihood and survival, did go beyond the procurement of necessities and often did result in the theft of high-ticket items. The chaos that ensued prevented police from effectively countering these crimes. Indeed, police were forced to use ineffective means of dealing with looters who were, in fact, stealing items from local stores; they often were forced to release the looter but would, as a weak attempt at enforcement, would take their photographs with the intent of issuing warrants for their arrest during later weeks that would follow (Baum, 2006).

Reports also made claim that marauding bands of gangsters were brandishing firearms and shooting at rescuers as well as snipers in the city who took shots at rescue helicopters. These claims all turned out to be false. In addition, local news channels in other areas of the state and throughout the nation made reports that gangs were roaming the streets shooting police officers as well as other survivors. This also turned out be largely untrue; only one police officer in New Orleans was ever shot (Police Officer Kevin Thomas) and this was not by a gang member. At no time were indictments brought forward against gang members in the city, demonstrating how many of the reports given to the public were extreme and mostly untrue. What is unfortunate is that the hysteria generated by these rumors and dramatized events simply added to the stress and difficulty that the New Orleans police experienced during the days after the hurricane. Many of these officers were fatigued, working day and night to save people from rooftops and such. The worry and tension is one reason given to explain several incidents where police engaged in unnecessary or excessive shootings, on occasion, during the course of events following the hurricane strike. Among the most sensational stories were those that contended that mass rapes and serial murders were occurring in the Superdome. However, many of these false accounts were dramatizations provided by people in trauma who spoke to the media, as well as various responders from the National Guard and other agencies, who had provided exaggerated or false stories that later could not be substantiated. For example, in an interview to the *Times Picayune* newspaper of New Orleans, a National Guardsman from Arkansas noted that a freezer room had been found with 30 to 40 dead bodies stored therein, most of whom had appeared to have been killed through acts of violence. Later, when a sweep of the Superdome was conducted, this pile of bodies was never discovered. Likewise, sensational comments made by Mayor Ray Nagin on the *Oprah Winfrey Show,* a national television program, referred to killings and raping that had occurred repeatedly over a five-day period in the Superdome (Roberts, 2005). Later, no official reports of sexual assault were ever made by persons who had dwelled in the Superdome and no witnesses to these events could be found. Furthermore, the Louisiana Department of Health and Hospitals counted a total of 10 people who had died in the Superdome during the aftermath of the storm, and 8 of these were due to natural causes; only 2 deaths were thought to have occurred at the hands of another person (Roberts, 2005). While two potential murders is certainly unfortunate and a notable tragedy, this is nowhere close to the headcount that had been often alluded to during the course of events that soon followed the storm. When asked about the wild accounts provided by Mayor Nagin, it was explained that his accounts were based on information that the mayor had been provided, information from sources he trusted, and from sources that he did not corroborate with prior to making statements on national television.

NOPD: Excessive Force, Misconduct, and Ethical Problems

One major issue of contention between many NOPD officers and the then-mayor, Ray Nagin, is the debate over whether officers were given instructions to shoot unarmed looters throughout the city as a means of gaining control of the population (Shankman, Jennings, McCarthy, Maggi, & Thompson, 2012). Many officers, including ranking officers, contend that this order was given and that it was even given by the mayor on one occasion when the mayor had personally addressed police personnel regarding the need to stabilize the city (Shankman et al., 2012). Regardless of these accounts, it is undeniable that, prior to the hurricane, the murder rate in New Orleans was 10 times higher than the national average, with higher-than-average rates of criminality in all categories. After the city was secured, criminal activity declined at significant rates and has thereafter consistently remained lower than pre-Katrina years. One could contend that much of the criminal population may have been displaced as a result of the hurricane.

In 2012, five former NOPD officers were sentenced to prison terms that ranged from six years to 65 years in length due to an incident where unarmed citizens were shot to death while crossing the Danziger Bridge. The incident reportedly occurred on September 4, 2005, during the early days that followed Katrina's landing. When police arrived, six people were crossing the bridge in search of food and supplies. Among them was Ronald Madison, a 40-year-old mentally disabled man, and 19-year-old James Brissette, who were both killed at the scene, with the other four persons being wounded by police gunfire. During the period of the reported lawlessness that followed the hurricane, police had been told that citizens had been shooting other citizens as well as Army Corps of Engineers representatives, rescue workers, and the police themselves. In addition, the confusion over whether looters were to be shot was also an issue for many in the department, though most officers simply refused to do so. All of the civilians who were victims of the aforementioned shooting were allegedly unarmed. The police involved in this incident, however, altered the facts of the scene to make the shootings appear justified, with officers conspiring to plant a gun, fabricate witnesses, and provide false reports of the events.

Ultimately, it was this case that would be showcased as grounds for cleaning up and revamping the New Orleans Police Department, and resulted in a series of U.S. Justice Department investigations. Interestingly, in 2013, a retrial was ordered for the officers responsible for the Danziger Bridge shooting cover up due to judicial ethics concerns among prosecutors who leaked information during several stages in the proceedings against these and other officers. Further, a series of charges have been filed against other NOPD officers related to conduct violations, including allegations of looting and the abandonment of posts. Most all of the allegations of looting among NOPD officers were determined to be unfounded or in accordance with policy under exigent circumstances, though some officers were reprimanded for failing to challenge bona fide looting that occurred around them as they procured necessary items. In addition, a series of hearings were held shortly after circumstances were stabilized, in which officers who abandoned their posts were questioned about their conduct. In many cases, these officers hoped to return to the force after explaining their situations. In some cases, officers left due to family members and loved ones being in jeopardy. In other cases, less honorable reasons were provided. Over time, nearly 85% of those officers who had abandoned their posts were ultimately dismissed from the NOPD due to their actions.

Last, it is clear that issues related to ethical conduct have plagued the city of New Orleans, just as is true-to-form for much of the state of Louisiana. In 2013, Ray Nagin, now retired from the position of mayor of New Orleans, was indicted for multiple counts of fraud and corruption related to the later renovation of the city. In general, these charges involve allegations that the mayor gained direct personal gain from a variety of contracts and agreements, which lined the pockets of both the contractor and also provided the mayor with financial incentives. Allegations of paid vacations and other benefits have also been leveled at the former mayor. These developments, along with several others since the Katrina catastrophe, have further cast a black eye on the city and served to further tarnish the reputation of the city and the state in which it is located.

Logistical Issues and External Assistance

Additional problems with the police agency's emergency plan included the lack of guidance regarding safe parking of emergency response vehicles. For instance, many of the vehicles were parked in low-lying areas of the city to protect them from the strong winds that had blown into the area prior to the storm's arrival. However, once the flooding started (remember that no one anticipated that the levees would break and/or that such little warning would exist), these vehicles were the first to be flooded.

In addition, basic provisions such as clean uniforms or routine supplies were not readily available, nor were contingencies in place for their eventual availability. Evidence from more than 3000 criminal cases was ruined by floodwaters at police headquarters and in the courthouse. Hundreds of guns, much of the NOPD ammunition, and other equipment such as bullet-resistant shields was ruined, as well. In total, it became clear that the NOPD had not been properly prepared for inclement weather conditions of the level that was experienced during Hurricane Katrina. Whether it is realistic to think that NOPD should have been prepared for such a catastrophe may be a matter of opinion. What is a matter of fact is that the department was nearly paralyzed during the immediate hours and days that followed the storm's landfall in New Orleans.

Outside Assistance

By the second week that followed Katrina's impact on New Orleans, over 1600 federal law enforcement officers had arrived to help in New Orleans (Roman et al., 2007). Under a variety of statutes, federal assets and personnel can be (and were eventually) used to support state and local officials with public safety issues during incidents that rise to a national level of concern. These additional sources of support were welcomed by the city of New Orleans, including the NOPD. However, federal law enforcement, in an attempt to not convolute the attempts of local law enforcement, created a command center that operated separately and was designed to aid with requests for response only until NOPD indicated that they would no longer need the aid from external agencies.

Though federal support did make conscientious efforts to work in tandem with local law enforcement, confusion related to specific law enforcement responsibility and authority did occur, both across levels of government and between different agencies. Some of this was exacerbated by the mismanagement and poor coordination of FEMA in integrating law enforcement resources into the overall response landscape. Indeed, it seemed to many that those agencies that did work in tandem with FEMA actually fared worse in providing assistance than those that just acted largely on their own; so burdensome were the regulations and sense of bureaucracy with the federally coordinated operations. One example is what Sobel and Leeson (2006) referred to as "the tale of two sheriffs," in which Sheriff Warren Evans of Wayne County, Michigan, and Sheriff Dennis Randle, of Carroll County, Indiana, both sought to provide assistance to the city of New Orleans. Their accounts are included below:

> Both sheriffs were eager to assist hurricane victims, and both had control over the necessary resources. Sheriff Evans ignored both FEMA and his governor's instructions to wait for FEMA approval and went to New Orleans with nine truckloads of supplies and 33 deputies to help. Sheriff Randle, on the other hand, followed procedure, was buried under mounds of FEMA paperwork, and faced an unnavigable approval process. He never made it to New Orleans. (Sobel & Leeson, 2006, p. 57)

As Roman et al. (2007) noted, there is no doubt that federal law enforcement response to Hurricane Katrina was a central facilitator in restoring the New Orleans Police Department's command structure as well as the larger criminal justice system. Yet, even with this being the case, the coordination was slow and the bureaucracy was excessive, potentially leaving many in precarious positions while preliminary issues were worked through. To further exemplify this point, consider that Mayor Nagin waited over 15 hours to request for assistance from the National Hurricane Center, from the time that the director of that organization had called Nagin to inform him that untold disaster was inevitable for New Orleans (Sobel & Leeson, 2006). Though federal agencies did provide substantial assistance, it was, in the words of Walter Maestri, Emergency Management Director of Jefferson Parish, the case that "for approximately six days... we sat here waiting" (Philips, 2005; Sobel & Leeson, 2006).

Although many attested to chaos within branches of the federal government during the first days after the storm, stakeholders stated that the cooperation between federal authorities and the local police was unprecedented. The NOPD welcomed the various federal law enforcement agencies that sought to help. This, in turn, has also resulted in partnerships that have continued between the Federal Bureau of Investigation (FBI) and the NOPD through various task forces that the federal agency typically had excluded from local police departments. The point being that the NOPD's willingness to accept aid and the sincerity to create partnerships have paid off in future benefits where they have been made privy to federal agency information and coordinated responses that usually are not allowed with most local agencies (Perlstein, 2007). Training activities as well as coordinated sweeps routinely occur where both levels of government work in a unified manner in areas ranging from drug enforcement to organized crime, and even counterterrorism operations.

Final Evacuations of Residents: The Texas Connection

Space and accommodations for those residents who had collected in and around the Superdome area in New Orleans, numbering in the thousands, was unavailable in many areas of Louisiana. Indeed, shelters were full and other areas of the state were either damaged or impacted by a great number of persons who had evacuated prior to the storm's impact with New Orleans. It was during this time that residents were eventually transported, across state lines, into Texas. The cities of Houston (with thousands of evacuees housed at the Astrodome) and San Antonio were, perhaps, the most prominent recipients of post-Katrina evacuees from the New Orleans area.

Thousands of refugees had relocated to the state of Texas from various areas of southern Louisiana, including New Orleans and other areas of the state that had been impacted by the hurricane. Among these refugees, it was thought that anywhere from 1300 to 1700 probationers and parolees had also fled to the Lone Star State, causing problems for both law enforcement and correctional staff throughout both states (Sandberg, 2006). It was also reported that local law enforcement officials often found that evacuees had criminal backgrounds, including acts of violence (Chau, Kaynak, & Foo, 2007). Even more telling is the observation that the number of homicides in the Houston area increased by 23% in less than six months after evacuees were relocated in that city. In many cases, these murders reportedly involved Louisiana evacuees as perpetrators or victims of the crime (Kennett, 2006).

The Texas Perspective

In response to both Hurricanes Katrina and Rita, the state of Texas received more than 250,000 evacuees (by September 2005). By December 31, 2005, an estimated 160,000 evacuees remained in the Houston region alone, thus creating unique issues for the city of Houston, as well as the state of Texas (Hughes, 2006). Although there were pressing issues to resolve pertaining to housing, food, water, and medical care, the primary issue for the affected law enforcement agencies of Texas was that of the rapid influx of evacuees. These displaced persons were largely from economically disadvantaged areas and had now been left destitute due to the hurricane.

Impact of Evacuees on Major Law Enforcement Agencies in Texas

It is relevant to examine the data related to law enforcement statistics collected both while evacuees were moving into Texas, and after they had settled in. Much of this data is the result of a series of surveys conducted by the Police Research Center at Sam Houston State University, and later published in a series of TELEMASP bulletins through the Bill Blackwood Law Enforcement Management Institute of Texas (LEMIT) (Pullin, 2006).

As of May 2006, 88% of the 52 largest police departments in the state of Texas were actively dealing with Katrina evacuees (Pullin, 2006). The number of evacuees that were reported in the major cities ranged from as many as 160,000 in Houston, to as few as six in Amarillo (see Table 9.1).

Table 9.1   Number of Evacuees in Jurisdictions as of May 2006

City	Number of Evacuees
Houston	153,000
Dallas	10,000
Plano	3000
Fort Worth	2500
Arlington	2450
Baytown	1500
College Station	1500
Pasadena	493
El Paso	300
N. Richland Hills	143
Montgomery County	100
Victoria	100
Abilene	35
San Marcos	25
Texas City	24
New Braunfels	20
Amarillo	6

Source: Pullin, M., (2006), *Impact of Katrina Evacuees upon Law Enforcement*, Huntsville, TX: TELEMASP Bulletin, Texas Law Enforcement Management and Administrative Statistics Program, Law Enforcement Management Institute of Texas.

This data does not include an analysis of every city in the state, and the numbers vary depending on data collection procedures. In this instance, the data were collected directly from law enforcement agency administrators regarding their existing data on Katrina evacuees.

Money Spent on Evacuees

In the years following Hurricane Katrina, a recurring question arose regarding Texas law enforcement costs associated with evacuees. Although all of the costs associated with this natural disaster are difficult to calculate with a high level of precision, some direct costs to law enforcement agencies were measured via documented expenses (e.g., overtime, fuel, etc.). Of the expenses involved, the Houston Police Department expectedly topped the list with a reported $4,732,529 in spending above and beyond what would normally have been budgeted during a similar period of time (Pullin, 2006). In fact, 73% of law enforcement agencies surveyed by LEMIT indicated that they had direct costs incurred by the agency as a result of Katrina evacuees. Table 9.2 includes a synopsis of money spent per agency (responding to the survey) as it relates to Katrina evacuees.

Arrests Associated with Evacuees

Six major cities directly measured and tracked arrests associated with Katrina evacuees. The two largest jurisdictions impacted, Houston and Dallas, counted a total of 603 arrests (as of May 2006) associated with evacuees.

Table 9.2   Monetary Expenses per Agency Related to Evacuees

City	Monetary Expense
Houston	$4,732,529
Arlington	$580,000
Garland	$91,200
Waco	$40,000
Abilene	$25,800
Duncanville	$16,350
Baytown	$12,800
Bedford	$3000
Amarillo	$713
Grapevine	$125

Source: Pullin, M., (2006), *Impact of Katrina Evacuees upon Law Enforcement*, Huntsville, TX: TELEMASP Bulletin, Texas Law Enforcement Management and Administrative Statistics Program, Law Enforcement Management Institute of Texas.

Table 9.3   Houston Police Department Arrests Associated with Evacuees

(a) 121 Petty offenses (i.e., public intoxication, traffic, criminal trespass, evading, other)
(b) 116 Violent offenses (i.e., unauthorized weapon, assault, homicide, family violence, other)
(c)   48 Property offenses (i.e., theft, burglary, auto theft, other)
(d) 160 Drug offenses (i.e., marijuana, controlled substance, intent to distribute, other)
(e)   27 Other offenses (i.e., forgery, felony warrant, parole violation, other)

Source: Pullin, M., (2006), *Impact of Katrina Evacuees upon Law Enforcement*, Huntsville, TX: TELEMASP Bulletin, Texas Law Enforcement Management and Administrative Statistics Program, Law Enforcement Management Institute of Texas.

Of these 603 arrests, Houston recorded 472, for which the arrest charges are presented in Table 9.3.

Issues Associated with Probation and Parole Supervision

A recurring theme in the media during the time following Hurricane Katrina related to issues of probation and parole supervision, and related negligence. Specifically, many politicians and pundits noted that parolees from New Orleans were not properly supervised upon their emergency release/evacuation, thus causing issues for Texas (as well as other states). Some reports have indicated that as many as 1700 probationers and parolees went unsupervised (Michaels, 2006). Once the media began actively reporting on this issue, the number rose to 3000 (Michaels, 2006). Many of the reports described the evacuees as dangerous felons and "freed killers." As an example, one article noted that "Texas officials, who welcomed Katrina evacuees, have spent months sparring with federal and Louisiana officials about the unsupervised parolees and probationers, including men and women paroled for murder, rape, and robbery" (Sandberg, 2006, p. A1).

This overwhelming negative and inflated media attention led to a backlash from many citizens in Texas, enough so to warrant the following statement from State Representative Ted Poe (R-Texas):

> When Katrina occurred, we got the good, the bad and the ugly from Louisiana. We'll keep some of the good and some of the bad, but the ugly got to go back. Texas did the neighborly thing by taking in these people. Now...the criminals need to go back to Louisiana. (Johnson, February 6, 2006, p. B1).

During this time, Texas officials had asked FEMA to provide a list or report of offenders on community supervision who had received some type of federal aid as a means of identifying these persons. Oddly enough, identifying these offenders only solved part of the problem; Texas officials were not able to detain or hold these individuals if they did not have a warrant from Louisiana. Because of the disruption to Louisiana's data system, the ability to fulfill this requirement was not routinely met, putting Texas law enforcement in an uncertain legal standing. Ultimately, it took over a year for Louisiana to begin a serious accounting of the 1300 criminals in Texas who had applied for federal emergency relief.

Within a year, it was clear that this influx of offenders had impacted areas of Texas. Many were reported to be members of over a dozen local gangs in New Orleans that had come from various housing projects operated by the New Orleans Housing Authority, with over 700 sites that housed around 49,000 residents (Kennett, 2006). These areas of New Orleans were also where most of the gang-related activity had originated and also constituted some of the primary problem areas for drug-related crimes. Houston was the venue for a large number of these evacuees, and, corresponding to this influx of evacuees, problems with gang offenders seemed to visibly and rapidly increase (Kennett, 2006). Within a few months of their evacuation to Houston, killings and robberies mounted as these gang members connected with old friends in Houston and sought to make a name for themselves within the criminal circles that already existed in the city. This led to the formation of a 10-member Gang Murder Squad in Houston. The squad also requested visits with several New Orleans police officers so that they could gain valuable intelligence on the various gangs and their membership (Kennett, 2006).

Suffice it to say that Katrina impacted criminal activity observed in Texas, particularly in the Houston area. The response by law enforcement in this region was relatively quick, particularly in combating gang members from Louisiana. Much of this likely had to do with the fact that Texas law enforcement officials have long had to combat a variety of criminal gangs, both on the streets and within the Texas correctional system. It would then seem that these officials were well equipped with the ability to target this threat. While it was likely inevitable that the crime rate would go up after Katrina, the law enforcement response ultimately was successful in curbing a continued and long-term increase in violent crime. This was also due to the fact that many of these offenders were also recovered by Louisiana law enforcement and community supervision personnel and brought back to their original jurisdictions.

The Role of Social Services

It is additionally critical to discuss the contributions of other partners in the disaster response. Among these were a variety of social and mental health service personnel who aided both law enforcement and correctional staff who were tasked with responding to the Katrina crisis. In many cases, these mental health workers provided services to the traumatized population but in other cases, they also provided assistance and support to law enforcement personnel, when or if necessary.

Further, many social service and/or mental health professionals worked in the Superdome and in shelters in outlying areas, providing services as volunteers with agencies such as the Red Cross or state relief agencies. In many cases, these professionals worked in areas of support that aided law enforcement who retrieved survivors during the days that immediately followed Katrina's landfall as well as weeks afterward. These individuals assisted with a myriad of issues and concerns for survivors, both in New Orleans and outlying areas where evacuees were sheltered. These services proved critical for law enforcement responders who found it difficult to render long-term services to a population with numerous preexisting medical, social services, and psychological needs (Zuckerman & Coughlin, 2006).

As has been noted, the sense of organization among police and other responders was severely impaired, leading to a number of barriers faced by survivors that included the following: (1) ineffective communications/coordination between the various governmental and other agencies; (2) inability to mobilize resources to the most devastated locations due to lack of or poor transportation options; (3) issues related to confidentiality and privacy; (4) unrecoverable medical records; (5) lack of sufficient medical supplies; (6) language and cultural barriers; (7) inadequate housing alternatives; and (8) the need to provide treatment beyond that of basic triage.

Relief workers, emergency responders, outside law enforcement personnel, and volunteer teams mobilized around the nation to deliver services to hurricane victims. Some teams were comprised of licensed counselors and social workers, previously trained in crisis intervention. Teams conducted needs assessments, made clinical diagnoses, and provided referrals to appropriate care providers (Hoffpauir & Woodruff, 2008). Nonprofessionals included people with administrative or technical skills, such as translators or computer skills. Mental health responders lacked many of the resources necessary to provide services, including adequately crisis-trained staff. Indeed, consider that 89% of psychiatrists left the greater New Orleans area when people were most in need (Lister, 2005). The higher rates of mental illness seen in Louisiana since the hurricane occurred clearly placed a strain on hospitals across Louisiana, also due to less mental health facilities and clinics being available (Donnelly, 2010). Jones, Immel, Moore, & Hadder (2008) found that although psychologists were only a small part of the relief efforts following Hurricane Katrina, their clinical, research, and applied skill sets significantly contributed to the ongoing recovery efforts in the Gulf Coast. These skill sets, according to Substance Abuse Mental Services Administration (SAMSHA), was critical in consulting with governmental agencies, providing additional assistance that went beyond initial response, and training crisis workers, counselors, and law enforcement in the area of disaster mental health and cultural competence. Like other emergency relief and recovery providers, many mental health professionals (and their families) were experiencing the added stress of being displaced right along with the hurricane victims they were assisting (Hoffpauir & Woodruff, 2008).

Community Relations, Diversity, and Mitigating Response

The following excerpt, from an essay by Margery Austin Turner with the Urban Institute, paints a clear and vivid picture of the people most impacted by Hurricane Katrina, that is, low-income African Americans. Based on this framework, an overview of how various social service providers responded to the crisis will follow:

> Long before the onslaught of Hurricane Katrina, the collapse of the levees, or the chaos of evacuation, the social infrastructure of New Orleans was failing many of the city's residents. Jobs and population had been leaving the city for decades; public school performance was dismal; and rates of unemployment, poverty, poor health, and hardship were high. Conditions were especially bleak in the city's poor neighborhoods, where decades of racial segregation, disinvestment, and neglect fostered severe isolation and distress. People living in these neighborhoods faced daunting risks and few prospects for economic security or advancement. Scenes from the Superdome and the flooded streets of New Orleans exposed the poverty and vulnerability of many African American residents. (Turner, September 8, 2006, p. 3)

In general, social services for the predominately low-income, African American population in New Orleans was a marginally effective, yet fragile, system of primarily local, state, and federal programs and resources (Lister, 2005). Thus, it is clear that impoverished and minority populations had already been given substandard assistance prior to Katrina.

The events during and after the hurricane illuminated this to state officials as well as other persons around the nation. Thus, after Katrina, numerous federal agencies, such as SAMHSA, provided funding to have mental health and social services workers assist in providing appropriate services to persons who were impacted by Katrina. Indeed, two of the authors of this chapter were involved with post-Katrina response, particularly in relation to drug abusing populations who had additional mental health disorders. In many cases, these services were provided in tandem with community supervision agency personnel. These personnel also faced numerous challenges related to mistrust among the minority population of state agency workers due to the poor rapport that these agencies had with minority communities prior to Katrina. Likewise, because many of these communities also had poor relations with police and child service organizations, mental health and social service workers developed an appreciation for culturally competent and culturally relevant services. A new interest in training and an emphasis on culturally competent interventions emerged in the region as a means of addressing the sense of mistrust that had only been exacerbated by sensationalized events during Katrina.

A year after Katrina, law enforcement agencies in the city of New Orleans as well as the Orleans Parish and Jefferson Parish areas have indicated that they had more calls for service related to domestic violence, suicide, substance abuse, and mental health commitments than before the storm hit the city. This is even more important when one considers that the overall population of New Orleans was substantially less after the storm than it was prior to the hurricane; meaning that the total number of calls (not per capita, but total calls) for these types of services were fewer prior to the storm when a larger population existed than was seen with a smaller population, a year later (Turner, November 2006). Indeed, the number of suicides in Orleans Parish tripled during the year that followed the hurricane (Turner, November 2006).

These developments as well as others throughout Louisiana have prompted police agencies throughout the state to embrace what is commonly referred to as Crisis Intervention Team (CIT) training. This training is for police officers and is intended to familiarize officers with various symptoms and issues associated with many of the more commonly encountered forms of mental illness and to provide them nonlethal tools to resolve circumstances in as peaceful a manner as the situation may reasonably present. The CIT training is also effective at improving police–community relations and can aid in avoiding outcomes like that observed on Danziger Bridge. The lead author of this chapter is a CIT responder and also a trainer and has seen firsthand how this type of officer approach can de-escalate encounters and also preserve a positive image within the community.

Police Trauma Assistance—Assistance Through Police Peer Support

The psychological impact of Hurricane Katrina also continued to have an impact on law enforcement responders during the early days of recovery. Indeed, it is clear that many police officials had suffered trauma from the rescue of stranded residents and working under chaotic conditions, but they did not tend to seek assistance for their trauma (Wellborn, 2006). As a result, it had repeatedly been reported that "officers are having trouble controlling their tempers and are getting into altercations with people on routine calls (Wellborn, 2006). Traditional cop culture generally does not support officers in seeking mental health assistance, thus many who have been affected with traumatic events do not report these concerns and problems in environments where it is appropriate and, instead, allow their careers and family life to suffer. As a result, many agencies have turned to Critical Incident Stress Debriefing, which is a service provided by other police colleagues to aid officers in trauma.

In Louisiana, the Southern Law Enforcement Foundation has spearheaded these types of debriefings and presently consists of hundreds of volunteers from various agencies who respond to debriefing needs. Though these debriefing teams will typically have a mental health expert as part of the team, the foundation makes it clear that these debriefings are not counseling and are not intended to be psychotherapy. Rather, on the foundation's Web site, the following statement can be found:

> Often misunderstood as a form of counseling, the tools we use are not designed to fix what's broken, but help mitigate the critical stress immediately following an incident. By learning new coping skills the officers learn how to lower the impact of critical incident stress. It's not counseling, it's support. It's cops helping cops. (Southern Law Enforcement Foundation, 2013)

The use of critical incident debriefing teams has continued in response to other potentially traumatic incidents. The lead author of this chapter is a trained team member and has served as the mental health member on debriefing teams associated with police and correctional incidents. These types of interventions can be very effective in aiding officers who respond to traumatic events like Hurricane Katrina and showcase how one cannot ignore the psychological impact of traumatic events for victims as well as our police officers who respond to those events.

Police and Corrections Partnerships to Address the Offender Population

During the time shortly after Katrina's landfall, when the flooding first began, it became apparent to law enforcement and correctional staff that inmates in many of the facilities around the city would need to be evacuated. The largest jail facility in New Orleans, the Orleans Parish Prison (OPP), was and still is operated by the Orleans Parish Sheriff's Office. This facility is not, in actuality, a true prison but is a jail. It is, however, one of the largest jails in the nation. The inmates of this facility were kept at the facility throughout the storm but, once the facility began to flood, their transfer was inevitable. These inmates were ferried, by small boat, a handful at a time, over a three-day time period, to an overpass of a highway in the area (Morton, 2006). After two days on the overpass under supervision of parish deputies, these inmates were bused to multiple facilities throughout the state. Many of the conditions under which inmates were temporarily kept were reported to be crude and primitive, with numerous incidents of violence, victimization, and maltreatment noted.

From this time of inmate relocation, a number of issues have developed over the years that followed. One key problem was that inmates who were labeled as gang members or associates were further intermixed throughout the larger correctional population in the state. Because internal tracking and data sources were destroyed, the ability to follow up on these inmates had been seriously impaired. This meant that institutions (including jail facilities that would eventually house inmates from New Orleans and outlying areas) would have unknown gang affiliations within their jurisdiction. While the official stance of the Louisiana Department of Public Safety and Corrections (LDPS&C) is that there is no gang problem within the correctional system, local gangs in New Orleans have existed for years, as well as members of the "Crips" gang who had arrived from California into Shreveport, where they have existed for over two decades. In fact, Shreveport is the hometown of Tookie Williams, a founder of the "Crip Nation," and he has made numerous visits to the city.

Proof of the gang problem in Louisiana can be found in numerous original courtroom documents (see *State of Louisiana v. Micheal A. Cooks*, 1998) where prosecutors note that defendants are members of the "Rollin' 60's Crips." During the late 1990s, a number of other arrests of gang members involved in the drug trade had been made in Shreveport, such as those involving the "Bottom Boys." In New Orleans, official arrests of members of the "Latin Kings," with ties to members in Miami, have been recorded by local and federal officials. However, the primary gang threat in New Orleans has consistently come from a variety of local-grown gangs. Consider the following excerpt from the National Drug Intelligence Center, which stated that:

> The "posses" or "crews" that are identified by neighborhood or public housing project, the Mosley Gang, Perry Francois Gang, Dillon Gang, and Got It Boys, are the larger, more active neighborhood street gangs. According to the latest estimates, there are approximately 16 gangs with 400 members in New Orleans. (National Drug Intelligence Center, 2001)

The simple fact is that in various areas of the state, gang task forces that include law enforcement and correctional personnel have been formed; certainly there is no need for such task forces if no gang problem existed within the state.

Members of these various 16 gangs, with membership over 400 strong, are what were purportedly thought to have evacuated to Texas, with most going into the Houston area. This is what is thought to have led to much of the spike in crime in the Houston region within a year after Katrina. Many of these gang offenders were among those individuals who were on community supervision in New Orleans and, because there was no plan for probation and parole personnel to track evacuated persons on community supervision, the eventual process of locating these offenders took well over a year. Even then, the process was hampered by the loss of two office sites in the city for supervising offenders in Jefferson and Orleans Parish.

During the initial few weeks after Katrina, many supervision officers with Louisiana Probation and Parole assisted other law enforcement personnel (in Louisiana, officers in Probation and Parole are sworn officers who routinely carry firearms) in search and rescue forays throughout the southern part of the state, aided fire departments, and also assisted 911 dispatchers in the aftermath of Katrina. Thus, it is clear that the community corrections segment of personnel in Louisiana worked directly with other law enforcement personnel; naturally this prevented them from maintaining their offender caseloads during this time, which exacerbated the problems that eventually emerged in various areas of Texas.

Later, after Katrina rescue efforts had ceased and the rebuilding of New Orleans began, a new gang problem emerged in New Orleans; one that city police and regional sheriff's deputies had not anticipated; this involved the emergence of the Mara Salvatrucha (MS-13) into the area (Nguyen, 2006). The arrival of these gang members was observed by law enforcement among an estimated 50,000 or so Latino workforce of contractors who were hired to aid in the rebuilding of the city. Among these workers were members of the MS-13 who, while working in construction, eventually set roots in the south Louisiana region. This obvious threat has been taken seriously by the Louisiana State Police who offered a gang awareness seminar in Baton Rouge for several law enforcement agencies (Nguyen, 2006).

Conclusion

It is clear that, for the state of Louisiana, Hurricane Katrina was a historical marker that tested the ability of that state's law enforcement and correctional system personnel, as well as various disaster response, medical, and other auxiliary emergency response services. However, it was not just Louisiana who had been put to the test, it turned out that it tested the entire nation. The outcome was one that exposed a number of weak spots in response services in the city of New Orleans, as well as the state of Louisiana and, ultimately, that of the nation itself.

In relation to the state of Louisiana, it was clear that policies and procedures on interagency coordination were in serious need of improvement to better address exigent circumstances. This included coordination in operations, as well as backup communication systems. Throughout the state, numerous agencies remained aloof as to the operation of other organizations, many of which were seeking to accomplish the same mission during the crisis. This caused serious lag time in response and impaired the ability to use resources in an optimal manner. This is true in regard to police agency collaboration with emergency response agencies as well as with other segments of the criminal justice system. Leadership in these agencies was forced to take ownership to facilitate this collaboration between and among agencies.

As to the city of New Orleans, it was clear that the operational readiness of police and other services was in need of improvement, both in terms of training and in terms of better technology and equipment. During the past eight years, improvements in technological data storage systems and communication processes have been made, often with the support of the U.S. Department of Homeland Security. In addition, significant efforts have been made to improve personnel standards within the NOPD through better hiring and vigorous training initiatives. In addition to an emphasis on responder practices, the reinforcement of ethical practices, culturally competent policing, and the need for effective police–community relations have been observed. While it is, of course, sad that such improvements were seen only after such a disaster, the strides that the city of New Orleans and the state of Louisiana have made to contend with these deficiencies do demonstrate that numerous agencies and their personnel, whether law enforcement or otherwise, are determined to not allow another similar incident to occur in the state of Louisiana.

References

Baum, D. (January 9, 2006). Deluged: When Katrina hit: Where were the police? *The New Yorker*. Retrieved October 14, 2013 from: http://www.newyorker.com/archive/2006/01/09/060109fa_fact

Chua, A., Kaynak, S., & Foo, S. (2007). An analysis of the delayed response to Hurricane Katrina through the lens of knowledge management. *Journal of the American Society for Information Science and Technology, 58*(3), 391–403.

Donnelly, B. (August 27, 2010). Katrina five years after: Hurricane left a legacy of health concerns. Retrieved October 2, 2013 from: http://www.foxnews.com/health/2010/08/27/katrina-years-hurricane-left-legacy-health-concerns/

Dowden, F. G. (2006). Hurricane Katrina: Managing Law Enforcement and Communications in a Catastrophe. Washington, DC: U.S. Senate Testimony (February 6, 2006). Retrieved October 1, 2013 from: http://www.gpo.gov/fdsys/pkg/CHRG-109shrg27025/html/CHRG-109shrg27025.htm

Hoffpauir, S. A., & Woodruff, L. A. (2008). Effective mental response to catastrophic events: Lessons learned from Hurricane Katrina [Electronic version]. *Family & Community Health, 31*(1), 17–22.

Hughes, P. R. (August 10, 2006). State sheds light on plight of evacuees. *Houston Chronicle*.

Jervis, R. (January 8, 2013). Former New Orleans mayor Ray Nagin indicted. *USA Today*. Retrieved September 28, 2013 from: http://www.usatoday.com/story/news/nation/2013/01/18/new-orleans-mayor-ray-nagin/1845617/

Johnson, K. (February 20, 2006). Katrina made police choose between duty and loved ones. *USA Today.* Retrieved September 28, 2013 from: http://usatoday30.usatoday.com/news/nation/2006-02-20-neworleanspolice_x.htm

Jones, R. T., Immel, C. S., Moore, R. M., & Hadder, J. M. (2008). Hurricane Katrina: Experiences of psychologists and implications for future disaster response [Electronic version]. *Professional Psychology: Research and Practice, 39*(1), 100–106.

Kennett, J. (March 3, 2006). Louisiana gangs that fled Katrina heighten Houston murder rate. *Bloomberg Press.* Retrieved September 29, 2013 from: http://www.bloomberg.com/apps/news?pid=newsarchive&sid=az6n8C6gsqf0

Lister, S. A. (October 5, 2005). Gulf Coast hurricanes: The public health and medical response. *Congressional Research Service.* Washington, DC: The Library of Congress.

Lister, S. (2005). Hurricane Katrina: The public health and medical response (CRS-24). *Congressional Research Service.* Washington, DC: The Library of Congress.

Lonergan, S. (1995). Population movements and the environment. *RPN, 18,* 1–4, http://www.fmreview.org.rmn181.htm

Michaels, D. (April 14, 2006). Katrina left flood of felons in Texas: DPS warns local police of Louisiana evacuees on parole or probation. *The Dallas Morning News.* Retrieved July 20, 2014 from: http://www.dallasnews.com/sharedcontent/dws/dn/latestnews/stories/041406dntexcriminals.1c6ce522.html

Morton, D. (August 10, 2006). Empire Falls: The rise and decline of the New Orleans jail. *The New Republic.* https://ssl.tnr.com/p/docsub.mhtml?i=20060814&s=morton081406

National Drug Intelligence Center. (2001). Louisiana Drug Threat Assessment. Washington, DC: United States Department of Justice. Retrieved October 10, 2013 from: http://www.justice.gov/archive/ndic/pubs0/666/cocaine.htm

Nguyen, C. (2006). Baton Rouge, state authorities prepare to battle gangs in Louisiana. *WAFB 9 News.* Retrieved September 29, 2013 from: http://www.wafb.com/story/4829962/baton-roue-state-authorities-prepare-to-battle-gangs-in-louisiana

Perlstein, M. (July 30, 2007). Staying above Water: Survival in the post-Katrina NOPD. *New Orleans Magazine.* Retrieved October 1, 2013 from http://neworleansmagazine.com/in-this-issue/articles/news/staying-abovewater-2506.html

Philips, S. (September 9, 2005). What went wrong in hurricane crisis? *Dateline NBC,* interview transcript.

Pullin, M (2006). Impact of Katrina evacuees upon law enforcement. Huntsville, TX: TELEMASP Bulletin, Texas Law Enforcement Management and Administrative Statistics Program, Law Enforcement Management Institute of Texas.

Riley, W. J. (2006). Testimony of Warren J. Riley, Superintendent of the New Orleans Police Department before the Senate Committee on Homeland Security and Governmental Affairs. Monday, February 6, 2006, 2:00 p.m. Retrieved July 20, 2014 from: file:///C:/Users/Owner/Music/Downloads/020606Riley.pdf

Riley, W. J. (2007). Testimony of Warren J. Riley superintendent of the New Orleans Police Department before the Senate Committee on Homeland Security and Governmental Affairs. New Orleans. LA: Dillard University.

Roberts, M. (September 28, 2005). Superdome crime more urban myth than real. *Houston Chronicle*. Retrieved October 14, 2013 from: http://www.chron.com/news/hurricanes/article/Superdome-crime-more-urban-myth-than-real-1479934.php

Roman, C. G., Irazola, S., & Osborne, J. W. (2007). *After Katrina: Washed away? Justice in New Orleans*. Washington, DC: Urban Institute.

Sandberg, L. (July 28, 2006). Katrina parolees on lam in Texas. Many criminals who evacuated Louisiana remain unaccounted for. *Houston Chronicle*. http://www.chron.com/disp/story.mpl/front/4078030.html

Shankman, S., Jennings, T., McCarthy, B., Maggi, L., & Thompson, A. C. (July 24, 2012). After Katrina, New Orleans cops were told they could shoot looters. *ProPublica*. Retrieved October 5, 2013 from: http://www.propublica.org/nola/story/nopd-order-to-shoot-looters-hurricane-katrina/

Sobel, R. S., & Leeson, P. T. (2006). Government's response to Hurricane Katrina: A public choice analysis. *Public Choice, 127,* 55–73.

Southern Law Enforcement Foundation. (2013). *Southern Law Enforcement Foundation*. Retrieved July 20,2014 from: http://www.slefoundation.org/

State of Louisiana v. Micheal A. Cooks. (1999), No. 97-KA-0999. Retrieved July 20, 2014 from: http://www.lasc.org/opinions/97ka0999.opn.pdf

Tanber, G. (September 23, 2005). Katrina: A criminal catastrophe. Arrested on misdemeanors, left to die in flooded jail. *The Toledo Blade*.

Turner, A. (September 8, 2006). 69% of poor evacuees are here to stay. *Houston Chronicle*.

Turner, D. (November 2006). Mental health problems for Katrina persist. *The Washington Post*. Retrieved October 19, 2013 from: http://www.washington-post.com/wp-dyn/content/article/2006/11/08/AR2006110802135.html

Wellborn, J. (November 2006). Interview with Dorie Turner in mental health problems for Katrina persist. *The Washington Post*. Retrieved October 19, 2013 from: http://www.washingtonpost.com/wp-dyn/content/article/2006/11/08/AR2006110802135.html

Zuckerman, S., & Coughlin, T. (2006). Initial health policy responses to Hurricane Katrina and possible next steps. Retrieved October 4, 2012 from: http://www.urban.org/UploadedPDF/900929_health_policy.pdf

About the Authors

Dr. Robert D. Hanser is a criminal justice professor and the director of the Institute of Law Enforcement at the University of Louisiana at Monroe. Dr. Nathan Moran is a professor of criminal justice and department chair at Midwestern State University in Texas. Professor Anissa Horne works at the North Delta Human Services Authority and Richwood Correctional Center in Louisiana.

Coordinating Police Responses to Critical Events in United Nations Mission Areas

10

MICHAEL R. SANCHEZ

Contents

Introduction

Coordinating critical incident response in a United Nations mission area is a much more complex endeavor than one might think. Effective response requires the coordination of four separate components. Each element possesses its own unique role, command structure, nationality, and leadership. There are frequently cultural, linguistic, operational, and doctrinal barriers to effective coordination of these separate components that must be overcome. Additionally, the political nature of a United Nations mission, issues of sovereignty, ethnic sensitivity, perceived bias, limited rules of engagement, and the restrictive nature of the mission mandate can severely affect critical incident response in a United Nations mission area. In order to conduct effective critical incident response in a United Nations mission, one must possess effective communications skills. The ability to communicate effectively and diplomatically is absolutely necessary in such a diverse environment.

Serving as a police officer in a United Nations Police (UNPOL) mission is quite different from domestic police service. In order to gain a clear understanding of critical incident response in United Nations mission areas, one must first explore the unique nature of an UNPOL mission along with each of the different critical incident response components. Each component has a definitive role to play along with unique capabilities and limitations. When it comes to critical incident response, these components are expected to cooperate and collaborate effectively.

The United Nations Mission in Kosovo (UNMIK) and the United Nations Stabilization Mission in Haiti (MINUSTAH) represent two different types of United Nations police missions that provide excellent contrast for analysis. Each of the mission areas has experienced critical incidents that permit greater depth of insight.[*]

The United Nations, Peacekeeping, and Police Missions

The United Nations engages in peacekeeping operations around the world. The composition of a United Nations peacekeeping mission is a mixture

---

[*] A portion of the information in this chapter is a result of the author's personal experience having served in upper level command positions in two different United Nations police missions. The author served the United Nations Mission in Kosovo (UNMIK) Police from 2005 through 2008 and ultimately served as the Director of Personnel and Administration for UNMIK Police. In this position, the author was a member of the UNMIK Police Commissioner's Senior Staff. The author also served as a regional commander for the United Nations Stabilization Mission in Haiti (MINUSTAH) Police in 2009 and 2010.

of civilian administration, military, police, and formed police unit (FPU) components (Benner & Mergenthaler, 2008). Each individual mission contains a unique blend of these elements based on the nature of the unrest or conflict that gave rise to the need for peacekeepers. The exact blend of components is also dependent on the mission mandate as defined by the United Nations Security Council (Hårleman, 2003).

The use of United Nations police in peacekeeping missions began in 1960 when the United Nations deployed international police officers to the Congo (Mobekk, 2005). Early United Nations police missions tasked the UNPOL officers with monitoring local police to discourage abuses. This monitoring task was part of the overarching goal at the time of simply preventing further violence (Levine, 2008). Even up to this point, the development, modernization, democratization, and capacity building of the host nations' police had not been attempted.

United Nations peacekeeping and policing went through several growth stages until 1999 when the United Nations Mission in Kosovo (UNMIK) and the United Nations Transitional Administration in Timor-Leste (UNTAET) were both formed. Both of these missions represented a transition into what is known as the "fourth generation" of peacekeeping missions (Silander, 2009). These missions utilized large UNPOL forces that were granted executive policing authority. Both missions were tasked with mentoring and capacity building of the indigenous police agencies. The shift to a larger more challenging role for UNPOL components indicates that UNMIK and UNTAET could also be considered the beginning of the modern era of UNPOL missions.

The need for the shift to larger more ambitious police missions has come from the realization that the stabilization of organic police components is crucial to the creation of rule of law and the development of the host nation (Bayley, 2006; Durch & England, 2010). Police are frequently a mechanism for oppression and must be reformed for a peacekeeping mission to have any reasonable chance of success. Democratic transformation of a country or province would seem to be an impossible goal unless one started by reforming the police. The modern era of UN policing focuses on reorganization of the police as an integral part of the mission mandate. The expansion of UNPOL's role in peacekeeping can be seen by the growth in UNPOL deployments over the past 20 years. In 1995, UNPOL officers comprised only 2% of UN Peacekeeping forces deployed worldwide. By 2007, this ratio increased sixfold to 12% (Smith, Holt, & Durch, 2007).

The modern era of peacekeeping missions included a fundamental shift in the strategic goals of the UN Police. In past missions, the UNPOL officers were assigned as monitors to *observe and report*. The modern era of peacekeeping has seen UN Police more actively engaged in assisting in the democratic reform, restructuring, and mentoring of local police. The UNPOL is now recognized as the primary engine of reform, training, mentoring, and capacity building of organic police forces (Smith, Holt, & Durch, 2007).

The advent of the modern era of UNPOL missions has seen large robust missions being fielded (Hårleman, 2003). In 1998 there were almost 3000 UNPOL officers deployed in missions around the world. In 2010, that number increased to 13,500 UNPOL officers representing 87 nations serving in 13 United Nations missions worldwide (Durch & England, 2010; Rotman, 2011) (Figure 10.1).

The modern era of large, robust, and technically challenging UNPOL missions is also a very expensive proposition. Consider the example of the UNMIK police mission in Kosovo. All UNPOL officers are paid a per diem by the United Nations of 68€ (approximately $91) per day. This per diem is referred to as a Mission Subsistence Allowance (MSA). The annual overall MSA cost alone for the UNMIK police mission had been estimated to be $115,000,000 (Muharremi, Peci, Malazogu, Knaus, & Murati, 2003). As with almost everything in the modern world, cost is an important consideration. Ultimately, cost has played a role in adjusting the composition of peacekeeping missions.

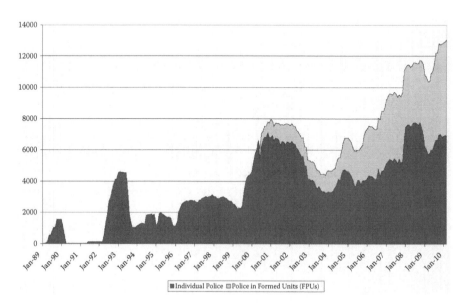

Figure 10.1 UN Police deployments, 1989–2010. (From Durch, W. & England, M., 2010, *Enhancing United Nations Capacity to Support Post-Conflict Policing and Rule of Law (revised)*, Washington, DC: The Stimson Center.)

The Creation of a Peacekeeping Mission and Establishment of a Mandate

The United Nations is a consensus building organization comprised of 192 sovereign nations that reach agreements through cooperation and collaboration (Fasulo, 2009). The UN Security Council (UNSC) debates and acts on matters of international security. A United Nations peacekeeping mission is normally created by passage of a UN Security Council Resolution (UNSCR) authorizing a specific mission. The resolution also defines the all-important *mandate* of a peacekeeping mission. The mandate is the overarching goal of the mission (Hårleman, 2003).

Each UN Security Council Resolution authorizing a peacekeeping mission articulates a separate mandate for the UN Police component. The individual standard operational procedure and operational doctrine of an UNPOL mission must conform to that mission's unique mandate. Each mission's authorization is completely different since the mandate reflects the status and needs of the beneficiary country or region. A Security Council Resolution can establish a police mandate that can activate thousands of UNPOL officers; however, the mandate itself can be deceptively simple and succinct.

The United Nations Mission in Kosovo

The United Nations Mission in Kosovo (UNMIK) mission was created as a result of the exit of the Serbian government from Kosovo in June of 1999. While Kosovo was a province of Serbia, the population of Kosovo was approximately 85% ethnic Albanians. Despite being a distinct minority, ethnic Serbs had monopolized all local and provincial governmental positions as part of a nationalist movement following the breakup of Yugoslavia. Backlash from a brutal 1998–1999 crackdown on ethnic Albanians by the Serbian military caused the international community to step in to stop the reported bloodshed. NATO forces engaged in a 79-day bombing campaign against Serbian troops in Kosovo and Serbia proper in order to force Serbia to withdraw its military presence from Kosovo. When the Serbian government finally relented and agreed to withdraw, the Serbs not only took the Serbian Army, but all of the governmental components that had been placed in Kosovo as well. Kosovo had thereafter essentially become a province without a functioning government. The UN Security Council Resolution that authorized the UNMIK mission was UNSCR 1244, which had been enacted in June 1999. UNSCR 1244, Article 11 described in specific detail the primary responsibilities of the UNMIK mission. Only one sentence pertains to the UNMIK Police, that is, paragraph "i" states that the mission is responsible for "(m)aintaining civil law and order, including establishing local police forces and meanwhile through the deployment of international police personnel to serve in Kosovo" (UNSCR 1244, 1999, p. 4).

The UNMIK police mission was fully operational from 1999 until 2008. During that nine-year time frame, the UNMIK Police deployed thousands of UNPOL officers throughout Kosovo. Over those years, security and rule of law has been reestablished in post-conflict Kosovo. The most resounding success story has involved the development, training, and formation of the Kosovo Police Service, a modern and relatively effective 8000 person national law enforcement agency.

The United Nations Stabilization Mission in Haiti

The MINUSTAH mission was created in 2004 by UNSCR 1529 in response to extreme lawlessness and noted instability within Haitian governmental institutions. Section 2, paragraph "c" of UNSCR 1529 authorized the deployment of an interim United National police mission for a period *not to exceed 3 months* to: "… facilitate the provision of international assistance to the Haitian police and the Haitian Coast Guard in order to establish and maintain public safety and law and order and to promote and protect human rights" (UNSCR 1529, 2004, p. 2). The mandate of the MINUSTAH mission has been consistently extended and is currently still operational (i.e., through 2014).

While the articulation of the mandate is quite succinct, the directive could be viewed as merely a strategic statement, since the determination on precisely *how* to achieve that objective has been left to the United Nations Department of Peacekeeping Operations (DPKO). Within the United Nations, law enforcement specific elements of a Security Council Resolution are normally administered by the Police Division of DPKO. One can note that these mandates both contain language designed to engage the UNPOL component in training, rebuilding, and mentoring. The modern era of UNPOL missions now includes the UNPOL officer performing a transformational role in peacekeeping (Durch & England, 2010).

Comparison of the UNMIK and MINUSTAH Mandates

It must be highlighted that the mandates authorizing the UNMIK and MINUSTAH missions had been very different. Key factors in the variations between these two directives and missions have influenced the dynamics of incident response in each mission area and make these two endeavors excellent for comparison and discussion, particularly as it relates to critical incident response.

The UNMIK mission had been established because Kosovo, which had still nominally been a province of Serbia, had been left without any functioning governmental institutions or services. In order to restore basic public services, rule of law, and civil order, the UNMIK mission had been created to become the de facto government of Kosovo. The UNMIK Police were vested with executive authority, which meant that they had been empowered to enforce the laws of Kosovo, conduct investigations, make arrests, and file criminal and civil charges. In addition, during critical incidents, the UNMIK Police, due to this executive authority, were tasked with the responsibility to restore order and to protect the citizens of Kosovo. As such, a sector of the UNMIK Police, including the Special Police Units, had been developed specifically to respond to disorder and unrest, and was responsible for reinstating order and making arrests if necessary.

The MINUSTAH mission in Haiti was created by the UN Security Council at the specific request and invitation of the Haitian Government. Unlike Kosovo, which had no functioning government, Haiti was and still is a sovereign nation. In comparison to the UNMIK police mission, the MINUSTAH Police were not granted executive authority, although they were armed for self-protection. It should be noted that many UN Police missions are unarmed. As a nonexecutive police force, the MINUSTAH Police *did not* have the authority to enforce the laws of Haiti, to investigate crimes, or to make arrests. Thus, the actions of the MINUSTAH Police would be subject to more restrictions and situational considerations than that of the UNMIK Police.

UN Peacekeeping Missions: Operational Elements in Critical Incident Response

There are four operational elements that have a role to play in critical incident response in a United Nations mission area. Each element is unique with its own capabilities and limitations. Each factor has its own particular role to play.

"Organic" Police Forces

While not a United Nations asset, local or "organic" police forces are central to the critical response capability of a United Nations mission. The UN Police essentially exist only to develop, mentor, and build the capacity of the organic police agencies in the mission area. The local police organizations are expected to manage critical incident response when the UNPOL mission leaves their country, so it makes sense that this force be developed into an integral part of disaster and disorder response while the United Nations Police mission is in place. It is obvious that the nature, composition, and capabilities of these organic police forces vary greatly from mission to mission.

Kosovo Police Service

The Kosovo Police Service (KPS) was not in existence when the UNMIK Police mission started in 1999; in fact, there were no functional public service organizations whatsoever in Kosovo. One of the unique aspects of the UNMIK Police mission was that for a considerable amount of time, the UNMIK Police *were* the de facto police in Kosovo. Part of the UNMIK Police mission mandate was the recruitment, vetting, training, mentoring, and capacity building of the KPS from scratch. This mandate was exceptionally challenging and represents the first time the United Nations created a national police service from its infancy. Since Kosovo unilaterally declared her independence in 2008, the Kosovo Police Service has been renamed the Kosovo Police (KP).

The KPS was recruited and vetted to reflect the cultural diversity of Kosovo. In a post-conflict region that was rife with ethnic tensions, there would be no other way to create a police force that would be seen as legitimate and accepted by the entire populace. After a full 14 years since inception, the KPS is now a modern multiethnic national police force on par with other federal law enforcement agencies located within the Balkan region.

Critical incident response capabilities within the KPS lie mainly with the Regional Operational Support Units (ROSU). As Kosovo is divided into six regions, each of them maintains its own Regional KPS Command, which includes a ROSU unit. These units perform a variety of functions, from high-risk arrests to serving warrants, and crowd and riot control.

During the tenure of the UNMIK Police mission, each ROSU unit had UNPOL officers assigned to it as coordinators and mentors. The ROSU units were initially trained by the multinational NATO Kosovo Force (K-FOR) military units operating in each respective region. This policy ultimately caused considerable problems because each of the six ROSU units had been trained by a military force from a different nation. As a result, each ROSU unit was instructed in a different crowd control philosophy and standard operating procedure. While this program appeared to function successfully on a regional level while the UNMIK mission was operational, by allowing the ROSU units to cooperate with the regional NATO national military units operating in their region, the policy was nevertheless shortsighted. During the final years of the UNMIK mission, as KPS was considering operating without UNMIK Police support, it was realized that having the ROSU units trained by their NATO regional counterparts also meant that the ROSU units could not easily cooperate or collaborate with each other. After independence in 2008, the ability of the Kosovo police to combine ROSU teams from different regions to deal with exceptionally large civil disturbances could prove to become challenging under volatile conditions.

Police Nationale d'Haïti (PNH)

For most of the 20th century, Haiti has been politically unstable. In 1995 the Haitian Army, which was the vehicle for much of the oppression and dictatorial excesses in Haiti, was disbanded (Library of Congress, 2006). With the assistance of the United States and the United Nations, the Police Nationale d'Haïti (Haitian National Police), otherwise referred to as the PNH, was created to replace the disbanded military in providing law enforcement and rule of law in Haiti. However, the PNH itself was problematic from its inception due to the fact that many of the original PNH officers were former members of the Haitian Army.

The current UN Mission in Haiti, MINUSTAH, was created in April 2004. Assistance, mentoring, training, and capacity building of the PNH were central to the mandate for the UNPOL component of the MINUSTAH mission. While in Kosovo, the KPS served a population of 2 million and numbered approximately 8000 police officers of all ranks, by contrast, Haiti's population is approximately 8.3 million and the PNH numbers approximately 2000. One could therefore consider the PNH as a far less robust police force than the KPS. To examine this phenomenon further, the Les Cayes (Sud) region of Haiti covers the southwest corner of the lower peninsula of Haiti. This region is approximately 1000 square miles with a population of 800,000. The PNH component for this region encompasses 23 police stations, called *commissariats*, and 365 police officers.

The PNH has regionally based specialized units, similar in concept to the KPS ROSU units, called *Unité Départementale de Maintien de l'Ordre* (i.e., the Departmental Unit of Maintenance of Order) or UDMO. UDMO units are, however, small, ill-equipped, and poorly trained. Similar to the ROSU units, UDMO officers engage in special patrols, high-risk arrests, raids, and riot control. Training of UDMO units has been conducted by the UNPOL officers assigned to the region. As a common practice, this task has usually fallen upon the French police officers deployed within the mission. The bridge between the local specialized riot police and international military forces that was observed within Kosovo has been absent in Haiti. There was no direct interaction between the UN military component and the UDMO officers. UDMO units were supposed to be the front-line units when civil unrest occurred; however, the units were not robust or substantially staffed enough to regularly undertake this role.

The United Nations Police (UNPOL) Program

UNPOL officers are considered by the United Nations to be experts in their field and are geared more toward monitoring and mentoring than active policing. As a general rule, UNPOL officers rarely engage in traditional law enforcement activities, except in missions that have an executive mandate. While UNPOL officers in UNMIK conducted a considerable amount of patrolling early in the mission, these duties had been transitioned to the KPS as soon as possible. The UNMIK UNPOL officers then focused on monitoring the progress of KPS and mentoring all levels of the organization. MINUSTAH UNPOL officers were largely involved in monitoring and mentoring of the PNH and engaged in no independent enforcement duties whatsoever.

UNPOL officers are deployed as individual police officers from their home country's national police force to serve in an UNPOL mission. This process is called *secondment*. Since America does not have a national police force per se, potential UNPOL officers are routinely recruited from across America, vetted, trained, deployed, and provided with administrative and logistical support by a private contractor. Specific private companies contract with the U.S. State Department to provide American police officers to the United Nations UNPOL program.

Unlike military officials deployed to conflict and post-conflict zones, UNPOL officers live on the economy of the mission area. They rent an apartment or hotel room, shop in local supermarkets, and eat in local restaurants. Living within the community has caused the UNPOL officer to be tied more closely to that community. To defray this individual cost, UNPOL officers are paid MSA directly from the United Nations. For many countries, MSA is a significant amount of money. The MSA for MINUSTAH UNPOL officers was $150 per day, which averaged out to approximately $4500 per month. For a police officer in Eastern Europe or Africa who makes $300 per month, MSA represents a financial windfall of epic proportions as well as a significant cost for the United Nations.

In the past, the primary role of an UNPOL officer in the field has been to monitor the local police force's activity and report. The idea being that organic police forces would make improvements if they knew that they were being observed and that their actions were being monitored. While being watched might motivate a developing police agency to change, it does not necessarily provide them with the support or training to make the needed revisions. The modern era of peacekeeping has seen the role of the UNPOL officer expand to that of adviser and mentor to the local police organization (Kember, 2010). Development and capacity building of the local police force is important because this agency will have to act on its own eventually. According to the MINSUTAH Standard Operating Procedure (2004), one of the primary responsibilities of an UNPOL officer is to: "(a)dvise the local police on the appropriate means to handle the situation, be persuasive and attempt to explain, demonstrate, and encourage the appropriate response. If necessary, verbally intercede and strongly recommend appropriate action" (p. 16). The MINUSTAH SOP (United Nations Security Council, 2004) goes on to say that if the unacceptable behavior of the local police continues, the UNPOL should prepare an "incident report" (p. 16).

In contrast, the UNMIK police had an executive police mission, which gave them the authority to take definitive action up to and including arresting an offender. As can be seen in the language of the MINUSTAH SOP (2004), the responsibilities and capabilities of a nonexecutive mission are far more restrictive. An UNPOL officer in the MINUSTAH mission does not have the authority to take over a situation that is out of control; they could only recommend a course of action to the PNH.

UNPOL officers also serve in support positions throughout the UNPOL mission organization. In both the UNMIK and MINUSTAH missions, there were UNPOL officers serving as administrative clerks, counselors, IT specialists, trainers, fleet management, and logistics positions. In comparison, relatively few UNPOLs actually serve daily in direct contact with the host country's police organization. More notably, UNPOL officers are rarely expected to be actively engaged in riot control activities. And UNPOL advisers to local police supervisors are engaged in mentoring and advising these regional and central headquarters commanders. UNPOL officers could be deployed to actively take part in anti-riot operations in extreme emergencies, and have done so in the past, but this has been very rare.

United Nations Formed Police Units

In post-conflict zones where there is still the threat of violence or instability, the United Nations has often deployed specific complements to deal with riot and disorder control and disaster response. These Formed Police Units (FPUs) are the crowd control and critical incident specialists in many United Nations mission areas. They are deployed as a complete company-sized unit comprised of between 120 and 140 officers. FPU units have proven to be highly effective when more manpower and force may be required and clearly more than regionally deployed UNPOL or local law enforcement officers can provide. FPU units are also capable of being deployed with more precision than a military unit might be (Durch & England, 2010). The FPU unit is considered to be an integral part of the security of a UN mission area; however, these units do also have their limitations.

The first FPUs used by the United Nations were deployed within the UNMIK mission area in Kosovo. FPUs have been conceived as a heavily armed, rapid deployment complement that could handle incidents that were too large or violent for executive policing UNPOL units. FPUs are cohesive units that are comprised of police officers; in most cases they include personnel from paramilitary police organizations, such as France's *gendarmerie* or Italy's *carabinieri*. The FPU role can be viewed to be a perfect fit for these paramilitary resources, since their national role is generally considered to be more tactical than community oriented.

The FPUs deploy and train as a unit, and live in the mission area within their own base. The strategic placement of FPU bases across the mission area would conceivably allow for quick response to emergencies and effective coverage of contingency events. It has been reported that this rapid deployment capability has made the FPUs a versatile and flexible component (Hansen, 2011) of the UNPOL deployment.

Traditionally, the FPU officers live in barracks and eat in their own mess facility. The equipment and vehicles that an FPU uses are normally leased to the UN by the host nation for the duration of the unit's deployment. Without the necessity of paying MSA, deployment and support of an FPU unit is less costly than it would be for an equal number of UNPOL officers or UN military units. This noted cost-effectiveness of UN FPU units has fueled an increase in deployments of FPUs by the UN over the past 15 years.

What separates the FPU unit from regionally deployed UNPOLs is that an FPU is a cohesive unit from a single country. In addition, the FPU unit had already trained together before the unit's deployment. These Formed Police Units have three main responsibilities:

1. Public order management
2. Protection of United Nations personnel and facilities
3. Supporting police operations that require a formed response and may involve a higher risk and above the general capability of individual United Nations police (UNDPKO, 2010a)

The primary duty of the FPU is public order. These units are highly trained in crowd control and riot response. The mere presence of an FPU company involves a strong and visible show of force that frequently maintains order simply through deterrence. While generally the FPUs support the local police organization in the public order role, they are also capable of operating independently when the mission mandate permits. On the other hand, some FPUs can encounter the problem of interoperability with FPUs from different nations. In the past, conflicting operational philosophies and crowd control methodologies has inhibited cooperation between units (UNDPKO, 2010b; Hansen, 2011).

The FPU is very flexible and can operate as a company, platoon, squad, or at the team level. The UN Guidelines on FPU Operations (2010) has established that the smallest tactical subunit of an FPU involves a minimum of 10 police officers. However, in the field, FPUs frequently work in highly effective teams of five officers. The five-man team can occupy a single vehicle, and has been shown to be highly mobile and effective in MINUSTAH. The success of five-man teams has also allowed the FPU to stretch its resources considerably. The FPUs have proven to be an excellent bridge between the capabilities of the local police forces with UNPOL advisers and the military peacekeeping component (Hansen, 2011).

FPUs have also excelled in providing area security and providing a strong, visible deterrent to violence (Bruno, 2007). FPU five-man teams have been used extensively to provide area and polling place security during elections in Haiti, which had previously proven to be difficult and challenging to secure. Violence and intimidation at these sites has consistently been a problem. As an example, the Les Cayes Region in Haiti officially has more than 150 polling places. Securing a project of this parameter has been shown to be complex and challenging. The FPU teams have been excellent at providing area security for the most problematic polling areas. In the UNMIK mission, FPUs have been used to conduct Vehicle Check Points (VCPs), thereby providing a high visibility deterrent to potential problematic or criminal behavior.

In conclusion, Formed Police Units have become a very popular and effective tool in peacekeeping operations. They are flexible, competent, and inexpensive. In the days of shrinking budgets, an FPU can be a very cost-effective tool. Deployment of a battalion-sized military unit for peacekeeping duties costs the United Nations approximately $30 million, while the deployment of a United Nations FPU costs on average $5 million (Anderholt, 2012). The effectiveness and economy of FPU units is why half of all police personnel deployed to UN Peacekeeping operations are now in the form of FPU units (Hansen, 2011).

United Nations Military Peacekeeping Forces

UN Peacekeeping military forces constitute the second largest military component deployed globally (Fasulo, 2009). The traditional role of military peacekeeping forces has been to act as a physical and peaceful barrier between fighting groups in conflict areas. Peacekeeping duties require a well-trained military cadre that is capable of operating under the unusual constraints of the UN Peacekeeping mandate. National military forces are conceived, designed, and trained to fight other military units. Traditional military brigades normally engage enemy targets, seize enemy territory, and destroy enemy equipment with the goal of driving off or defeating the opposing force (Durch & England, 2010). Such training runs counter to the role of a peacekeeping force, which is expected to use force carefully and only as a last resort.

This philosophy gap can best be illustrated through an example. In 2006 in Kosovo, a committee was developed to review and revise the UNMIK mission's emergency plans. Representatives of the NATO K-FOR military component, UN Civilian Administration, UN Security personnel, and the UNMIK Police were assigned to this working group. A significant aspect of this plan involved the coordinated response of all mission components to a potential complete breakdown of civil order, war, or anarchy. In the event of a flare-up of hostilities or a serious breakdown of public order in a UN mission area, the UN philosophy is one of protecting UN personnel and evacuating from the mission area until the unrest or warfare quiets down. For this reason, UN personnel have been directed to never allow their UN vehicle's gas supply to fall below half a tank of fuel in order to ensure that there is enough in case of the need of evacuation. Recall, rally, and evacuation drills are common in UN missions. Due to the number of UN personnel present in a peacekeeping mission, evacuations would most likely take place by convoys of UN vehicles protected by FPU and military components.

The first order of business of this committee was to review the NATO security plan for the UN headquarters compound. Quite surprisingly, when the NATO K-FOR representatives revealed their defense plan for the UN facility, their intended secure perimeter had excluded two key aspects, the evacuation helipad and the fueling station. Queries about the omission of these vital resources were responded to by military officials by stating that the exclusion of these resources would make the perimeter more defensible and provide better "fields of fire." They continued that there was no need for vehicle fuel if UN personnel would remain inside of the defended perimeter, and as there was only one helipad, it could not be used to evacuate all UN staff by air. From the UN perspective, NATO was incorporating purely military logic. From the UNPOL perspective, helipads could have evacuated VIPs and wounded, as well as bring in ammunition and supplies. In addition, the UNMIK Police Close Protection Unit had been tasked with extracting UN personnel trapped in their accommodations and with bringing them to the UN headquarters site. As the entire UN contingent could conceivably have to be evacuated by convoy, it would have been difficult to conduct those operations without fuel.

It must be emphasized that UN or NATO military peacekeeping forces are not used for policing in peacekeeping missions. They are not trained for that role, but must nevertheless cooperate and collaborate with the UNPOL and FPU components. There are times, such as the first few months of the UNMIK mission in 1999, when the military component had been used to maintain basic order until UNPOL forces are able to deploy and operate effectively (Hills, 2007). As such, the military component is a critical aspect of a peacekeeping mission. The deployment of military resources to a peacekeeping site can provide a strong resource as they have been shown to present a capable and tactical option to support the public security operations that occur every day in a UN mission area.

Military peacekeeping forces do engage in routine and targeted patrol activities to increase visibility and deterrence across the mission area. The ubiquitous presence of a military component has been shown to ensure the free movement of the civilian population and has aided in keeping public order (UNDPKO, 2012). Of note is that international peacekeeping requires a military force to be highly disciplined. The rules of engagement are highly restrictive and regulated by the mandate. The level of force available and to be considered in any one situation has been shown therefore to be dependent on the mandates of the mission.

Finally, UN military peacekeeping personnel train extensively in riot and crowd control. Their training includes rapid deployment for intervention in a demonstration that has begun to spiral out of control. They are a critical supplement for the UNPOL FPUs if a situation were to get out of hand. In addition, most military peacekeeping components usually have armored personnel carriers and are more heavily armed than the local police, UNPOLs, or FPUs.

Coordination of Response to a Critical Incident

Coordination of the four components in response to a critical incident is accomplished in layers. The first layer is comprised of the local police resources with their UNPOL advisers embedded with them. The second layer is normally comprised of one or more UNPOL FPUs. The highest level involves the deployment of UN Peacekeeping military forces.

Coordination of these components usually occurs at the UNPOL regional level through the UNPOL Regional Commander, although higher levels of command can become involved depending on the mission and the nature of the disturbance. The coordination of military and FPU assets can be difficult. Military components and FPUs have independent chains of command, but the same mandate to help the UNPOLs when needed. For example, a UNPOL Regional Commander cannot order a military or FPU component to assist; rather, he or she can merely request assistance. This type of relationship is highly dependent on having a regional commander with diplomatic skills. If there is an issue or disagreement, the highest ranking member of the UN mission in the country can provide specific directives to the various mission components. One noteworthy exception to this arrangement was observed in the UNMIK mission, as the military component of the mission did not involve UN troops, but rather NATO personnel. As such, the K-FOR cadre answered to their own commanding general who was responsible to NATO headquarters, not the United Nations Secretary General. At times, this arrangement did lead to communication and collaboration issues.

The coordination of assets clearly can only occur when the nature and extent of the incident is known. A UNPOL Regional Commander can coordinate with the local police resources to prepare the first line of response. The regional commander can then relay updates to the UNPOL FPU and to military component commanders, or more frequently their respective operations officers, in an effort to develop a strategy for elevation to the second and third layer options. Not every situation requires that all components be present and equipped, as their presence could conceivably exacerbate an otherwise nonviolent demonstration.

Haiti: Example of Operational Coordination

A demonstration in Haiti in March 2010, after the January 2010 earthquake, can provide an example on how coordinated planning within a UN mission area can be accomplished. UN Police command staff had received word from the PNH that there was going to be a demonstration (called a *manifestation* in Haiti) to take place in downtown Les Cayes. The UNPOL Regional Commander and Deputy Regional Commander met earlier with their PNH command counterparts and were advised that a march and manifestation were being planned a few days in advance. Approximately 300 to 500 participants were expected to take part. The demonstrators were scheduled to march a route through Les Cayes, and end up at a Haitian official's office, where the bureaucrat would address the crowd. The demonstration was intended to be peaceful; however, in Haiti, every manifestation has the potential to spiral out of control due to the action of a small number of agitators.

Through discussions with PNH counterparts, it was agreed that the "UDMO" would not be present at this demonstration. The UDMO was an aggressive police component and was very feared by the public. It was considered that their presence might enflame the crowd. This perceived assertiveness and reputation should not be considered negatively since it has been observed that a single UDMO officer could break up a demonstration of 40 people when a group of regular PNH officers could not. It was agreed by both the PNH and UNPOL that four joint teams of three officers would be deployed to directly monitor the crowd. This was a minimal presence that would exhibit a police presence, but likely would not be viewed adversely. The Deputy Regional Commander would be one of the four UNPOL officers to provide direct command assessment.

Next, the UNPOL command team coordinated with the regional FPUs. Postearthquake, one additional FPU unit was temporarily assisting the assigned FPU in that region. In this case, the extra FPU was from Nigeria. The regular regional FPU unit was from Senegal. Both were viewed positively, but had been already overtasked due to postearthquake incidents and conditions. The Nigerian FPU had agreed to provide a 40-person platoon to support the demonstration monitoring. The FPU unit was to be kept out of sight of the crowd approximately two blocks away. Staying out of sight until needed would ensure that the FPU's presence did not enflame the crowd, but also allowed for quick response if the situation started to spiral out of control. The regional commander (the author) would be posted with the FPU to make the final determination if they were to be deployed.

The next meeting of the regional UNPOL command staff involved the counterparts from the regional military component from the Uruguayan Army (URUBAT). Given the nature of the manifestation, and the intelligence that the gathering was intended to be peaceful, the decision was made not to deploy URUBAT's well-equipped anti-riot platoon. It was requested that this complement should be on standby at the URUBAT base, available for immediate deployment should a situation evolve that the FPU could not handle.

In the end, the march and manifestation were both peaceful. The primary duty of the PNH and UNPOL officers had been to look for agitators and excise them from the crowd before they could stir up trouble. No agitators were present at this manifestation, so the teams simply observed and kept track of the pulse of the crowd. The FPU and URBAT teams were not needed on this day.

Haiti: Integrated Security Operation for Election Security

Elections in Haiti are always tempestuous and problematic. With so many polling stations and limited resources, maintaining security throughout the Les Cayes Region was a complex operation that utilized an integration of resources rather than a layered approach. Haiti had an election in February 2010. This election was ultimately postponed by the earthquake, but the operational planning process for providing security during this election nevertheless can provide an excellent example of an integrated operation for a preplanned large-scale event.

Intelligence Gathering

The Les Cayes Region alone had over 150 polling places scattered throughout the region. It was impossible to provide security to every single polling place, so intelligence gathering was essential. The results of this information collection would determine how to deploy and utilize the resources available. Months prior to the scheduled election, integrated intelligence gathering teams had been created. It was decided that each intelligence team would consist of an experienced UNPOL officer (usually the Zone Commander), several FPU officers, and an URUBAT soldier. This cadre would be assigned a specific area and would gather information and data for all of the polling places in that district.

Each team would travel to their respective area and pick up a PNH officer who was permanently assigned to that neighborhood. The officer's institutional and personal knowledge of that community was considered crucial. The teams would also pick up a representative from the election commission who was to be deployed to that location.

Each of the intelligence teams would visit each polling place in their zone of responsibility. They would discuss the relative level of political tension, activism, and potential for violence with polling representatives, citizens, PNH officers, and the election officials. The URUBAT soldiers would map out response routes to each polling place, some of which were extremely remote and only accessible by foot or donkey. Precise GPS coordinates would be recorded for each polling place in the event that a reaction force from MINUSTAH headquarters in Port au Prince would be required.

Coding and Documenting the Polling Sites

Each polling site was color coded as green (little or no risk for violence), yellow (moderate risk), and red (high risk). Each polling place was then noted on a large regional map. The color coding of each polling place, and the subsequent mapping, allowed for a visual representation of the high-risk areas of the region.

It came as no surprise that red areas tended to cluster together and that yellow polling sites were positioned on the fringes of those neighborhoods labeled red. One could reasonably track the potential location of agitators through this mapping process. The Les Cayes Region had three zones, and it took three intelligence gathering teams a little more than a month to gather all of the requested information and data. Once the intelligence collection and mapping had been complete, the next step would be operational security planning.

Operational Planning

Operational planning for an election with so many polling stations and limited resources could be exceedingly challenging. Regional election security was planned using a method that was a hybrid between layered and integrated approaches. The allocation of resources had to address the high-risk areas directly, the medium-risk neighborhoods through proximity, and the low threat communities indirectly.

For such an operation, the regional UNPOL component was augmented with UNPOL officers temporarily reassigned from Port au Prince. These provisional officers were generally from headquarters support units that did not actively engage in field duties and could thus be spared from their daily duties for a few days. Such augmentation allowed for greater UNPOL oversight of the election security operation.

In the end, UNPOL officers would team up with PNH officers and would directly monitor high-risk polling stations. If there was a cluster of high-risk polling stations, this team might be responsible for patrolling a group of polling stations. The PNH also assigned individual officers to monitor the high-risk stations. These PNH officers were in contact with their PNH colleagues who had been placed with the UNPOL teams.

Five-man FPU teams were assigned strategically to clusters of high-risk areas, whenever possible. The FPU teams were responsible for responding to a set group of polling stations should they be called. Thus, there was a mixture of PNH, UNPOL, and FPU officers and teams deployed across identified critical locations. The FPU were layered so that they could rapidly back up the PNH and UNPOL officers at any polling site if required.

The military URUBAT component was divided into five-man teams as well. These teams were also located in the neighborhoods with high-risk polling stations for deterrence and visibility; however, they also had a larger response zone and would be made available to respond to problem areas. Their arrival would likely not be as rapid as the FPU, but their presence would provide the option of a higher threat of force should a situation unravel.

Furthermore, URUBAT's excellent anti-riot team was on standby with armored personnel carriers to respond if their military teams could not maintain control. It was considered that the response of the URUBAT riot control teams could be as long as four hours, depending on the location of the unrest.

The final layer of protection involved a mobile crowd control team of Brazilian soldiers located in Port au Prince who would be transported by helicopter. This unit was on call for quick response to any area of Haiti should the situation require additional manpower. The availability of this complement had been the reason for carefully recording the accurate GPS coordinates of each polling station during the intelligence gathering phase. There were some polling stations in the mountains that were only accessible by a four- to six-hour hike on foot over very rough terrain. It was determined that the mobile unit could prove to be extremely valuable should there be severe problems at one of these extremely remote locations.

It can be observed that the planning of an operation within a UN mission area requires an extreme amount of flexibility and accurate planning. No two operations are quite the same, and the operational planning process relies heavily on accurate intelligence, clear communication, and insightful application of the available resources.

It should be noted that in the MINUSTAH mission, there was an intelligence unit at the UN headquarters in Port au Prince that mainly dealt with national or Port au Prince specific threats. Each region did not have an intelligence unit per se. Intelligence was gathered by the UNPOL officers through their daily contact with the PNH, and was then collated by the regional commander or deputy regional commander. Thus, successful operational planning also hinged on each UNPOL officer having a trusting and open relationship with their PNH counterparts.

Two Operational Case Studies

One could learn tremendously from the lessons revealed in two large-scale incidents, one of which occurred in the UNMIK mission in Pristina, the capital of Kosovo; and the second which took place in Les Cayes in Haiti under MINUSTAH. In one case, it can be seen that the limitations of the mission mandate could make adequate response difficult. Normally, law enforcement officers are experts in accomplishing their tasks, under all types of conditions. Responding to a critical incident in a United Nations mission area requires commanders to have deep insight into the nature of the mission, the mandate, issues of sovereignty, as well as an understanding of social and political repercussions of their actions.

The "Vetëvendosje" Protest in Kosovo in February 2007

On February 10, 2007, a planned protest took place in Pristina, the capital of Kosovo. This protest was sponsored by the Vetëvendosje movement. This movement advocated freedom and sovereignty for Kosovo, along with the removal of the United Nations administration and personnel from the area. Recall that Kosovo was under the protection of the United Nations, though it was still nominally a province of Serbia. However, the vast majority of Kosovars, who were ethnically Albanian, wanted independence from Serbia. Even before it commenced, the Vetëvendosje protest was expected to be a large-scale protest with the potential for violence. A layered approach to security arrangements had been planned. The KPS were responsible for the first line of defense in securing the protest area. An FPU unit from Romania was present as a second line of defense.

As the protesters approached the Kosovo Assembly and Government Building in the city's center, the street was barricaded with steel barricades that were manned by KPS officers with their UNMIK police advisers. At approximately 1500 hours, individual protesters attempted to remove the barricades and were confronted by KPS officers. The crowd became agitated and began to throw objects at the police (Ombudsperson in Kosovo, 2008).

As control of the situation began to slip away, the UNMIK FPU was deployed and fired tear gas to disperse the crowd. The crowd retreated but refused to disperse. While the FPU was attempting to disperse the crowd, KPS officers were excising agitators and placing them under arrest. The FPU then fired more tear gas and incrementally increased that level of force by firing rubber bullets at the crowd. The crowd then lost its cohesiveness and dispersed down side streets. The entire protest was dispersed by 1730 hours (Ombudsperson in Kosovo, 2008). In this case, the FPU involvement proved sufficient to quell the disturbance.

The planning and execution of this operation was a layered approach that worked as intended. When the Kosovo police complement had been overwhelmed, the FPU component stepped in. In this case, the FPU's involvement was sufficient to regain control so military components were not needed.

On the other hand, the incident did result in tragedy as two of the protesters who had apparently been shot with rubber bullets by FPU personnel eventually died. A large-scale international investigation was initiated and the UNMIK Police Commissioner resigned under pressure after this incident. A UN investigative report ultimately determined that the protesters had been shot with outdated rubber bullets that caused excessive injury and ultimately death. Subsequent to this incident, the use of rubber bullets was banned from UN crowd control doctrine.

Analysis

With the exception of the unfortunate deaths of the two aggressive rioters, this operation unfolded as planned and highlighted the potential success that can be achieved using the concept of layered components. This protest was not spontaneous, so sufficient time was available for planning and preparation. The appropriate resources were in place and were reasonably well coordinated.

The timing of the use of the FPU component could be viewed as being effective. The deployment of the FPU had also freed up the KPS officers from trying to hold back the crowd and allowed them to arrest some of the aggressive instigators. The lesson learned is that each point of coordination should be carefully and thoroughly articulated to avoid confusion. This process can be time-consuming and tedious; however, it should be noted that an UNPOL, FPU, or UN military component will likely revert to their national training in the absence of adequate coordination. Their national operational doctrine might not be appropriate for the emerging critical incident, so clear, concise, and unified coordination is extremely important.

The Les Cayes Prison Riot of January 2010

After the January 12, 2010 earthquake in Haiti, almost every prison in Haiti experienced a certain level of disorder, rioting, and a large number of escapes. The only two penitentiaries that did not experience the complete loss of inmates were in Cap Haitian and Les Cayes. On January 17, 2010, the Les Cayes UNPOL Regional Headquarters received a telephone call that there was a full-scale riot in progress at the Les Cayes Prison. The prison was located in Les Cayes proper right behind the PNH Les Cayes Regional Headquarters and main PNH commissariat for Les Cayes City. Upon arrival of UNPOL supervisors, the facility was experiencing a full-scale riot. Haitian prisons were operated by the Direction de l'Administration Pénitentiaire (Directorate of Prison Administration) or DAP. The prisoners had overpowered the DAP guards and taken over the prison. Fortunately, the DAP officers escaped without serious injury; however, they left the 467 inmates in full control of the entire facility. With the site surrounded by police, the inmates had gathered in the prison yard, were throwing rocks out of the prison at the police. The prisoners were actively seeking a means of escape.

To counter this threat, FPU and UNPOL teams formed a secure perimeter around the facility. There were approximately 11 PNH officers present, but there were no UDMO officers among them. Of the approximately 365 PNH officers assigned to the entire Les Cayes Region, approximately 70% of them were absent from duty as they had traveled to the center of the earthquake in Port au Prince in search of relatives. PNH manpower at the time was minimal and could easily be described as being inadequate.

As UNPOL arrived on scene, some of the PNH officers had been attempting to throw tear gas containers into the recreation yard of the prison. A number of prisoners threw some tear gas canisters back at the police. Tear gas should be deployed tactically as a part of a coordinated operation.

When additional responding units arrived, the entire complement consisted of approximately 11 PNH officers, 15 UNPOLs, a 40-person FPU, and a 40-person military URUBAT team. The URUBAT soldiers were split approximately in half between regular soldiers and riot control soldiers, who were carrying batons, but no side arms. The postearthquake security challenges had clearly drained considerable manpower, more so from the regions outside of the capital city.

The PNH Regional Commander specifically requested that UNPOL send the FPU and URUBAT teams into the prison to restore order. This was clearly a very complicated request. FPU units have a mandate to maintain civil order; however, a prison riot does not constitute civil disorder. To enter the prison and restore order would mean that UN components were enforcing and reestablishing Haitian law within the facility. This request exceeded the UN mandate. Remember that the mission directive for the UNPOL of the MINUSTAH is to "assist" the PNH. Interestingly, had this incident occurred in Kosovo, where UNMIK had executive authority, the request could have been granted. In addition, to have UN Police components restore order in a Haitian facility could be considered a violation of

Haitian sovereignty. The UNPOL Regional Commander refused the request to restore order in that fashion.

The PNH Regional Commander was not content, but it was highlighted that the FPU/UNPOL cordon around the prison could take into custody any inmate who attempted escape, because they could be considered a threat to public order. An operation to retake the prison would obviously have to be planned carefully, and UN components could not take the lead. A joint operation to restore order, between PNH, UNPOL, FPU, and URUBAT would have to discussed and planned very carefully.

Next the PNH Regional Commander inquired if the UN representatives would consider placing the URUBAT soldiers on the roof of the prison as a show of force and deterrent. The URUBAT Commander agreed to go up on the roof with the PNH Deputy Regional Commander to discuss the option. They joined a team of UNPOL officers on the roof, which had been protected from flying rocks by riot shields and who were observing the prison yard. The URUBAT Commander came down off the roof almost immediately after stating that the PNH Deputy Regional Commander had asked him to order his soldiers up on the roof and then to fire their weapons down into the crowd of prisoners. The URUBAT Commander clearly refused this request and further refused to post his soldiers on the roof.

The UNPOL Regional Commander, the PNH Deputy Regional Commander, the FPU Commander, and the URUBAT Commander jointly discussed a tactical strategy that would restore order, but that also would conform to the constraints of the UN mandate. As this meeting was taking place, a Haitian government official arrived. He had identified himself as the Department Deputy (i.e., the Haitian equivalent of a member of Congress).

A few minutes after the arrival of this official, the Haitian Regional Commander announced that he would be ordering the PNH Deputy Regional Commander and 10 PNH officers to make entry into the prison and restore order. Obviously, the UNPOL Regional Commander disagreed and advised against it in the strongest possible terms. Again, the constraints of the mission mandate prevented UNPOL officials from ordering the PNH to abort this potentially ill-fated operation. Remember, the MINUSTAH Policy and Procedural Manual (2004) stated that UNPOL officials could only "...be persuasive and attempt to explain, demonstrate, and encourage the appropriate response. If necessary, verbally intercede and strongly recommend appropriate action" (p. 14).

Despite fervent protestations, the PNH were determined to make entry into the prison, although they were dramatically outnumbered. UNPOL commanders opted to remove UNPOL representatives from the roof and pulled resources back. Quite quickly the PNH officers entered the prison and immediately a fusillade of shots rang out. In the end, the PNH officers had shot 11 prisoners dead, with the remainder hastily surrendering. The riot was over. The URUBAT Commander later allowed only his unarmed riot control team to enter the prison to assist the PNH. This was a wise move as any armed UN personnel in the facility could have directly or through association incurred blame for the shooting. At the very least, any armed UN personnel inside the prison, even during the aftermath, could have been dragged into the inevitable fallout and recriminations.

In the end, all of the PNH officers who made entry into the prison ultimately wound up in prison themselves for murder, including the PNH Deputy Regional Commander. The fallout from this obvious violation of human rights could have been politically disastrous for the MINUSTAH mission had they actively participated. An accusation of UN Police or military components shooting unarmed prisoners could have sparked countrywide violence against the UN and its personnel. UN entanglement in the fallout was avoided only through careful adherence to the mandate and excellent command decision making.

Analysis

This incident was a case that clearly identified the prospective constraints imposed by the UN mandate and highlighted the limitations that have been placed on the UNPOL, FPU, and military components of the Haitian mission. Not only were the UN Police restricted in their ability to respond to the riot, it should be noted that UNPOL had also been limited in the ability to stop the PNH from following a course of action that led to disaster. The United Nations Police did not have the authority to dictate to the PNH in their own country.

Sound decision making had been exercised by the commanders in the field. Under these circumstances, guidance from national UN headquarters, had it been needed, was not available. UN Police headquarters in Port au Prince was in abject chaos after the earthquake. The UNPOL Police Commissioner and the SRSG had been killed in the earthquake. The Deputy Commissioner was out of the country. Communication was limited at best.

It was made clear that many of the UNPOL and FPU officers, being professional law enforcement officers, desperately wanted to restore order. It is in a police officer's blood to address such a situation. But this specific scenario clearly exemplifies why UN Peacekeepers must be highly disciplined. United Nations Police and military assets must also have commanders who are thoroughly versed in the UN philosophy and have a comprehensive and broad understanding of the mission mandate and its limitations.

Conclusion

Critical incident planning and deployment in a United Nations mission area is a complex and multidimensional undertaking. Factors that must be taken into consideration in planning for a known event or in responding to a spontaneous event are:

- Recognizing the resources available:
  - The capabilities of each component
  - The limitations of each component
  - The national training and philosophy of each component
  - Maintaining positive communication within and between each component
- Understanding of the mission mandate:
  - What the mandate allows
  - What the mandate restricts
  - How the mandate meshes with the operational objective
  - How the mandate affects and restricts each component
- Communication:
  - A strong cooperative relationship with the local police component is essential
- Accurate intelligence collection will provide important information for the planning of any critical incident response:
  - Friendly, professional, and respectful communication with the commanders of other components
  - Diplomatic skills
  - The ability to communicate in a clear, concise, and simple manner
  - A deep understanding of multiculturalism
- Keeping an open mind:
  - It is only natural that each participating nation would believe that their approach and methods would work most effectively. One must remain open to consider different approaches and choose the tactic that best fits the situation.

Coordinating police responses to critical events in United Nation mission areas is a challenging task that requires careful coordination of multiple international law enforcement and military components. Planning and executing an operation in this environment is all the more complicated because no single element has total command and control. The success or failure of an operation depends largely on the patience, diplomacy, and communication skills of the incident commander and his supporting team. Each of the four components (i.e., local law enforcement, the UN Police, the formed police units, and the UN military components) must be coordinated through cooperation and collaboration.

Responses to major events in a UN mission are usually organized and coordinated by the UN Police Regional Commander. However, tactical command can shift to commanders of other components if the event starts to unravel. Careful coordination is required to transition tactical command of the operation to different components and to different supervisors depending on the circumstances of the situation. Planning and managing an operation of this sort is highly complex. Each component has its own unique capabilities, strengths, and weaknesses. These factors must be woven into the operation plan to ensure that the strengths of each component are maximized while their weaknesses are minimized. Coordinating police responses in UN missions is all the more challenging because the stakes are often very high. In one's home country, a botched law enforcement operation could result in violence or political unrest. In a post-conflict United Nations mission area that is steeped in ethnic tensions, a botched operation could renew hostilities.

References

Anderholt, C. (2012). *Female participation in formed police units.* Carlisle, PA: U.S. Army Peacekeeping and Stability Operations Institute.

Bayley, D. (2006). *Changing the guard: Developing democratic police abroad.* New York: Oxford Press.

Benner, T., & Mergenthaler, P. (2008). *Doctrine development in the UN peacebuiliding aparatus: The case of UN constabulary police, 1999–2006.* San Francisco: Paper prepared for the 49th Annual International Studies Association Convention.

Bruno, L. (2007). *Formed police unit tasks.* Vicenza, Italy: International Network to Promote the Rule of Law.

Durch, W., & England, M. (2010). *Enhancing United Nations capacity to support post-conflict policing and rule of law* (revised). Washington, DC: The Stimson Center.

Fasulo, L. (2009). *An insider's guide to the UN.* New Haven/London: Yale University Press.

Hansen, A. (2011). *Policing the peace: The rise of United Nations formed police units.* Berlin, Germany: Center for International Peace Operations.

Hårleman, C. (2003). *An introduction to the UN system: Orientation for serving on a UN field mission.* Geneva: United Nations Institute for Training and Research, Programme of Correspondence Instruction.

Hills, A. (2007). The inherent limits of military forces in policing peace operations. *International Peacekeeping, 8*(3), 79–98.

Kember, O. (2010). *The impact of the Indian formed police unit in the United Nations mission in Liberia.* Washington, DC: Georgetown University.

Levine, D. (2008). *African civilian police capacity and international peacekeeping operations.* Washington, DC: The Henry L. Stimson Center.

Library of Congress. (2006). *Country Profile: Haiti.* Washington, DC: Library of Congress—Federal Research Division.

Mobekk, E. (2005). *Identifying lessons in United Nations international policing missions.* Geneva SUI: Geneva Centre for the Democratic Control of Armed Forces.

Muharremi, R., Peci, L., Malazogu, L., Knaus, V., & Murati, T. (2003). *Administration and governence in Kosovo: Lessons learned and lessons to be learned.* Pristina, Kosovo: Centre for Applied Studies in International Negotiations.

Ombudsperson in Kosovo. (2008). *Ex Officio No. 008/2007: Regarding the incidents that occurred during the "Vetëvendosje" protest on 10 February 2007.* Pristina, Kosovo: Ombudsperson Institution in Kosovo.

Rotman, P. (2011). First steps towards a police doctrine for UN peace operations (2001–2006). *Policing and Society: An International Journal of Research and Policy, 21*(1), 84–95.

Silander, D. (2009). The United Nations and peace building: Lessons from the UN transitional administrations in East Timor and Kosovo. *Social Alternatives, 28*(2), 23–28.

Smith, J., Holt, V., & Durch, W. (2007). *From Timor-Leste to Darfur: New initiatives for enhancing UN civilian policing capacity.* Washington, DC: The Stimson Center.

United Nations Department of Peacekeeping Operations (UNDPKO). (2010a). *Formed police units in United Nations peacekeeping operations.* New York: Strategic Policy and Development Section, Police Division, UN DPKO.

United Nations Department of Peacekeeping Operations (UNDPKO). (2010b). *Formed police units in United Nations peacekeeping operations* (revised). New York: Strategic Policy and Development Section, Police Division, UN DPKO.

United Nations Department of Peacekeeping Operations (UNDPKO). (2012). *United Nations infantry battalion manual.* New York: United Nations Department of Peacekeeping Operations, Department of Field Support.

United Nations Security Council. (1999). *United Nations Security Council Resolution 1244.* New York: United Nations Security Council.

United Nations Security Council. (2004). *United Nations Security Council Resolution 1529.* New York: United Nations Security Council.

About the Author

Michael R. Sanchez is pursuing a Ph.D. in business administration with a concentration on criminal justice at Northcentral University in Arizona, and is former police director in the UNMIK Police in Kosovo and former regional commander in the United Nations Mission in Haiti.

Effective Planning for Major Events and Incidents

11

Examining the New York City Police Department Protocols and Guidelines

JAMES F. ALBRECHT

Contents

Introduction

Whether you talk about the September 11, 2001 attack, Hurricane Sandy, the Thanksgiving Parade, or a New York Yankees World Series baseball championship game, the city of New York has had plenty of experience planning for and responding to large-scale events. The New York City Police Department "Patrol Guide," the agency's primary policy and procedural manual, contains thousands of pages and hundreds of guidelines and protocols to address potential scenarios that law enforcement officers could encounter during their daily routines. Three full sections of this guidebook, specifically "NYPD Patrol Guide Section 212—Command Operations," "NYPD Patrol Guide Section 213—Mobilization/Emergency Incidents," and "NYPD Patrol Guide Section 220—Citywide Emergency Management System (CIMS)" outline in detail the steps that NYPD supervisors and resources should take under specific situations, most of which would involve critical incidents or large-scale events. Much of this material has been incorporated into the U.S. Department of Homeland Security's National Incident Management System mandates, which were developed after the September 11, 2001 attacks and which delineate standardized measures for critical incident response for first responder agencies across the United States. And finally, the city of New York, which created the New York City Office of Emergency Management in 1996 as an interagency mechanism to synergize the deployment of numerous organizations to large-scale events, also has constructed the Citywide Incident Management System to ensure that incident response is properly coordinated.

The New York City Police Department: Policies and Procedures

The New York City Police Department, created in 1845, has possessed a rules and regulations manual since its inception. This guidebook has over the decades evolved into the NYPD Department Manual, one of a trilogy of official instructional volumes that also include the NYPD Administrative Guide, the NYPD Organization Guide, and NYPD Patrol Guide (New York City Police Department, 2013), all of which continue to provide procedural guidance to the agency's personnel across the organization. In addition, many of the NYPD's investigative bureaus and divisions also maintain their own procedural manuals. These documents, whose pages well exceed the thousands, are also complemented by "Interim Orders," "Operational Orders," "Finest Messages" (sent through the teletype), and NYPD bureau level memos that provide contemporary and at times temporary revision to agency protocol. Add the New York State Penal Law, the New York State Criminal Procedural Law, the New York City Charter, the New York City Administrative Code, the New York State Vehicle and Traffic Law, the New York City Traffic Regulations, and the NYPD Legal Division Bulletins, which detail relevant appellate court decisions, and one can easily note that the resources of the NYPD have a plethora of detailed information that guide their daily actions.

The NYPD Patrol Guide (New York City Police Department, 2013), divided into 19 "series" or individual topics within the table of contents, includes three sections, "NYPD PG Section 212—Command Operations," "NYPD PG Section 213—Mobilization/Emergency Incidents," and "NYPD Patrol Guide

Section 220—Citywide Emergency Management System (CIMS)" dedicated exclusively to the detailed steps and protocols that NYPD supervisors and resources should follow when responding to critical incidents or planning for large-scale events. In addition, each of the approximately 100 New York City Police Department commands, officially called *police patrol precincts, transit (subway) districts,* or *housing (project) police service areas,* maintains an "Unusual Disorder Plan." Combined with the NYPD Patrol Guide protocols, each of these Unusual Disorder Plans contains a wide range of information that easily permits commanders and police station supervisors to respond to a plethora of potential incidents, whether planned or spontaneous. It is the substance of these two phenomena that will be examined in comprehensive detail in an effort to properly understand how a large metropolis like New York City* can address the thousands of events that occur within her boundaries on an annual basis.

Preparation for Preplanned Events

Properly preparing for a large-scale parade or demonstration, or even a weather-related disaster, involves intensive evaluation and planning. As much information and intelligence about the event and participants should be obtained in advance, particularly if there are indications that the event has the potential to result in disorder or criminal activity. It is imperative that the planning officer or team should:

- Review past history of the participant group(s) and location
- Peruse agency intelligence records and all available open source material, including information available via social media
- If the need arises, engage intelligence personnel prior to the event
- Contact and coordinate with other agencies and organizations that could potentially complement the response and enhance preparation
- Monitor news and media sources in real time before, during, and after the event

If possible and as soon as feasible, the planning team should arrange and attend meetings with:

- The event operator
- The event sponsor
- The private security coordinator
- Leaders of participating groups, particularly if more than one have competing agendas

---

* The latest U.S. Census data estimates the New York City population at approaching 8.4 million residents, who are joined by more than 3 million commuters who travel there from outside the city on a daily basis.

- Neighborhood and community leaders and groups
- Law enforcement agency HQ planning representative(s)
- Planning representatives from public service, medical, first responder, public transportation, and other relevant organizations

Any intelligence that could potentially enhance the safety and security of event participants, community residents, and business representatives should be conveyed prior to the start of the event. Media outlets should be requested to convey critical information as soon as it becomes available, specifically as it relates to the potential for or incidence of criminality, violence, disorder, vandalism, crowding, and traffic restrictions.

Proper preparation by the police planning panel should include efforts to acquire information about each of the following matters:

- The anticipated number of persons expected to participate
- A floor plan of the site or facility
- A map of the localized area
- Detailed criminal history of the location
- Previous history of disruption or disorder at that site or at similar events
- The availability of alcohol (e.g., beer sales or tailgating)
- The expected demographics of the anticipated crowd
- The potential for anarchist, disorderly, or criminal behavior
- The presence of armed or other security personnel
- The possible presence of dignitaries, notables, and political figures
- The need for government permits (e.g., sound device or permit for demonstration)
- Anticipated traffic issues (e.g., parking) or possible obstruction of area roadways
- Medical aid/EMT/triage locations
- Evacuation and emergency response routes
- Secondary large-scale events occurring in the surrounding communities or region
- Weather conditions
- Other pertinent information

Response and Coordination at Significant Spontaneous Incidents

When responding to the scene of a spontaneous critical incident, the first priority must be to provide medical assistance as needed, and then to restore safety and security to the site as quickly as possible. The first arriving police personnel must "take command" and request the needed resources until the arrival of an agency supervisor. Communication of all pertinent information must be conveyed through the chain of command in real time. Since responding units would be preoccupied with response activities, the intelligence and information gathering may have to be coordinated by resources at the nearest police station, at regional headquarters, by centrally located administrative or investigative personnel, or at a temporary field command post. In these types of scenarios, all critical information must be conveyed in both directions of the chain of command, as field resources may not have the time or potential to gather detailed intelligence or collect information away from the incident site. In addition, police representatives must initiate outreach to community leaders and residents. Media outlets should be utilized to collate information and updates, and to enhance the immediate exchange of vital information to the public. The need for the creation of inner and outer perimeters for first responders, and secondary safety zones for media representatives and area residents must be taken into immediate consideration.

The command post staffing and operations should be implemented in line with National Incident Management System guidelines.* In addition, separate police and interagency command posts should be developed, but the interagency incident commander would be in overall control of the coordinated response.

Incident Command Team

The command team for any critical incident should be staffed to ensure that all of the following responsibilities are being addressed:

1. Incident Commander is in overall command of coordination, deployment, and decision making at the scene.
2. Administrative/Planning Officer is responsible for documenting significant information and events in an incident command diary, for highlighting unfolding occurrences, for recommending potential future actions, and for preparing an assessment and critique of the agency's response after the incident has ended.
3. Operations Officer is the chief tactical advisor to the Incident Commander.
4. Intelligence Officer is the primary investigation and intelligence coordinator.
5. Personnel Officer will maintain all staffing, assignment, and deployment records.

---

* National Incident Management System guidelines are available online at FEMA: http://www.fema.gov/national-incident-management-system

6. Logistics/Finance Officer will retain records on all equipment deployed or available at the scene and maintain documents on financial considerations, including potential and actual overtime costs and damage to jurisdictional property.
7. Public Information Officer will convey relevant information to media sources and community leaders.

According to the National Incident Management System model (Federal Emergency Management System, 2014), the incident command staff should include at the minimum the following positions:

1. Incident Commander
2. Operations Section Chief
3. Planning Section Chief
4. Finance/Administration Section Chief
5. Logistics Section Chief

The protocol also recommends a number of support positions in line with the responsibilities outlined above.

The rank of the incident commander and staff officers should be commensurate with the scope and size of the task at hand. If dealing with a small demonstration or facility strike, then the incident commander could be one of the lowest ranking front-line supervisors in the agency, for example, sergeant. On the other hand, if the event is significant or has drawn media attention, a higher ranking officer, possibly even the agency head, could be designated the incident commander. In addition, at small-scale incidents, some of the command staff officer tasks could be combined, that is, a Personnel and Logistics Officer.

In addition, the Administrative/Planning Officer is responsible for preparing a summary report at the conclusion of the event that should include a critique including information received not only from police supervisors involved, but also based on feedback from government officials, media representatives, members of the community, and other sources. This report, including recommendations for enhanced performance in future similar scenarios, should be forwarded through the chain of command and maintained on file for later reference.

Police Resources and Deployment

As a general rule, approximately 70% of police resources at the scene should be deployed and 30% of the available personnel should be retained in reserve. Potential assignments could include:

- Perimeter maintenance
- Crowd dispersal
- Mobile response to unfolding incidents

- Arrest duty
- Directed and foot patrol
- Protection of vulnerable, critical, and sensitive locations
- Escort duty for public utility company personnel and fire department and emergency medical resources
- Checkpoint duty

Police resource units should be deployed in teams normally consisting of one front-line supervisor (e.g., sergeant) responsible for a complement of 4 to 10 properly equipped police officers* deployed in uniform. In addition, reserve teams should be fully prepared for immediate deployment as directed, and could be situated at locations in the area as a visible presence or deterrent.

Supervisory Competence

One of the most critical decisions to be made prior to any preplanned or during an impromptu incident is to determine if the incident commander possesses the appropriate competence and ability to coordinate all actions of police personnel and other resources at the scene. If there is any doubt, then this assessment must be resolved immediately.† The highest-ranking agency official available must communicate directly with the specified incident commander and conduct an evaluation of managerial capability. It is imperative that the designated incident commander possess the requisite leadership and decision-making capabilities to accomplish the task. Effective deployment and performance must remain paramount, particularly when safety, security, life, and limb may be at stake.‡

The NYPD "Unusual Disorder Plan"

Each of the more than 100 New York City Police Department police stations, which are responsible for routine street patrol, subway and commuter safety, and community security within the federally subsidized housing developments, is required to maintain a comprehensive report that will be used to

---

* The number of police officers on a specific team would rely on their particular assignment. Normal NYPD teams consist of one sergeant and eight police officers, while arrest teams would be comprised of one sergeant and four police officers.
† Some issues that could potentially hamper the ability of a supervisor who finds themselves in the middle of a large-scale event could include: lack of sufficient patrol experience, absence of prior experience involving similar events in the past, incidental trauma, restricted motivation, or a sense of overwhelming exposure.
‡ As a former certified NYPD and Federal Emergency Management Agency Incident Commander and Regional Commanding Officer, I have learned that one must be more concerned with efficacy in critical incident response and coordination than in avoiding embarrassment or "hurt feelings."

assist in planning and responding to critical incidents and significant events. This report is called the *Unusual Disorder Plan.*

The Unusual Disorder Plan is a document maintained in a secure but readily available file at each police station that includes all of the following pertinent information:

1. Introduction with overview of history, demographics, and geography of jurisdiction, and highlights of prior major critical events.
2. List of sensitive and vulnerable locations including: religious institutions, military facilities, weapons shops, medical hospitals and clinics, schools, chemical factories, hazardous material storage sites, public utilities, power supply stations, government offices, diplomatic residences and consulates, and so on.
3. Potential predesignated staging and mobilization points capable of parking hundreds of emergency vehicles and organizing thousands of rescue personnel.
4. Special tactical and deployment plans for previous major events and critical incidents.
5. Equipment available, including list of vehicles, K-9s, cell phones, and portable radios.
6. Alternate detention facilities.
7. Contact information and addresses of key community representatives, school administrators, area nursing homes, and regional medical emergency rooms.
8. Contact details for representatives from government, public service, and private agencies needed for interagency cooperation.
9. Contact information for all assigned police personnel.
10. Potential helicopter landing sites and waterfront marinas.
11. Potential morgue locations, triage sites, and first aid stations (including floor plans of any area hospital emergency rooms).
12. Location of other law enforcement facilities, court buildings, prosecutors' offices, jails, prisons and detention facilities.
13. Alternate fueling sites.
14. Location of response and evacuation routes with preidentified traffic control posts along those routes to expedite emergency travel.
15. Potential indoor rest locations for emergency responders.
16. Color-coded maps of jurisdiction for use at the incident command post, which highlight sensitive and vulnerable locations, response and evacuation routes, potential mobilization and staging sites, and noting other key information.
17. Numerous copies of a detailed map of jurisdiction for distribution to personnel from intra-agency jurisdictions and other responding agencies.

Numerous copies of the entire package are maintained in each specific police station concerned, with one copy secured in the vehicle of the patrol supervisor, and another copy at the police station shift supervisor's desk. Additional copies are permanently filed at the regional and central agency headquarters and at the interagency command center, the New York City Office of Emergency Management, which is under the supervision of the mayor. Clearly this information must be properly secured, but at the same time, the Unusual Disorder Plan document must be readily available in time of urgent need.

Jurisdiction-Wide Mobilization Plan

In order to ensure an orderly response to the site of what may be a chaotic and evolving scene, the New York City Police Department has long utilized highly coordinated and preplanned regional and jurisdiction-wide mobilization plans, which have commonly been referred to as the "Rapid Mobilization" system.

The first major arrangement is that for each of the three primary work shifts (i.e., 7 A.M. to 3 P.M., 3 P.M. to 11 P.M., and 11 P.M. to 7 A.M.), there are designated "duty captains," "duty inspectors" (similar in rank to colonel), and a "duty chief" who are responsible for the coordination of any major incident that occurs within their area of assignment.* A supervisor from one of the police stations would contact the designated duty captain in real time of any major occurrence, for example, person shot, homicide, bank robbery, police-involved shooting, and so on. Notifications would also be made to the NYPD Operations Unit at the central NYPD headquarters and to the regional (i.e., borough) patrol headquarters.

If additional resources outside of the local police station are needed to deal with the incident or spontaneous event, the patrol supervisor on the scene can request additional personnel and equipment by reporting via portable radio that there is a need for a "Level 1 Mobilization." The duty captain can make the decision to request additional resources by calling the NYPD Operations Unit and requesting a Level 2, 3, or 4 Mobilization.

The levels of the "Rapid Mobilization" mechanism involve a four (4) tiered response protocol. A "Level 1 Mobilization" would require the response of the regional duty captain and all available patrol personnel from the regional "Patrol Borough Task Force," a separate unit located in each of

---

* A duty captain would be responsible for coordinating any major incident within their borough of assignment, for example, Manhattan South, Queens North, and so on. A duty inspector would be responsible for events occurring within a fixed number of boroughs. The duty chief would have citywide authority for all major incidents that occur on that specific shift.

the eight patrol regions, which is specifically trained and equipped for crowd and disorder control incidents. A "Level 2 Mobilization" would require the response of the regional duty captain, three pre-identified lieutenants, and one sergeant and eight police officers from each of the police stations within the "Patrol Borough" in which the incident occurred. The duty captain could request resources from outside the specific Patrol Borough in which the incident has occurred by calling the NYPD Operations Unit and requesting a "Level 3 Mobilization" and by specifically stating the number of additional police officers needed (e.g., 80 police officers who would respond with a number of lieutenants and sergeants). The NYPD Operations Unit would be responsible for hastily determining from which of the eight Patrol Borough Task Forces the police officers would respond from. A duty captain could direct a citywide response by conferring with the duty inspector and duty chief and requesting a "Level 4 Mobilization" via the portable radio or by calling the NYPD Operations Unit. This rare directive would involve the response of personnel from all Patrol Borough Task Forces, all duty captains, pre-designated lieutenants, and one sergeant and eight police officers from each of the approximate 100 police stations across New York City. In addition, resources from the Community Affairs Division, Traffic Division, Special Operations Division (e.g., tactical and rescue personnel and equipment, Aviation Unit, HazMat Unit, Harbor Patrol, etc.), Detective Bureau, Highway Patrol, and other units would be directed to respond as specifically needed. In addition, as soon as a specific mobilization level has been requested at any time or location, a "Readiness Level" is conveyed to all personnel across the city in order to expedite the response of additional personnel should that need arise.

Each police officer receives a pocket-sized copy of the "Rapid Mobilization" protocol, which must be carried while in uniform. More importantly, before the start of each of the shifts, all NYPD resources, which would be part of each of the rapid mobilization level requests, are pre-identified and advised of this status at the start of their respective shift. This protocol ensures that not only can sufficient personnel respond to the scene of a critical incident or significant event in a timely fashion, but also that an adequate complement of police resources are available to continue to conduct routine patrol and investigative functions. One final note is that Rapid Mobilization requests made on the night (i.e., 11 P.M. to 7 A.M.) shift would involve a smaller cadre of pre-identified personnel, and as a result, patrol supervisors and duty captains may have to resort to higher mobilization levels during that time period to ensure the response of sufficient resources. It is also imperative that patrol supervisors and duty captains be acutely familiar with the police station and regional Unusual Disorder Plans to ensure awareness of the potential staging and response locations, and designated response and evacuation routes.

Off-Duty Mobilization Plan

Under circumstances in which an unplanned large-scale incident or event has occurred, it may become necessary to request the response of off-duty police personnel. Normally, this decree would be decided by the top NYPD leadership and be conveyed via the NYPD Operations Unit. However, the ranking supervisor at the police station involved, after conferring with the commanding officer, whether on- or off-duty, could "recall" specific nonworking police personnel under extreme circumstances.* Administrative personnel working in the police station would be utilized to contact the designated resources using contact information available in the Unusual Disorder Plan and other files. When a recall is conducted on a region- or citywide scale, it would prove useful to use local media outlets to assist in conveying this request.

Normally, recalled personnel should respond to their permanent assignment locations. However, when circumstances exist in which traffic, transit, or other impediments exist, then one of the potential staging or response sites identified in one of the nearby police station Disorder Control Plans could be utilized as a collection point for off-duty personnel. In this case, it would be prudent to have police department or public transportation buses or vans available at the site to transfer these resources as needed. In addition, since these police officers would be responding from home, additional protective equipment (e.g., bullet resistant vests, gas masks, ballistic or crowd control helmets, flashlights, batons, etc.) and identifiable "Police" traffic vests and baseball caps should be made available in order to ensure that these law enforcement officers would be immediately recognizable as NYPD personnel.

Citywide Incident Management System

The New York City Office of Emergency Management has been in existence since 1996. In order to properly coordinate an interagency and multijurisdictional response to a critical incident that occurs within the confines or near the borders of the city of New York, the Citywide Incident Management System (CIMS)† was implemented by the mayor in 2005 (New York City Office of Emergency Management, 2014). The CIMS is in full compliance with the federal government's NIMS protocol.

---

* On both September 11, 2001 and on November 12, 2001, when a passenger plane crashed in Queens, the author was on duty and designated as the NYPD Duty Captain for the NYC borough of Queens. A decision was made to immediately recall key police station supervisors and patrol personnel who were not working and have them respond to work.
† New York City Citywide Incident Management System definitions and protocols are available online at: http://www.nyc.gov/html/oem/html/planning_response/about_cims.shtml.

The key components of CIMS include:

- Outlining how citywide emergencies or multiple large-scale incidents will be managed.
- Defining specific agency roles and responsibilities at different emergency incidents.
- Establishing the NIMS incident command system standard as the format for staffing the interagency incident command post and for coordinating critical incidents within New York City.
- Establishing the means of integrating regional, state, and federal agencies into the response to a major event or disaster.
- Delineating the operational implementation of CIMS.
- Defining how incident operations, including rescue, criminal investigation, site management and recovery, and safe and expedited restoration to normalcy are to be prioritized, and articulating when these procedures can be concurrently undertaken.
- Establishing a procedure for post-incident review, evaluation, and the critique of emergency responses.
- Developing a report of lessons learned and recommend best practices.
- Formulating the implementation of training requirements for city agencies that could be deployed in response to a large-scale incident or event.

Of significant importance is that CIMS guidelines specifically mandate that the New York City Police Department is in charge of incident command and site management, while the New York City Fire Department would be accountable for rescue functions and responsibilities related to first aid and medical assistance. The protocol also explicitly outlines which public service and utility companies would be required to respond to specific types of events. More particularly is the definition of the NYPD as the incident command agency in any occurrence in which terrorism or criminality is suspected. The CIMS protocol identifies the respective core competencies and explicit expertise of public service agencies and utility companies that operate with New York City.

Providing overall guidance and coordination would be the New York City Office of Emergency Management (OEM). The New York City OEM would monitor on-scene coordination by:

- Ensuring that the CIMS incident command structure is being utilized.
- Making certain that interoperable communications are functioning.
- Relaying real-time, accurate information to the OEM command center and to the mayor.
- Supporting logistics and communications needs of agencies at the scene.

- Facilitating the identification of the incident command agency and resolving any interagency differences and discrepancies.
- Determining when to activate New York City's interagency Emergency Operations Center.
- Coordinating the post-incident evaluation and critique and forwarding to agencies involved.
- Developing a CIMS training curriculum for all pertinent response agencies located in New York City.

Some of the more difficult challenges encountered in the past have involved jurisdictional issues. Specifically, what role do the CIMS or NYPD critical incident response protocols play in a situation in which the federal government, for example, FBI, claims that it has taken overall authority for incident control and investigation? This could prove to be politically sensitive since the NYPD and other New York City agencies are better trained, equipped, and prepared than federal agencies are to deal with terrorist and large-scale incidents. Another factor to be addressed is how to deploy National Guard troops, New York State Police Troopers, retired NYPD personnel who may show up to assist,* NYPD auxiliary police personnel,† and law enforcement resources who may respond from regional or out-of-state police agencies. The long-term friction between the NYPD, the FBI, and the U.S. Attorney General's Office could clearly hamper effective response, criminal investigation, rescue and recovery, and other related follow-up activities.

A final issue involves counseling and trauma-related assistance for rescue and recovery personnel, area residents, local business persons, victims and their relatives. Posttraumatic stress and mental health debriefings have proven to be difficult, particularly in scenarios which require an extended response and the involvement of all available resources. A staggered and multistage trauma debriefing approach could prove to be most valuable, as many negative effects are often experienced well after the incident and response period.

The NYPD Response on September 11, 2001

While the terrorist attack on the World Trade Center on September 11, 2001 ended in the death of 2749 victims in New York City on that tragic day, the NYPD's critical incident response protocol had proven to be practically effective, even in such a large-scale event. The "Rapid Mobilization" protocol,

---

* More than 50,000 retired police personnel continue to reside within New York City and the surrounding region.
† The number of NYPD auxiliary police officers exceeds 4000.

which on that date involved a Level 4 citywide mobilization response, resulted in the prompt and coordinated response of more than 3000 on-duty NYPD officers.* Designated response routes permitted expeditious travel into Manhattan from the outer boroughs and directly to the identified response and staging locations. In particular, all tunnels to and from Manhattan were used exclusively for emergency response vehicles. Designated evacuation options, specifically all Manhattan bridges, were utilized for pedestrian flight to the outer boroughs. From the start of the incident, NYPD traffic police and civilian enforcement officers were posted at key sites to control access and to direct first responders onto the specific response routes. In addition, all off-duty personnel were recalled through direct contact or via local media outlets.

The Unusual Disorder Plan for the NYPD First Precinct, in which the World Trade Center is located, proved to be instrumental in rescue coordination. Given the short time period available for the evacuation of the two World Trade Towers, it must be highlighted that more than 30,000 persons were assisted from the buildings by rescue personnel; this included essentially all of the employees and visitors who had been below the terrorist attack impact floors. It has been noted that more than 500,000 persons were evacuated from the World Trade Center complex and surrounding neighborhood during the first hour after the attack, more than 1 million people were directed out of the Manhattan downtown zone within two hours, and more than 3 million persons were evacuated from the island of Manhattan within three hours. Not only did the pedestrian evacuation option prove to be successful, but the impromptu decision to request available watercraft to respond to the lower Manhattan Hudson River waterfront permitted the hasty movement of an estimated 500,000 persons to New Jersey and the outer New York City boroughs.

In addition, the existence of the detailed disorder control plans at each police station permitted the respective commanders to quickly develop the unforeseen counterterrorism plans that tactically and strategically secured the city's residents, infrastructure, all identified critical and vulnerable sites, and potential terrorist targets.† This instantaneous deployment permitted the people of New York City and most businesses outside of the World Trade Center rescue and recovery zone to return to normalcy within a few days. Clearly this event was the greatest to impact the great city of New York up

---

* The author, a retired NYPD Captain, was the designated duty captain for the borough of Queens and immediately responded to the World Trade Center with Queens police personnel and firefighters. He was assigned by the incident commander to the Incident Command staff and coordinated the initial rescue operations.

† The author, at the time a police station commander, was able to convert the Unusual Disorder Plan into a comprehensive regional counterterrorism plan within 24 hours of the initial attack on the World Trade Center.

to that point. All indications are that the critical incident planning that had taken place before this tragic day played a significant role in the effective nature of the rescue and evacuation efforts. One can only hope that nothing of this nature will ever occur on American soil again.

Conclusion

It is quite apparent that practical and effective planning and routine emergency response drills, specifically involving the participation of all potential participating agencies, should enhance efficacy in an actual critical incident. Interagency and cross-jurisdictional cooperation, comprehensive preparation, and the need for community insight and input cannot be overly emphasized. And other major tragic events, for example, Hurricane Katrina, Hurricane Sandy, Mississippi River flooding, and so on, that have since occurred have provided many important lessons, and the respective post-incident evaluations have resulted in numerous recommended best practices. It is imperative that no jurisdiction take the position that something of that scale or nature could not happen there. The principal lesson identified in many of these and other critical incidents is that, regardless if your primary emergency response plan and related drills have emphasized civil disorder or a natural disaster, having the basic but comprehensive plans in place will better prepare the agencies in that area to respond to any type of incident, whether involving a toxic chemical spill, a terrorist incident, an active shooter, or a building collapse. Practice will not necessarily make one perfect, but can significantly enhance emergency incident response and hopefully save lives.

References

Federal Emergency Management Agency. (2014). *National Incident Management System*. Retrieved February 5, 2014 from: http://www.fema.gov/national-incident-management-system

New York City Office of Emergency Management. (2014). *Emergency Response: Citywide Incident Management System*. Retrieved January 25, 2014 from: http://www.nyc.gov/html/oem/html/planning_response/about_cims.shtml

New York City Police Department. (2013). *NYPD patrol guide*. New York: New York City Police Department Printing Section.

About the Author

James F. Albrecht is a retired NYPD Captain and Commanding Officer, who was a certified NYPD and Federal Emergency Management Agency Incident Commander. James was on the NYPD Incident Command staff at the September 11, 2001 attack on the World Trade Center and has been the incident commander at a considerable number of critical incidents, including the passenger airline crash in Queens on November 12, 2001. Jimmy Albrecht is presently a professor of criminal justice and homeland security at Pace University in New York.

Intriguing Paradox
The Inability to Keep South Africa Safe and the Successful Hosting of Mega Global Sporting Events

12

CHRISTIAAN BEZUIDENHOUT

Contents

On the one hand, South Africa is hailed as a country that has successfully hosted several global events such as the Rugby World Cup, the FIFA Confederations Cup (FCC), the 19th FIFA Soccer World Cup, the 29th Orange African Cup of Nations (Afcon), the Indian Premier League (IPL) cricket tournament, the British and Irish Lions rugby tour, and recently the funeral of the late national icon Nelson Mandela. His funeral attracted leaders from across the globe and no noteworthy incident occurred. On the other hand, South Africa cannot keep its citizens safe, has one of the highest murder rates in the world, and is notorious for violent strikes and police brutality. This I see as the paradox of the inability to keep South Africa safe, but conversely successfully hosting mega events.

—Christiaan Bezuidenhout

Overview: The National Crisis

South Africa (SA) is a country with high violent crime rates, and many potential international visitors are cynical and uncertain whether it will be safe to visit SA. Also many SA citizens live in fear and can concur that SA is a violent high-risk country where man-made threats flourish. A high number of SA citizens immigrate to countries such as Australia to move away from the violent crime issue. However, SA has hosted several global events without any substantial incident occurring. Clearly, a few dynamics are at play and it is important to sketch an overview of current political, social, and policing issues in SA to encapsulate why we are able to host large-scale events with success.

After the previous political dispensation had been toppled ("apartheid"), SA underwent major constitutional changes with the commencement of the interim Constitution of 1993, Act 200 of 1993. Thereafter, on May 8, 1996, the Constitutional Assembly adopted the current Constitution of the Republic of South Africa, Act 108 of 1996, which had commenced on February 4, 1997. The aim of the Constitution is to accommodate every human being and to protect human rights at all cost. On top of this tall order, SA consists of nine provinces, which exclude two countries within the boundaries of SA, namely Lesotho and Swaziland. There are 1152 police stations in the nine provinces, which cover a land surface of 1,219,090 square kilometers. There are about 199,367 police members (157,518 sworn officers and 41,849 civilians) in the police service who must serve a population of 51.19 million people. South Africa harbors 11 official languages and countless different cultures and customs that demand special attention in the Constitution and in policing.

During the finalization stages of the Constitution, the National Crime Prevention Strategy (NCPS) was launched in May 1996. It was hailed as a holistic national strategy for reducing crime in South Africa and keeping South Africa safe. A team of multidisciplinary experts from government and civil society were tasked to develop a long-term strategy to assist government on addressing the root causes of crime in South Africa. The crime prevention strategy is a multidimensional approach that accommodated different important role-players and aimed to reduce crime (Bezuidenhout & Little, 2012; Newham, 2005). The NCPS strives for the coordination of the activities of government departments, other tiers of government, and non-state agencies engaged in crime prevention. Up to date, several programs have been formulated under the NCPS, each falling under one of four pillars: the criminal justice process; environmental design; community values and education; and finally transnational crime.

However, against the backdrop of the grand prevention strategy, dramatic increases in levels of crime in post-apartheid SA have placed the issue of crime prevention and control firmly on the political itinerary. The NCPS strategy propagated a developmental approach to the prevention of crime (Newham, 2005). This required that crime be seen as a broader social challenge rather than purely a security issue for the police. While the NCPS attaches a lot of importance to environmental design, it reveals a limited appreciation of what this actually entails, and its potential impact on crime levels. Consequently, crime reduction in its true sense meant addressing the socioeconomic and environmental factors that gave rise to crime, rather than only enforcing the law after it had occurred by means of reactive policing.

The initial noble idea with the NCPS was to reduce and control crime in SA. Some political advocates even advocated total prevention. Two methods of maintaining social order and addressing crime are crime prevention and crime control (Roelofse, 2011). Many are unaware of the fact that there is a difference between these two methods of social control. Generally speaking, crime prevention is about responsibilities and crime control is about activities. A core part of crime prevention involves society's responsibility to socialize people in such a way that they respect each other and respect each other's property. Ideally, this should happen through a coordinated effort by the government (all its departments), the criminal justice system, and civil society (e.g., the involvement of primary socializing agents like parents and teachers). This effort would therefore focus on influencing and directing people's behavior not to commit crime or to harm another person. Prevention therefore implies that the crime is unconditionally prevented and no one has the motivation to commit the crime again. Absolute prevention is probably only possible in a utopian world and will probably not be achieved with regard to violence and serious crime in SA.

Crime control, however, involves the activities of those who are responsible to enforce the law, as well as those who control community activities (Roelofse, 2011). These activities focus on controlling those people who are regarded as "predisposed" or gullible to commit a crime like a farm attack, a house invasion, participate in a violent strike, or poach an endangered rhino for its horn. There are actual interventions or involvements in terms of time and space to control the wrongdoer's behavior. These interventions employ strategies in the environment in which crime happens (environmental strategies), as well as strategies related to the way in which crime is committed (operational strategies) in order to control the behavior of those people who are inclined to commit the crime. Thus crime prevention is a long-term strategy that usually extends over several generations (transfer positive socializing practices over to another generation with the hope that high-quality individuals will cease to commit any crime and change their perceptions), while crime control can happen both in the long term and the short term. Long-term interventions could include a concerted long-term political will and policy change as well as prioritized initiatives to make an impact on a dilemma. Short-term interventions include sporadic foot or vehicle patrols, a zero tolerance stance, or employing a "shoot-to-kill" dogma by the security forces. The aim is to reduce specific crimes with specific interventions with immediate effect.

By the year 2000, the overall vision of the NCPS had dissipated as the state responded to the pressure from a crime-battered population by declaring a "war on crime." The four pillars of the NCPS were all crumbling, which resulted in governments' primary focus and resources being directed to the different bodies of the criminal justice system, and the term *crime prevention* has thereafter become synonymous with policing (Newham, 2005). Governments react differently to the challenges crime poses to their ability to achieve social control (Hagan, 1994, p. xiii). In this regard, David Garland opines in his book, *The Culture of Control: Crime and Social Order in Contemporary Society* (2001), that different governments across the globe, including the United States of America (U.S.) and the United Kingdom (UK) started experiencing problems with governance as early as the 1970s due to the welfare approach they were following toward crime and criminals. To address this problem, they introduced a more punitive approach. According to Garland, the "welfarist" approach, adopted by many first world countries after World War II, focused on the improvement of rehabilitation services, the reduction of oppressive control mechanisms, and the recognition of the rights of suspects and prisoners. The objective was to criminalize less, to minimize the use of custody, to humanize prisons, and to reintegrate prisoners into the community. However, during the 1970s crime rates increased dramatically in the United States and the UK. Consequently, the "welfarist" approach fell into disrepute with the middle class elite (Garland, 2001). Garland thinks that many governments experienced a policy predicament, and in addition started losing their ability to control crime. This forced them to change their policies and they had to adapt their approach to crime control. Over many years to date, many governments, SA included, face a predicament with regard to social control and crime control. Garland believes that this predicament is nestled on two major social facts, namely "the normality of high crime rates and the acknowledged limitations of the criminal justice state" (Garland, 2001, p. 106). In this regard, Garland says that "until recently, and with consistency rarely seen in other social data, recorded crime statistics showed an annual increase, in most crime categories, in virtually every year for more than thirty years" (Garland, 2001, p. 107).

Although a few governments successfully have relative social control over the populace and fight crime with specific inherently autochthonous tactics, many criminal justice systems in the globe came to be viewed primarily in terms of their limitations and propensity for failure rather than their prospects for future success (Garland, 2001). He believes that governments responded to this "nothing works" attitude by introducing new ways of controlling crime, such as the better management of risks and resources and more expressive penal measures. Thus high crime rates, which are common in many countries, and the limitations of many criminal justice systems (CJS) chiseled away at the myth of the sovereign power and control over the modern society. Many governments have no sovereignty and control over the populace as many governments face an inability to deliver the expected levels of control over crime and criminal conduct. The state responds to this predicament by either denying it or by becoming expressive in its actions. Common expressive principles are: "three strikes and you are out;" "zero tolerance;" and more drastic punitive measures. While crime and punishment become highly charged political issues, politicians use the crime control predicament to their advantage by advocating a tougher stand on crime and expressing their concern for public safety. Instead of acknowledging the limitations of the sovereign state and adapting to these limitations, a more punitive approach is usually adopted. Legislative measures of this ilk are described by Garland as a form of "acting out." The typical approach is to formulate and promulgate harsher legislation concerning manageable issues. He feels that sudden punitive initiatives such as the drug dispute, sexual predator statutes, and pedophile registers, mandatory sentencing as well as the "three strikes and you're out" law is "impulsive and unreflective" acting out behavior by governments as they circumvent burning issues like violent crimes (Garland, 2001, p. 132). The punitive measures are concocted with guile as politicians talk tough in the media on specific issues such as traffic offenses, drug-related issues, or traffic crimes and try and persuade the populace that they will be tough on crime. If one dissects this acting out response one will find that the real crime problems such as murder, rape, and robbery are not really on the agenda of this punitive approach as government is actually not in control of these difficult to control criminal activities and do not have resolutions to this predicament.

The foregoing is exactly what is happening in SA. SA introduced a "welfarist" approach after apartheid was toppled in 1994. The newly elected government under the leadership of the late Nelson Mandela (first democratically elected Black president of SA and leader of the African National Congress, ANC) focused on the abolition of the death penalty, the improvement of rehabilitation services, the reduction of oppressive control mechanisms, and the recognition of the rights of every SA citizen including suspects and prisoners. The objective was to criminalize less, to minimize the use of custody, to humanize prisons, and to reintegrate prisoners into the community. A restorative justice approach was adopted at the same time that crime rates increased dramatically after democratization. Violent crimes are currently out of control and ominously high in SA. To compound the government's predicament of a "welfarist" approach, the previous police commissioner of South Africa, General Bheke Cele, suddenly opted for a more forceful approach to crime prevention in South Africa. In 2009 he stated in public that he wants the law to be changed to allow police to "shoot to kill" criminals without worrying about "what happens after that" (Bezuidenhout, 2011; Goldstone, 2009).

His abrasive approach to crime fighting, namely that he and the SAPS will get tough on criminals, is somewhat out of sorts with the initial scope of the NCPS and the vision that President Mandela had for SA. Not long after Bheke Cele's announcement of more vigilant abrasive policing, a group of eight policemen were shown on national television news channels while they were beating and shooting a protester, Andries Tatane, during a protest to address poor service delivery by local government in Ficksburg in the Free State. He was also shot with a rubber bullet at close range and died of his injuries. Faull (2011) maintained in this regard that Cele's "fight fire with fire" approach may increase, rather than diminish police killings. An average of about 100 police officials are killed in SA every year in the line of duty. Criminals who believe that they are more likely to be killed than arrested by the police will arm themselves more heavily in response and will be more willing to shoot at the police in a bid to escape arrest. Many criminals also lead SA police officials into ambushes to kill them and to steal their firearms. The problem is that law-abiding civilians also experience this type of heavy-handed approach by the police and increasingly become afraid of police. As a result, they will be unlikely to cooperate with the police or provide them with information about criminal activities.

Since the "Tatane" incident of apparent unnecessary use of force, the police have been criticized on different forums for their brutality and poor relationships with the community. In reaction to this criticism, the SAPS said it had seen a rise in the "deliberate" killing and maiming of police officers across the country. SAPS insists that the community continues to show a lack of support and insensitivity to the number of policemen who are killed in the line of duty in SA. Different factors contribute to this breakdown in the relationship between the community and the police and the intolerance communities show toward police officials. Factors that compound the poor relationships and probably contribute to the high number of police killings in SA include poor management, poor training, and incorrect application of police procedure during police patrols. In addition the culture of intolerance and violence in SA has a significant effect on current community–police relationships. If these problems could be addressed successfully both police and public safety, along with police service delivery, may improve in future (Faull, 2011). After the Tatane incident, several brutal attacks by police officials have followed, which have rocked the nation and the international community. Reports of police brutality in South Africa have more than tripled in the last decade and have increased by 313%. Sadly, only one in 100 cases against rogue officers results in a conviction. When one contemplates these actions and figures, it would seem impossible for SA and the SAPS to ensure the successful hosting of a mega event. However, in some way, SA has hosted these large-scale events successfully in spite of the reported brutal activities by the police and the ongoing problems within the community. Recently, a series of high-profile police brutality cases, for example, the shooting of striking mineworkers at Marikana Lonmin mine, have left the reputation of the police service in tatters. Cases of police brutality leapt from 416 reported cases during 2001–2002 to 1722 cases in 2011–2012 (Smith, 2013).

Currently, South Africa's internal stability is threatened by a melting pot of violent strikes, showdowns within the police, and exorbitantly high crime rates. The 2012 Marikana miners' strike or Lonmin strike was a wild-cat strike at a mine owned by the Lonmin mining company in the Marikana area, close to Rustenburg, in the North West Province, South Africa. The event garnered international attention following a series of violent incidents between the SAPS, Lonmin security, the leadership of the National Union of Mineworkers (NUM), and strikers themselves, which has resulted in the deaths of 44 people, the majority of whom were striking mineworkers killed on August 16, 2012. At least 78 additional workers were also injured during this incident. The total number of injuries during the strike remains unknown. The press dubbed the incident as the "Marikana-massacre" as it was the single most lethal use of force by the South African security forces against civilians since the Sharpeville massacre in 1960 during apartheid.

In addition to the Lonmin strikers, there has been a wave of regular strikes across the South African mining sector and protests to rebel against poor service delivery by municipalities. In Brits, not far from Rustenburg where the Lonmin incident took place, protesters in Mothutlung and Damonsville (villages/townships in Brits, North West Province) used barricades, petrol bombs, and burned tires in the streets to show their dismay with the local municipality. They clashed with the police and the police killed two people and wounded another two during the protests in Mothutlung and Damonsville. The residents have reportedly been without water for a significant period. Residents started protesting about a water shortage and poor service delivery from the local government and some protesters lost their lives because of police brutality to pacify the situation.

In another incident in a town known as Tzaneen, the shops of foreign shop owners trading in Relela and Kubjana villages outside Tzaneen in the Limpopo Province were looted. The looting took place after a woman was murdered and her hand removed (probably for muti). Some traditional healers use human organs or bones in preparation of a concoction (a traditional muti). In this regard, Bhootra and Weiss (2006) state that "body parts for medicinal and ritualistic purposes are removed while the victims, mostly women and children, are still alive" (p. 255). This means that it actually necessitates a ritual, during which a victim who complies with particular requirements, such as a young woman or a child or a virgin, is chosen in order to obtain specific body parts, such as the hands, eyes, and genitalia. These body parts are generally used for medicinal purposes after they had been boiled or mixed with other substances, such as herbs. Generally the body parts, which are removed from the victim, may only be used for muti purposes if taken while the victim is still alive. This is due to the belief that powerful medicine cannot be made from the flesh of a human who is already dead. As a result, victims are not murdered before their organs are severed. They usually die as a result of their wounds. The purpose of requesting a concoction with human content or "blessed human limbs" is usually to improve an individual's situation (for example, burying a "blessed" human hand at the entrance of the business to attract more customers— symbolically waving them closer). This type of crime is not uncommon in South African squatter camps, informal settlements, townships, villages, and in the rural areas. In this case, that eventually disrupted into mayhem, the lady's cellular phone and house keys were placed inside her stomach, which had been ripped open. The local residents started protesting as they demanded the police to arrest the people who brutally killed the 20-year-old woman. Life in the two villages had come to a standstill with some schools closed, police satellite stations nonoperational, and taxi routes disrupted. During the same time frame, residents of the Kubjana village torched the house of a businessman suspected of kidnapping three boys. However, the three had locked themselves in the car while playing for hours and they were found by the owner when he got back from work. The owner noticed that the car's lights were on and he called the police. One boy was found dead in the boot of the man's car. Two other children were found unharmed in his vehicle. Residents clashed with police at the scene and threw stones at the police. The police fired live ammunition into the crowds and three people have died amid the protests in the area. During this protest and other protests that immediately followed the Tzaneen protest in different areas of SA, scores of police officers have been injured in the unrest, and police vehicles and property (police stations) have been damaged (Niehaus, 2009).

African Christian Democratic Party (ACDP) president Kenneth Meshoe condemned the regular clashes between the police and community members, saying police and protester clashes had become a regular occurrence in South Africa. Meshoe stated in this regard "it is like SA has become a war zone between the police and citizens. The ACDP firmly believes that where respect is given, respect is earned. Unfortunately, our

SAPS, while it has many fine officers, has [sic] not earned the respect of SA citizens." He further stated that incidents such as the "Marikana Massacre," Mothutlung service delivery protest shootings, and the Daveyton "dragging" scandal, have resulted in the police not being trusted. With regard to the Daveyton "dragging" scandal, Mido Macia, a 27-year-old taxi driver from Mozambican descent was tied to the back of a police vehicle and dragged along the street in Daveyton, on the East Rand in the Gauteng Province. Macia was seen tied to the back of a South African Police Service (SAPS) vehicle and dragged down the street for about 400 m. Amateur video footage was taken and nine police officers were suspended. After the dragging, Macia was later assaulted in police custody and passed away because of this ordeal. During January/February 2014 yet more serious protests erupted in different towns, cities, and villages across SA. For example, in Bronkhorstspruit, a town in Gauteng Province, more than 50 people were arrested after a library and a house were set alight by disgruntled residents. In villages nearby violent service delivery protests also erupted as protesters torched the Zithobeni satellite police station and municipal offices and the clinic in Rethabiseng. The city of Tshwane Municipality said residents of Bronkhorstspruit, Rethabiseng, and Zithobeni in Region Seven had been protesting because they were unable to buy prepaid electricity (www.news24.com on July 3, 2014).

The South African Institute for Race Relations executive, Frans Cronjé, warns that the SAPS has shot dead 30 rioters over the previous three years, but during January 2014, they had already shot dead eight and wounded many more. This countrywide protest movement already is a larger political movement than the ruling African National Congress Political Party who came into rule after apartheid was toppled. He said that violent riots by large mobs in villages such as Mothutlung, Damonsville, Relala, and Kubjana are an indication that the people are fed up and feel their lifestyles have not improved under the ANC government. At the start of 2014, there were several spontaneous riots that had flared up, and it is said that there are about four riots per day in different regions across SA (Van Rooyen & Swanepoel, 2014).

Service delivery protest marches, wage strikes, and other mob violence events such as the horrendous xenophobic attacks that emerge frequently give the SAPS more than enough to cope with (Burger, 2007). These incidents have managed to cause chaos in some parts of the country and the riot police have had to deal with several tough situations throughout the hosting of any mega event in SA. The riot police in SA are known as the Public Order Policing (POP) unit. Currently, several POP members are undertrained and lack discipline. There are about 33 POP units countrywide and approximately 6500 POP members countrywide (Geldenhuys, 2011), which are hopelessly too little for the continuous problems during strikes and protests. In addition, they do not always have the necessary nonlethal equipment (water cannons, pepper spray, barricades, etc.) with them when they police a strike or protest action. In cases when police are threatened by local communities they can only fall back on their live ammunition to protect themselves. In addition, vigilante justice is rife in SA. Many communities opt to take law into their own hands by arresting, summoning, and torturing or killing alleged offenders in communities.

Should the SA government not be able to keep the citizenry content, one can predict serious unstable times for SA. The next step probably will be huge coordinated protest actions countrywide and large-scale antigovernment rioting. POP will not be able to deal with a national problem of this magnitude. The Human Rights Institute of SA said it was deeply concerned as some civilians were killed while exercising their constitutional rights to express their frustration with the government. The citizens are fed up with the government, and their frustrations could be attributed to negative feelings that the advent of democracy had not delivered basic rights and did not deal with basic needs.

The unprofessional policing of protests, the regular violent clashes between the police and citizens, a lack of trust in the police, and the regular atrocious stories about police brutality that make media headlines are currently shaking the majority of the SA populace in its core. Safety and security for an average citizen is already not a given because of our crime situation, and this is even worsened by the regular brutal interventions by the police. Many citizens do not trust the police and rely on vigilante justice (especially in informal settlements and villages) or private security companies to protect them. The private security industry in SA provides guarding, monitoring, armed reaction, escorting, investigating services, target hardening gadgets, and other security-related services to citizens who can afford the service. SA's private security industry is one of the largest in the world with nearly 9000 registered companies and 400,000 registered active private security guards. This is attributed to the country's very high levels of crime, poor public–police relations, and a lack of public funds from government toward the improvement of SAPS. Government is also outsourcing certain security functions away from police responsibility. It is estimated that an approximate ratio of one public police officer for every 2.6 private (1:2.6) security officers exists in SA. However, some scholars state that the ratio is closer to four private security officers for every one public police officer (Annual Report: PSIRA, 2012/13; Kempen, 2010e).

The use of unwarranted violence on communities by police officers, who are meant to protect the communities they serve, have been deplored by several concerned parties. South Africa is termed the *Rainbow Nation* because it is home to many different racial and ethnic groups with their own cultural practices. This, however, often leads to confusion and tension between people from different cultural backgrounds who do not subscribe to the same cultural practices as well as with the formal system and its stance on indigenous practices and trends. The SA government therefore has a difficult task in attempting to balance indigenous laws and rules with the laws of modern civilization. They have lost their sovereign social control over the populace, and it is difficult to believe that they can ensure safety for all the citizens. It is therefore a myth that the SA government is in control of its populace and in command of the prevention of crime. SA is notorious for its violence, xenophobia (especially between local Black African people toward Black African people from other African countries), and the extreme levels of corruption. To add to the complications of the demands of the rainbow nation, politicians make impossible promises to local community members, which cannot be fulfilled in the timelines they promise. Some promises are impossible to execute. These promises to the poor and marginalized are usually part of their political campaigns before elections. Currently (2014), politicians are campaigning in the poor marginalized communities and they are making some of these farfetched promises. In addition, some political figures use this opportunity to mobilize youths and to refer to the revolution in their efforts to win supporters. However, local communities become fed up with the underperforming national government and local municipalities who are paid outrageous salaries for doing nothing. Nepotism and corruption are rife in these national and local governments, and many SA communities have had enough. They will continue to use riots, strikes (labor related), and protests (lack of services related) as their actions are covered by the media and politicians usually attend to matters once they are broadcasted on local and international news channels. The year 2014 is an election year in SA and politicians are currently trying everything to get votes. However, it can also be referred to as "strike season" as communities know politicians want votes and will promise anything during election periods.

To complicate matters is the fact that a significant majority of the SA population are from different Black ethnic groups, each with their own unique cultural practices and indigenous rules of law. In fact, in the latest publication of Statistics South Africa (2013), the SA population is estimated to be 52,982,000 million. According to this publication the Black Africans are in the majority (42,284,100 million) and constitute just more than 79.8% of the total South African population. The White population is estimated at 4,602,400 million (8.7%), the colored population at 4,766,200 million (9%), and the Indian/Asian population at 1,329,300 million (2.5%) (Statistics South Africa, 2013). The indigenous practices of many cultural groupings are therefore difficult to understand and accommodate against the backdrop of the democracy of SA, which is often hailed as the country with one of the most liberal constitutions in the world. There are so many different expectations from the different groupings and the government cannot produce the necessary services and support to all its citizenry. Aside from the diversity and differences in cultural and ethnical groupings, the current main list of items on most citizens' lips that are certainly not or never addressed are high crime rates, poor or no service delivery, a significant lack of legitimate job opportunities, as well as a deep anxiety regarding personal safety and security.

Crime is extraordinarily high in South Africa, and although it appears to dominate the domestic agendas of government it does not, as civil society seems to be more concerned about these concerns weighed against government concern. There are also legitimate concerns from civilians that levels of violence associated with crime in this country are on the increase. Ample evidence exists of the long history of human involvement in aggression and violence in South Africa. Today, South Africans are still under the constant threat of violent crimes such as murder, rape, robbery, assault, and the like. The result is increased fear of crime, and a growing distrust in the police and government officials in general to effectively deal with crime. Keeping South Africa safe for the local citizen is therefore seen through different lenses compared to the international visitor who attends a mega event and only sees the virtuous side of public stability at the major event.

Many South Africans are confronted by violent crime on a 24-hour basis. Relative to the rest of the world, violent crime in SA is higher than most countries. A high percentage of people are murdered, raped, tortured, and robbed daily. To contextualize the magnitude of the crime problem, 18,000 house invasions (owner and or family still in the house), and about 15,000 car hijackings occur each year. On a daily basis, about 50 murders, 152 rapes, and 350 robberies take place in SA (based on reported cases). Distressingly, a woman is killed about every eight hours in SA according to the Medical Research Council (MRC). Also, it is not uncommon to hear of a crime incident where gratuitous violence (excessive unnecessary violence) was used against the victims. Gratuitous violence is currently causing tremendous trauma for society in general, but more specifically during farm attacks and home invasions. The perpetrators will torture and maim the victims long after their instrumental goal of the attack was achieved (e.g., thieving a laptop and a mobile phone). In addition, if one does not become a direct victim the possibility exists that vicarious victimization (usurp others' victimization) takes place. The relentless media reports of the brutal murders, farm attacks, house invasions, rapes, and robberies force people to usurp each other's victimization. This in turn fuels the fear of crime and instability even more. Also as discussed earlier, the police are daily confronted by angry mobs because of poor service delivery or strikes for the reason of wage negotiations. In South Africa, a belief system exists among many citizens that crime is out of control, and because of this many citizens and especially the vulnerable groups such as the farming community and minority groups in terms of the population statistics live in fear behind a façade of false security (e.g., carrying of a firearm at all times, carrying pepper spray, keeping guard dogs, installing burglar proofing, alarms, armed response, electric fencing, and electronic monitoring). One reason for this is that the mistaken belief in security acts as a defense mechanism to cope with the strains caused by regular incidences of violence in general society in SA. Many factors can fuel the fear for personal safety, namely the mass media, the lawlessness of many groupings of citizens, gangs and syndicates, mob violence, and emotionally colored statements of politicians, as well as the absence of an effective criminal justice system (Bezuidenhout, 2013; Burger, 2007; Geldenhuys, 2011).

The government should with immediate effect provide better service delivery, root out the corruption, and they need to address crime, poverty, and the high unemployment rate in SA. Against the backdrop of the social control assumption of David Garland, politicians have accepted a strategy of ignorance and wrong priority. Politicians tend to prioritize traffic offenses and sex crimes but other burning issues such as the high murder rate, farm attacks, home invasions, car hijackings, and rhino poaching do not get the same prioritized treatment as the implementation of the E-toll system (paying per kilometer to use the highways in Gauteng Province) or traffic violations (e.g., national projects on drinking and driving or a "zero-tolerance for a traffic violation" projects in certain provinces). Even the South African Revenue Service (SARS) has massive campaigns to ensure that each South African gets the message that if they are liable for tax they should submit a tax return or bear the brunt of the justice system. The same level of enthusiasm is absent to address the concerns of the citizens. To support the belief that Garland's proposition is relevant to SA, namely that the state responds to this predicament by either denying it or by becoming expressive in its actions, several politicians have made some inappropriate statements concerning the crime problem in SA. In 2006, the then Minister of Safety and Security, Charles Nqakula said: "they can continue to attack everything we do... and be as negative as they want; in the end it is the people out there who for many years have been crying for peace and stability who determine who rules this country ... they can continue to whinge until they're blue in the face, they can continue to be as negative as they want to or they can simply leave this country." (To contextualize the problem, his remarks and some comments from citizens can be viewed on YouTube at www.youtube.com/watch?v = WwXSIDp3RSM.)

Considering the national safety conundrum, one can ask the question: How did SA manage to host several mega events in the past relatively safely with no major incident to report? Against the aforesaid backdrop, it is difficult to fathom what forces are at play to ensure the safety of visitors to mega events. Today, our constitution implies that we are the apotheosis of racial morality, equality, freedom, fairness, and political correctness, yet South Africans are living in a very politically charged, imbalanced, unfair, and violent society and, on paper, we should not have been able to host a global event like the FIFA Soccer World Cup successfully.

The Successful Hosting of International Mega Events: The South African Anecdote of the FIFA Soccer World Cup

As SA has hosted many large-scale events with success, only one example will be used to guide the discussion on the hosting of a mega event in a crime-burdened country. The FIFA World Cup (Football/Soccer World Cup) is probably the biggest spectacle in global sport; and in 2010 SA hosted the 19th edition of this event with relative ease, despite all the challenges the police entertain on a daily basis, as highlighted in the foregoing discussion. It is even bigger than the Olympic Games, due to the number of spectators that usually visit the host country to support their teams, and due to the global media coverage that this event attracts. The FIFA World Cup was a month-long soccer tournament decided by 64 matches, played in ten stadiums spread over nine SA cities. Approximately 450,000 visitors came to SA to watch the games live. About 3.3 million tickets were sold for these matches. Any country wishing to host the FIFA World Cup has to deliver 17 guarantees to FIFA. In essence, these guarantees are provided by various government departments and include ease of access to SA; a supportive financial environment; intellectual property and marketing rights; safety and security; health care services; transport; and telecommunications. These guarantees are so important that they were consolidated into the 2010 FIFA World Cup South Africa Special Measures Act of 2006 in September 2006, as per FIFA requirements. In addition, a Memorandum of Understanding was signed between the Minister of Finance and the President of FIFA on October 27, 2006, to close the deal.

When a mega event of this magnitude comes to SA, the National Joint Operational and Intelligence Structure (Natjoints) usually develops and coordinates a comprehensive security protocol. The Natjoints was established as the operational arm of the Justice, Crime Prevention, and Security Cluster, following a Cabinet decision. Natjoints reports to and is directed by the JCPS cluster (Justice, Crime Prevention, and Security) at both Cabinet and Directors-General level. All the various role-players, including relevant government departments, implement, execute, and monitor all interdepartmental and cross-provincial operations affecting safety, security, and stability in the Republic of South Africa. The track record of the Natjoints speaks for itself, thanks to the integrated approach which has been adopted and implemented and which is the result of a high level of cooperation and coordination between various government departments and lessons learned from past mega events. These departments include, among others, the SAPS, the South African National Defense Force (SANDF), the Department of Environmental Affairs and Tourism, SA Weather services, Department of Agriculture and Forestry, the Metro Police, the Department of Trade and Industry, the Department of Health, and the Department of Sport and Recreation. SAFA (South African Football Association) and FIFA were also present on the planning and priority committees. All the departments or the Local Organizing Committee (LOC) (relevant departments and role-players of the applicable country) are held responsible to manage any safety and/or security incidents and/or related accidents. It was the responsibility of the LOC to ensure safety and if something would have happened, FIFA would not have been held responsible, but the LOC would be accountable. During the past 13 years and based on previous experience, this structure has been responsible for ensuring safety at the mega events that SA has successfully hosted. Also the SAPS was working closely with foreign intelligence agencies through the newly established Intelligence Coordinating Committee (ICC) and they were prepared for any national or global threat.

The National Joint Operational Centre (Natjoc) is housed in the Capital of SA, Pretoria. As soon as a large-scale event is announced and SA is identified as the host; planning and protocols would commence by Natjoints and implementation would commence at the Natjoc. Natjoc is operational 24/7 and the structure is duplicated at the provincial level in all the nine provinces and is referred to as the provincial JOC. Also the provincial JOCs were supported by Venue Operation Centers (VOCS). Natjoc's highly successful operational security brief and master plan was applied during the 2010 FIFA World Cup and covered the following areas:

(A) Ports of Entry (POE)

An integrated approach is followed by the relevant government departments deployed at POEs to ensure smooth facilitation of the arrival and departure of all guests, but without compromising safety and security. SA is bordered by two oceans, namely, the South Atlantic and the Indian Oceans. Representatives from the country's 32 ports of entry also received training in operating the First Defender, which is used for rapid, accurate identification of unknown chemicals at a POE. SAPS personnel at the airports were trained to be able to handle any situation at the airport such as handling of dangerous goods. They were also trained in customer care, identification of forged documents, and assistance protocol in crisis situations. At the main SA airport—O.R. Tambo International Airport—a new CCTV control room was also installed for the mega event and the control of the large number of visitors. In the cargo section security was also beefed up to monitor incoming and outgoing cargo.

(B)   Railway Policing

The Railway Police are deployed to ensure crime prevention on all trains used for transportation to and from the soccer venues. SA has many problems on rail facilities such as train overcrowding and train surfing.

(C)   Route Security

Police members perform visible policing and crime prevention duties on major routes and soccer teams are escorted by security teams.

(D)   City Security

The aim was to create a safe environment in host cities, especially at places of interest where fans gather, such as restaurants and tourist attractions. The police presence was visible but subtle, not to spoil the festive mood of the fans.

(E)   Securing Commercial Partners

As far as possible the police are vigilant on the policing of counterfeit goods and black market tickets. Thus as far as possible "FIFA's" rights and brand name were protected.

(F)   Social Responsibility and Domestic Concerns

The Department of Social Development was involved, especially to manage lost minors at stadiums. Different nongovernment organizations (NGOs) like Child Line participated in this part of the plan and specific designated areas were allocated to deal with lost children and other relevant social issues.

(G)   Venue Protection

The outer perimeter security measures at stadiums are the sole responsibility of law enforcement, while private security officers assisted law enforcement with protecting the inner perimeter. In addition, plainclothed law enforcement officials and informants were placed among spectators to quickly identify and deal with hooligans in the crowd. K-9 Units were also on hand to secure the venues. Explosives experts also swept the venues beforehand and all vehicles (e.g., catering trucks) were examined at a different location before they were allowed into the venues. Members of the Explosives Unit underwent additional training and were equipped with new technologically advanced devices. The United States assisted SA in antiterrorism training as part of the U.S. Department of State's Bureau of Diplomatic Security program. The training forms part of the State Department's Antiterrorism

Assistance program, known by its acronym ATA. In addition, different types of technologies such as infrared material analyzers, pole-climbing cameras, and undervehicle surveillance systems were employed to ensure safety at venues.

(H) Team Security

Each soccer team was closely protected by a security brief that provided 24-hour escort and protection services. In addition, safety measures were beefed up at the venues that were used as "base camps" (e.g., hotels or spas). The author is an employee of the University of Pretoria who hosted Argentina. A month before the World Cup the security measures were evident. Even our own access and parking facilities were scrutinized on a daily basis. Many students had to forfeit general parking areas as they became overall checking points of trucks and delivery vehicles as the University of Pretoria is located 800 meters from Loftus Versfeld, a venue where several games were played.

(I) World Cup Courts and Investigative Capacity

Apart from deploying 41,000 police (and 10,000 reservists) around stadiums, fan parks, hotels, and tourist sites the government also temporarily established 56 dedicated World Cup courts across the country. These courts were staffed by more than 1500 dedicated personnel, including magistrates, prosecutors, public defenders, and interpreters. This ensured that cases were speedily finalized in court. It is worth mentioning that the actual crime statistics reduced during the Soccer World Cup tournament. Some believe it was because of manipulation of the statistics while some scholars believe it was due to the swift and effective functioning of the World Cup courts and more dedicated investigative muscles during that month.

(J) Crowd Management

Some SAPS members successfully completed an additional crowd management training program before the World Cup. Resources such as airplanes, helicopters, water cannons, and other equipment to defuse crowds were always in the ready. In addition the Mounted Units also underwent additional training as they had a vital role to play in crowd management. Horses are extremely effective in crowd management and their high visibility is an effective deterrence and prevention tool for potential hooliganism and misbehavior at events. Senior management also requested all police officials who worked during soccer events to act professionally at all times. The author knows several police officials who opted to partake in the World Cup security initiatives. They were allowed to work overtime during the event (e.g., securing and guarding a secluded airstrip near the host city). One officer who secured an airstrip during the event said they worked long hours and were only paid the overtime stipend six weeks after the hosting of the FIFA World Cup. With regard to soccer hooliganism some countries assisted SA and compiled lists of known hooligans for the SAPS. For example, the UK government had pledged to keep their own hooligans out of SA for the duration of the World Cup tournament. A list of approximately 3000 names of known British hooligans was compiled, and the government endeavored to confiscate all the passports of these individuals to prevent them from traveling to SA. The UK sent a team of 12 English police specialists to support the SAPS during the World Cup.

(K) Restricted Airspace

Airspace restrictions were in place around stadiums during matches and compliance was enforced by the South African Air Force. However, SA has many airstrips with no radar coverage (e.g., game lodges). Getting into and out of SA is actually an easy assignment for informed pilots as many airstrips are open for landing at night.

(L) Naval Environment

The SA Navy deployed offshore patrol vessels and designated boats were in place for harbor protection. Police divers also underwent an underwater explosives incident countermeasures course, which aimed to provide specialized underwater technical training to law enforcement personnel in preparation for the World Cup. The course was facilitated by the U.S. ATA program.

(M) Interdepartmental Reaction Teams

Each of the nine host cities had an interdepartmental reaction team consisting of members from the Special Reaction Forces, SAPS, SANDF, Metro Police, Traffic, Health, and Emergency Services. These teams were assembled and structured according to the city's risk profile. It is important to take note that SA has insignificant pressure from natural disasters at this stage. It is highly unlikely that a tsunami or a natural earthquake will devastate SA. SA has many man-made risks such as violent crime and political corruption but has a low risk pertaining to natural disasters.

(N) Rapid Response Teams

Special high-risk units from the SAPS known as the Division Operational Response Services (ORS) were always at the ready. They included the Special Task Force, the Counter Assault Team, POP, the Air Wing, the Border Police, and the National Intervention Unit (NIU), and other special units from the SANDF were also on standby to react to any emergency situations anywhere in the country.

These policing initiatives were put in place without interrupting everyday policing in the troubled communities of SA and probably should be deemed as the basis of hosting a mega event of this magnitude (Geldenhuys, 2008a,b, 2009, 2011; Kempen, 2010a,b,c,d,e, 2013; Papp, 2010).

Policing the FIFA World Cup

The bulk of the resources (i.e., human and material) for the Soccer World Cup security operation came from the SAPS, with additional resources deployed by the Metro Police Services, the SANDF, the intelligence community, disaster management, and others like the special courts that were set up by the Department of Justice and played a significant role in the hosting of this mega event. It is estimated that approximately 51,000 members of the security services, excluding private security, were deployed to protect the integrity of the event, visiting heads of state, and to ensure the safety of all the spectators, sportsmen, and their management. About 41,000 of the 51,000 security services members were operational members of the SAPS.

The actual policing of the event was the responsibility of approximately 31,000 functional police members and an additional 10,000 reservists who were drawn from their usual functional duties at the local policing level. An additional 10,000 reservists were on standby (1000 in every host city), ready for deployment in case of emergency, which adds up to the total of 51,000.

Other law enforcement agencies such as the Metro Police departments, the railway police, and the different emergency services, like the fire brigade, rescue services (ambulances), and disaster services were also on standby. These other law enforcement agencies formed the so-called second line of defense. SAPS was also assisted by the private security industry, which assisted in performing safety functions at controlled access sites at the ten stadiums, fan parks, training venues where teams trained, and banqueting venues.

Before the World Cup commenced, the government promised to expand the SAPS personnel to address the crime conundrum in SA and to ensure racial and gender representation in the police. The government introduced an en masse recruitment drive in part to address the legacy of apartheid by promoting racial and gender representativeness in the SAPS. In so doing, they facilitated entry into the civil service by a significant number of Black African police officers. The success of this drive is commendable but open to doubt. Later on, the government insisted that this massive recruitment drive was necessary to enable the SAPS to better implement sector policing and that this would increase the visibility of and access to police officers, particularly in disorganized marginalized

BOX 12.1   A RESERVIST'S OPINION ABOUT THE RESERVE POLICE INVOLVEMENT DURING THE FIFA WORLD CUP

Reservists and the Soccer World Cup in South Africa 2010—A Reservist's Opinion.

It's a little-known fact that if it wasn't for the reservist component of the SAPS the 2010 Soccer World Cup would have gone very differently. A big problem the SAPS faced during this time was manpower in securing the various soccer stadiums around South Africa. Many foreigners who attended the matches were impressed by the police presence at the stadiums. They would frequently voice their approval, saying "how comforting it was to have so many police members guarding them, especially after all the terrifying crime stories they had heard before coming to SA." What they did not realize though is that it was an extremely delicate balancing act to bring so many police members out of the areas they normally worked in. Many police stations around the country were faced with operating with skeleton staff because of this month long tournament. As such, permanent police members would typically only supplement the stadium numbers on their off days (and also typically only on match days). But for the rest of the time, a large number of reservists were called up to secure the stadiums. These reservists were paid, but only half of what the permanent members were paid (and was also not provided with daily food vouchers), and had to work much longer hours than most permanent police officers. For example, at Cape Town stadium, a group of reservists with a minimal permanent member component (particularly commanders and members on management level) were responsible for establishing perimeter security around the stadium well in advance of the first matches. Reservists typically worked a 2-day shift—this is the 2-day 2-night on and 2 days off pattern, which is more intensive than the usual police shift schedule during this time, which has 4 rest days in their schedule. While the safe and successful hosting of the World Cup plans was certainly a team effort between the specialized units, permanent police members and other role-players the pivotal quiet role reservists played in success story of the Soccer World Cup in South Africa is unimaginable. (Author interview with a reservist)

areas where crime levels are high. In 2000–2002, the SAPS consisted of approximately 120,000 members. In 2005–2006, the police service was 155,532 strong. At this time, the government propagated that they had no choice but to employ more police officers. Next, they conveniently used the World Cup as one of their main motivations for the ongoing en masse recruitment drive. In 2008–2009, they were about 183,000 strong and in 2012–2013 they were 199,367 strong (157,518 sworn officers and 41,849 civilians). Although the eventual governmental target was 210,000 members by 2010 to coincide with the 2010 World Cup event, these targets were never reached in time. One could ask the question whether the insecure government was building a force to protect their political integrity. The number of Black police officers in the service has now increased to about 79%, which is on par with color quotas of the current population. A massive recruitment of this type over the last decade has required a substantial investment of public funds. The SAPS budget increased at an average annual rate of 13.6% from R36.5 billion (± US\$3.65 billion) in 2007–2008 to R53.5 billion (± US\$5.35 billion) in 2010–2011. The problem is that this budget is mainly usurped by an increased expenditure in compensation of the new unsuccessfully trained employees in SAPS. In addition to the poor training, the haphazard recruitment practices also had its drawbacks, as many police officers had been and continue to be involved in crime activities and are members of crime syndicates. In addition, police brutality in SA soared because of various factors (i.e., poor training, poor vetting of new recruits, and the influence of incidents of inter-organizational arrogance).

In addition to having more personnel for 2010, the SAPS were also forced to procure additional and sophisticated equipment that enhanced their operational capability during 2010 and beyond. Their managerial decisions are questionable as many pieces of equipment did not reach the end goal of usage after the World Cup. For the World Cup, an additional R665 million (US\$63.3 million) was included in the World Cup security budget, and has been spent on the procurement of special equipment including crowd-control equipment, crime scene trainers, unmanned aircraft (drones), helicopters, mobile water cannons, vehicles for highway patrol, and up-to-date body armor vests, bomb squad equipment, satellite imaging systems, and so on. The equipment is currently wanting in the strike and protester actions. However, during the Soccer World Cup approximately 300 mobile cameras were procured, which were linked to special mobile command centers. These centers featured hi-tech monitoring equipment, which was able to receive live footage from the airplanes, other drone cameras, and static cameras in strategic places. On top of the recruitment drive and procurement of specialized equipment, specialized training specifically to deal with crowd management and possible hostage situations also formed part of the SAPS preparations for the mega event. Should these initiatives still be in place, policing should have triumphed after the Soccer Cup. All of the above resources were deployed as part of an extremely comprehensive operational plan that provided inter alia, for crime prevention and combating operations, VIP protection, borderline security (including air and sea security), transport and route security, tourism security, and contingency planning for specific security threats. However, after the event these initiatives dissolved over time, and regular challenges became "normal" again. Please note that there are two landlocked countries within the geographical borders of SA, namely, Lesotho and Swaziland. Also in the north, northwest, and northeast land borders SA has four neighboring countries, namely Mozambique, Zimbabwe, Botswana, and Namibia.

Since the 2004 announcement that SA would be hosting the FIFA World Cup, the South African Police Service actively prepared for the event. Although SA showed that they could host mega events safely before the FIFA Soccer World Cup, FIFA required a very specific stringent security protocol. SA therefore had to submit a security concept to FIFA for approval no later than two years before the opening match of the 2010 FIFA World Cup. This comprehensive security plan was submitted on schedule June 30, 2008 (Bruce, 2013; Burger, 2007; Kempen, 2010b).

The Successful Results and Eventual Regression

The aftermath of hosting what has been hailed by one and all as a successful 2010 FIFA World Cup left the government and the security players involved with a sense of pride, confidence, optimism, and belief. It remains a great feat for a country whose ability to host an event of this magnitude was repeatedly under scrutiny by the global community. Many fans expressed their fears to come to the crime-invested country like SA. However, after the tournament many fans hailed SA and indicated that they would like to return to the warm and friendly rainbow nation. Even FIFA was impressed and paid the government significant bonuses for the successful hosting of the event.

The special World Cup courts did not remain after the event and the intensified policing of cities, airspace, borders, and harbors dissipated soon after the World Cup. The global event brought about synergy and an elaborate security effort, which curbed crimes around the intensified policing areas for that period of time. Crime apparently reduced during the tournament month and it is as if the offender population "cooperated" during the event. Crimes were still high in the rest of SA but according to official statistics crimes were less during the event. Maybe offenders also took some time off to enjoy the spectacle or the SAPS and government successfully secured the event with a multidimensional master plan.

Since the World Cup Games

At the present time, there is a deep public concern about the state of policing in SA. The consistent cases of police brutality and the significant denunciation of the police by the public are tangible. Government has responded with the help of the Justice, Crime Prevention, and Security (JCPS)

Cluster SAPS's Strategic Plan for 2010–2014. It is an outcome-based model, as well as an evaluation and monitoring tool, in order to realize the broad strategic outcome of the government: "All People in South Africa Are and Feel Safe."

This outcome contains various focus areas such as:

Goal 1: Ensure that all people in South Africa are and feel safe.

Goal statement: To provide police services that will ensure safer communities by:

(A)   Reducing the number of all serious crime incidents, contact crime incidents, and trio crime incidents;

(B)   Increasing activities to prevent and combat border crimes;

(C)   Increasing the percentage of court-ready case dockets for all serious crimes, contact crimes, and trio crimes;

(D)   Increasing the detection rate for all serious crimes, contact crimes, and trio crimes, including organized crime and the crimes against women and children; and

(E)   Increasing the conviction rates for all serious crimes, contact crimes, and trio crimes.

Goal 2: Ensuring adequate availability of, and access to the SAPS's service points.

Goal statement: Improve the levels of service delivery and accessibility to services by bringing the SAPS's service points closer to the communities.

This goal has been prioritized in the development of the SAPS's Medium-term Infrastructure and Capital Asset Plan, which forms part of the Long-term Infrastructure and Capital Asset Plan, and the Access Strategy for determining the construction of access or service points, (i.e., police stations, satellite police stations, fixed and mobile contact points), which is based on the analysis of geographical location and input from community engagements. Although there are other facilities and access points identified in some geographical areas, particular emphasis is put on constructing police stations and access points in the rural environment (Annual Report: South African Police Service, 2012/2013).

The government has also implemented the National Development Plan (NDP) 2030, titled "Our Future—Make It Work." The plan contains a number of far-reaching recommendations, which, if implemented, could see dramatic improvements not only in policing but throughout government. It was developed by the National Planning Commission (NPC) in the Office of the Presidency and was endorsed by the South African Cabinet at a lekgotla (political indaba) in September 2012. The ANC subsequently adopted it in December 2012.

This document is potentially the most important government policy directive in recent years. It comprises 15 chapters covering a range of developmental issues broadly aimed at accelerating progress, deepening democracy, and building a more active and inclusive society. It is therefore significant that one of its 15 chapters is dedicated to "building safer communities." The NDP recognizes that reducing crime and violence requires far more than what the police alone can achieve. Nevertheless, the plan does recognize the deterioration in police professionalism, following years of poor appointments of both senior and middle managers. It recommends, inter alia, that:

(A) The national commissioner and deputy national commissioners should be appointed by the president on a competitive basis. Unlike the current situation where the president tends to appoint political loyalists with inadequate skills and experience, the NDP recommends that a panel select and interview a short list of candidates based on objective criteria. The president would then use the list of appropriately skilled professionals to appoint the national commissioner and his/her deputies.

(B) A national policing board with multisectorial and multidisciplinary expertise should be established to set standards for recruitment, selection, appointment, and promotion, and should also develop a Code of Ethics for the police.

(C) All officers should undergo a competency assessment to gauge whether they meet the required standards for their current ranks. Officers who do not meet these standards should not be considered for promotion until they attain the required level of competence for that rank.

(D) In the next five years a two-stream system should be developed to create high-caliber officers and recruits. One stream would be for appointing noncommissioned officers and another for commissioned officers. Appointment into the officers' stream should be based on set criteria, probably developed by the national policing board.

(E) In the short-term, the existing Code of Conduct of the SAPS should be included in its disciplinary regulations and performance appraisal system. Periodic checks should be conducted to establish the extent to which the code is understood and practiced. Members who fail this test should be suspended or even dismissed.

(F) The NDP strongly recommends that the SAPS be demilitarized and that this should happen as soon as possible. It also recommends that the organizational culture of the police should be reviewed to assess the effects of militarization, demilitarization, remilitarization, and "the serial crises of top management." (Annual Report: South African Police, 2012/13; Burger, 2013; National Development Plan, 2011).

Before 1994, the South African Police Force (SAP) was defined as a paramilitary institution. After democratization in 1994, the ANC government demilitarized the national police agency. They changed the name to the South African Police Service, amended the rank structure (e.g., the head of the police was referred to as *commissioner* and not *general*), revised the uniform, and changed the insignia and the color of the vehicles. This they thought will defuse old negative attitudes toward the police; clearly it did not!

Statements by the president, politicians, the minister of police, and the national commissioner over the past few years have made it clear that the SA government intends to remilitarize the police again. In this regard, Burger (2013) stated "in fact, militarization in this context bordered dangerously close on establishing an alternative military institution. However, except for the ranks, none of the other intended changes materialized" (p. 1).

Since 2000, the police service started to revert back to a paramilitary organizational structure. This process was highlighted with the reintroduction of military ranks in 2010. This took place against the backdrop of a government that has lost control, experienced the predicament of minor social control, and which was seen as "acting out." Politicians and police chiefs are talking tough in the media, but violent crimes are increasing and the frustrations of the communities are snowballing. The government thought this remilitarizing initiative would command greater respect from the communities (National Development Plan, 2011). During 2010, the former SAPS National Commissioner, Bheki Cele, communicated to all the SAPS commanders that the new rank structure "should facilitate the enhancement of discipline, instilling public confidence and the upliftment of morale within the police ranks" (in Burger, 2013, p. 1). So far it seems very unsuccessful as the relations between the police and the community is currently in tatters and considered highly volatile.

Concluding Thoughts

From the forgoing discussion, it is clear that a paradox exists when it comes to keeping SA as a nation safe and the successful hosting of a mega event within the country's borders. SA is in dire straits concerning violent crime and keeping the populace safe. The government's "social contract" with the people can be viewed as being nonexistent, and the government is grappling to gain some form of control over the populace and to contain crime in SA. On top of this, corruption, nepotism, and inequality add to this government predicament of keeping the people in the boundaries of SA safe. The attitude and tone of senior police officials and politicians calling for police to "shoot to kill" is not helping the cause. The police have many systemic problems and the cyclical militarization and demilitarization processes only contribute to the confusion. Furthermore, the police leadership is not setting an example as the two previous chiefs of police have been implicated in allegations of inappropriate and unbecoming behavior and have been forced to leave office because of it. The current commissioner is also under a magnifying glass because of disputed behavior. The SAPS clearly has leadership issues and an endemic culture of nonrespect is clear across the rank and file structure. The poorly conceived en masse recruitment process, the lack of proper professional training, and dysfunctional command and control organizational mechanism can be viewed as exacerbating the issue. Police brutality and general violence in society have become "normalized," and it will take a concentrated effort by government officials and policy makers to defuse this time bomb. The problem is inherent to the current system, and the changing of rank structures or the policing approach will likely have little effect. Mutual respect between the police and the communities being served can be viewed as being absent. It is apparent that organizational respect can only be earned through a new professional police approach advocated and administered by properly qualified, well-trained, and open-minded staff. The problem in SA lies deeper than the changing of a rank structure. It is deeply rooted in political dogmas, attitudes, social inequality, and economic marginalization. Apartheid has become a convenient scapegoat notion, but the truth lies much deeper than this. Additionally, crime is rife in SA, and a culture of violence is intrinsic to SA. The political rhetoric to blame apartheid for everything is becoming hollow.

It is therefore an astonishing feat that SA has hosted several large-scale global events amid the prominent domestic dispute between the populace and the police. Consider the myth of sovereign control by the government and the high crime figures, as well as the troubled police–public relations, one can only state that the successful hosting of mega events are actually something to marvel about. It is as if the domestic problems had faded away for the duration of the mega event and then resurfaced as soon as the event was over. This phenomenon is difficult to explain, but the nation's track record of successfully hosting these overwhelming international events speaks for itself.

The current police force approach may be the correct approach in a violent crime ridden country, and perhaps the NDP may be the answer in developing a professional, accountable, respected police "forced" service. Society as a whole should change, and the responsibility does not only lie on the shoulders of the government and the police (see Box 12.2 hereafter).

Whether apartheid should still be blamed for the frail police service and scores of violent crime after 20 years of democracy is debatable. The actions of some politicians, many leaders in key positions, and a number of communities have often been deplorable. The ongoing protest actions and strikes in SA are shameful, but this is the only way these groups get the attention of

---

**BOX 12.2   OPINION OF THE SOUTH AFRICAN
PRESIDENT ABOUT THE POLICE**

Zuma blasts "trigger-happy" police (2014-02-08 12:50).

Johannesburg—President Jacob Zuma condemned the response of "trigger-happy" police to recent violent service delivery protests, the *Saturday Star* reported. In an interview with *Independent Newspapers*, Zuma said that protesters also needed to refrain from violence. "No, I am not happy. I don't think anyone can be with trigger-happy police. It's not good at all," Zuma was quoted as saying. "The police need to be trained, especially given the fact that SA is prone to protest. In a place where protest is a daily occurrence, police need to be ready. "Protesters who 'carry pangas and burn tyres' also shared the blame for violence, and South Africa had yet to address the 'culture and the legacy of apartheid violence,'" he said. One such example was the violence on 16 August 2012, in Marikana, North West, where 34 people, mostly striking miners, were shot dead when the police fired on a group gathered at a hill near the mine. "The fact of the matter is that you had miners on strike carrying every other weapon, actually ready to kill. In fact, they had killed 10 people before the police shot at people," Zuma said. While he did not want to pre-empt the findings of the Farlam Commission of Inquiry which is probing the deaths, Zuma said there were indications that the police were not the only party at fault.—SAPA (www.news24. com/SouthAfrica/News/Zuma-blasts-trigger-happy-police-20140208 on February 8, 2014)

---

the guileful political role-players who are in a predicament to keep SA safe. A sustainable political will and impeccable leadership hold the key to future progress. Allowing young militants and disgruntled community members to rule the country cannot be allowed. Also ongoing strikes and the mobilization of militant young people in impoverished areas will drive the current predicament of the mismanaged government to a pinnacle. This raises the question whether the mobilization of the youth in indigent areas could in some way be the forerunner of something similar to the revolutionary wave of demonstrations, protests, and civil unrest in the Arab world since 2010, that is, the so-called Arab Spring.

Empty promises will not change the government's predicament. Proper governance by respected leaders and the implementation of a professional police organization will pave the way to making SA a safer milieu to live in.

As for mega events, it would appear that South Africa is the "champion" of hosting successful super events of any nature. We have learned that hosting these global events is not an oxymoron but within the national capabilities. Why the government suddenly focuses all their attention on the hosting of these large-scale events when selected to do so, but later ignoring the national predicament is open to discussion. It is however unclear why the government does not extrapolate the successful "public safety recipe" experienced during the mega events and expand these lessons and efforts to the greater public in an effort to create a safer society for all.

Who knows if South Africa will bid for the Olympic Games in the near future, and possibly be selected as a host nation due to the successful track record of hosting mega events, even amid our domestic conundrum?

References

Annual Report: South African Police Service. (2012/2013). Department of Police. www.saps.gov.za

Annual Report: PSIRA (2012/2013). Private Security Industry Regulatory Board (PSIRA). www.psira.co.za

Bezuidenhout, C. (2011). Sector Policing in South Africa—Case Closed—Or Not? *Pakistan Journal of Criminology, 3*(2) & (3), April–July 2011, 11–25.

Bezuidenhout, C. (2013). Oorsig van plaasaanvalle in Suid Afrika en die potensiële uitwerking daarvan op die samelewing. [Overview of farm attacks in South Africa and the potential influence thereof on society] Part 3: Studies regarding farm attacks, pp. 437–459). In D. Hermann, C. van Zyl, & I. Nieuwoudt (Eds.), *Treurgrond: Die realiteit van plaasaanvalle, 1990–2012*. Pretoria: Kraal Publishers.

Bezuidenhout, C., & Little, K. (2012). Juvenile justice in South Africa: Challenges and existing processes. In P. C. Kratcoski (Ed.), *Juvenile justice administration*. Boca Raton, FL: CRC Press (Taylor & Francis Group).

Bhootra, B. L., & Weiss, E. (2006). Muti killing: A case report. *Med. Sci. Law, 46*(3), 255–259.

Bruce, D. (2013). New blood: Implications of en masse recruitment for the South African Police Service. *SA Crime Quarterly, 43*, (March 2013).

Burger, J. (2007). A golden goal for South Africa: Security arrangements for the 2010 FIFA Soccer World Cup. *SA Crime Quarterly, 19*, (March 2007).

Burger, J. (2013). Blaming militarisation for police brutality is aiming at the wrong target. *ISS Today* (March 21, 2013). Retrieved February 9, 2013 from: http://www.issafrica.org/iss-today/blaming-militarisation-for-police-brutality-is-aiming-at-the-wrong-target

Faull, A. (2011). *Preventing police killings requires improving police professionalism*. Pretoria: Institute for Security Studies. www.issafrica.org

Garland, D. (2001). *The culture of control: Crime and social order in contemporary society*. Oxford: Oxford University Press.

Geldenhuys, K. (2008a). 2010—Preparing for the world: A combination of horse- and manpower. *Servamus: Community Based Safety & Security Magazine, 101*(9), 10–12.

Geldenhuys, K. (2008b). 2010–Preparing for the world: OR Tambo International airport (Part 2). *Servamus: Community Based Safety & Security Magazine, 101*(12), 14–19.

Geldenhuys, K. (2009). Crowd control in SA: French style. *Servamus: Community Based Safety & Security Magazine, 102*(1), 6–7.

Geldenhuys, K. (2011). Operational response units of the SAPS: Public order policing. *Servamus: Community Based Safety & Security Magazine, 104*(11), 36–41.

Goldstone, C. (2009). Police must shoot to kill, worry later—Cele. Retrieved February 4, 2014 from: http://www.iol.co.za/news/south-africa/police-must-shoot-to-kill-worry-later-cele-1.453587

Hagan, J. (1994). *Crime and disrepute.* Thousand Oaks, CA: Pine Forge.

Kempen, A. (2010a). Preparing for the FIFA World Cup: Guaranteeing the world's visitors' safety (Part 1). *Servamus: Community Based Safety & Security Magazine, 103*(2), 12–13.

Kempen, A. (2010b). Preparing for the FIFA World Cup: The role of the private security industry (Part 3). *Servamus: Community Based Safety & Security Magazine, 103*(4), 30–31.

Kempen, A. (2010c). Preparing for the 2010 FIFA World Cup: The use of technology to safeguard fans and citizens alike (Part 5). *Servamus: Community Based Safety & Security Magazine, 103*(6), 30–33.

Kempen, A. (2010d). Final preparations for the 2010 FIFA World Cup: Training in technology (Part 6). *Servamus: Community Based Safety & Security Magazine, 103*(7), 30–31.

Kempen, A. (2010e). The 2010 FIFA World Cup: The grand finale. *Servamus: Community Based Safety & Security Magazine, 103*(8), 8–13.

Kempen, A. (2013). Securing a SAFE: AFCON 2013. *Servamus: Community Based Safety & Security Magazine, 106*(2), 50–51.

National Development Plan; Vision for 2030. (2011). Our future—Make it work. National Planning Commission. Department: The Presidency, Republic of South Africa. Retrieved February 9, 2014 from: www.gov.za

Niehaus, I. (2009). Beyond the utility of violence: Interpreting five homicides in the South African lowveld. *Focaal,* (54), 16–32.

Newham, G. (2005). A decade of crime prevention in South Africa: From a national strategy to a local challenge. Research report written for the Centre for the Study of Violence and Reconciliation. www.csvr.org.za

Papp, I. (2010). Football hooliganism: A threat to the world. *Servamus: Community Based Safety & Security Magazine, 103*(6), 34–36.

Roelofse, C. (2011). Crime prevention and control. In C. Bezuidenhout (Ed.), *A Southern African perspective on fundamental criminology.* Cape Town: Pearson [Heinemann].

Smith, D. (2013). South Africa reports of police brutality more than tripled in the last decade. *The Guardian,* (August 22). Retrieved October 2, 2013 from: http://www.theguardian.com/world/2013/aug/22/south-africa-police-brutality-increase

Statistics South Africa. (July 2013). Mid-year population estimates 2013. Statistical release P0302. www.statssa.gov.za

Van Rooyen, F., & Swanepoel, E. (2014). "Groot geweld kom dalk": Optrede is nou al "groter as die ANC" [Major violence on the cards. Actions is already larger than the ANC]. *Beeld* Newspaper. Retrieved February 4, 2014 from: http://www.beeld.com/nuus/2014-01-30-groot-geweld-kom-dalk

About the Author

Dr. Christiaan Bezuidenhout is a highly respected professor in the Department of Social Work and Criminology at the University of Pretoria in South Africa. He can be contacted via e-mail at: cb@up.ac.za.

Police Leadership and the Strategic Management of Mega Events

13

Policing the 2012 London Olympic and Paralympic Games

PERRY STANISLAS

Contents

Introduction

The Great Exhibition held in the Crystal Palace, London in 1851 was the first in what was to become "World Fairs" featuring some of the most important cultural, scientific, and technical innovations that would come to represent the modern age, and the first mass popular attractions of their type. These events represented amazing spectacles where host nations could demonstrate their global standing as the world's most advanced societies. The Great Exhibition was also a showcase for Peel's new police to demonstrate its capacity to manage an event of this kind (Emsley, 2005, p. 72). The success of the Great Exhibition and the Metropolitan Police in responding to this challenge draws attention to some of the unique characteristics of policing a particular type of event, which only a small number of international law enforcement leaders have experienced. The policing of these extraordinary events and some of the contemporary challenges involved were highlighted in the staging of the London 2012 Olympic and Paralympic Games (OPG).

This chapter will examine the preparations for the London 2012 OPG (or "Games") and the critical role of police leaders in making this important global event a success. It will highlight the function of the National Olympic Security Coordinator, his role and how he carried out his work, and some of the challenges faced in policing the OPG based on in-depth interviews held in 2013. The interviews also included the head of the Metropolitan Police's Serious and Organised Economic Crime Unit. These findings will not be presented here. The chapter highlights the human resource dimension of the preparations for the OPG, the key stakeholders involved, and the strategies used to enable them and others to effectively carry out their roles during the Games.

Understanding Mega Events

Mega events, according to Hesloot and Boin et al. (2012), refer to incidents that have widespread global implications given the difficulties in limiting their consequences. These incidents are significantly different in terms of their scale to the types of problems governments and agencies are accustomed to, which contributes to the uncertainty and extreme urgency associated with them. Examples of these are public health pandemics, environmental catastrophes, or international terrorist attacks. These events reflect the postmodern world, its structural interdependency, and technologies which make it difficult to isolate their effects (Bowling & Sheptycki, 2012; Brownword & Yeun, 2008), and have a major impact on public sentiment given the power of the contemporary media. The speed at which information is communicated in today's world creates a serious challenge for institutional leaders in being able to respond effectively and avoid being caught off guard (Stanislas, 2014).

Mega events carry significant reputational consequences for decision makers. This is illustrated by the fallout of Hurricane Katrina and the widespread criticism of the Bush administration and the Federal Emergency Management Agency (Parker & Paglia, 2012). The management of such events often requires international cooperation and skillful domestic coordination in order to mitigate the potential tensions between organizations at different levels of operation. The leadership challenges of mega events are very significant as indicated by Weston (2011) in his examination of inter-agency coordination for national emergencies.

Jennings and Lodge (2012) apply the concept of mega events to the staging of particular short-term activities which have long-term consequences for cities that hold them in terms of infrastructural developments and the creation of new facilities. An important feature of this type of activity is government commitment to make significant investment in these areas, which distinguishes these types of events from other larger incidents; as well as the potential disruption to the lives of citizens affected by them (Batty, Desyllas, & Duxbury, 2003).

A particular characteristic of mega events is their susceptibility to multiple risks and potential vulnerabilities, which can be interrelated and caused by a number of things; ranging from simple human error or purposive actions designed to cause disruption such as political and other forms of protests, or attacks on critical infrastructure (Evans, 2011). Given the complex structural interdependencies required to successfully coordinate and manage such major events, areas of risk can include communication failures, problems with transportation, or venues inter alia (see Swain, 2011; Weston, 2011). Consequently, the ability to operate effectively in a potential crisis environment is an important quality of leaders called on to either stage or respond to mega events (Leonard & Hewitt, 2012).

Policing Issues and Large-Scale Events

The type of matters state police are called on to address in policing large-scale events in liberal democratic societies, such as Britain, reflect the whole gamut of issues they are expected to tackle at any given time, which are crystallized around the planning and staging of a discrete and finite set of activities and highlight the totality of the "Peelian" concept of policing (Batty, Desyllas, & Duxbury, 2003, p. 1576; Crisp, 2013). This can involve preventing crime, the protection of important buildings, or managing flows of people and traffic, and being present to provide pastoral care and friendly assistance to visitors and citizens alike.

The police also play a vital role in supporting and facilitating the work of other emergency services (Alison & Crego, 2008; Batty, Desyllas, & Duxbury, 2003, p. 1576). Large-scale events draw heavily on what has been described as the "harder" policing functions, such as public order specialists and covert teams targeting groups such as pickpockets (Horn & Breetzke, 2009, p. 23). Critical in the preparation for many major events are the political policing of Special Branch and various personal protection specialists, such as the Royal and Diplomatic Protection Group and Tactical Support Groups (see Silke, 2011; Weston, 2011). In short the policing of large-scale events brings together most generalist and specialist functions of state policing in any country and draws heavily from the experiences of those institutions and the individuals within them.

The Security and Policing Environment and Context of the Modern Olympic Games

Two important events have changed the way the preparations of the modern Olympic Games are seen by government, the police, and other key stakeholders. The first was the attack on the Munich Games in 1972 resulting in the murder of Israeli athletes and coaching staff (Jennings & Lodge, 2012), and the bombings during the 1996 Atlanta Games (French & Disher, 1997). The emergence of terrorism has had a significant effect on the Games and how it is viewed by the police and security leaders. The Munich attacks exposed the lack of training and capability of the German police in a number of key areas of tactical response, which was to provide important lessons for future host nations (Jennings & Lodge, 2012, pp. 137–138).

A defining outcome of these events has been the increase in the number of stakeholders involved in the security of the Games beyond just the state police, to now include the intelligence and secret services, and many branches of the armed forces and the private sector, who have become an increasingly important stakeholder in obvious areas such as providing stewards (Wakefield & Button, 2013), and not so obvious areas of security such as cyberpolicing (Evans, 2011, pp. 172–173). Foreign security and intelligence personnel and private policing are also involved in protecting their own respective nationals, dignitaries, and clients (Evans, 2011, pp. 168–169; Jennings & Lodge, 2012). The scale of the security preparations involved was illustrated in the Athens Games, which included NATO and the International Atomic Agency (Jennings & Lodge, 2012).

The Athens Olympic Games were particularly important in creating the modern security template, due to this event being the first post 9/11 Summer Olympics, which many have described as leading to the total securitization of society. This is characterized by an overproliferation of state and private forms of surveillance both obtrusive and unobtrusive, and is closely linked to improvements in technology that potentially undermine the rights of citizens to live as free agents, and an exemplar case study for advocates and critics of securitization discourse alike (Bowling, Marks, & Murphy, 2008; Jennings & Lodge, 2012). The Athens Olympics was also crucial in highlighting the financial costs for securing the Games in the new era, which rose from an estimated £.2 billion to £6.3 billion by the time the event had commenced (Jennings, 2011, p. 150). The majority of the security costs for the games are normally borne by the host government, which contributes to the zero tolerance attitudes to risk and fear of disruptions to such a costly and resource intensive event.

The Policing and Security Context and the London OPG

The discussion and planning for the London OPG took place in an environment which provided much optimism and concern in equal measure. The police agency, like other public services, had been the subject of major budget cuts (Wakefield & Button, 2013, p. 256) and several important organizational reviews (Stanislas, 2013, pp. 66–67). An important dimension of these discussions revolved around the size of the public sector and the need for a more efficient and effective police organization, which had been increasingly called to share and devolve functions that contribute to what some have described as the shrinking state thesis (O'Malley, 1997). Another important set of broader considerations in thinking about staging the OPG was the crime rates in London and other areas in the country that had been identified as potential Olympic event venues (Batty, Desyllas, & Duxbury, 2003, pp. 27–28; Horn & Breetzke, 2009).

Crime and fear of crime clearly have a detrimental impact on the image of major events, attendance figures, and the safety of foreign visitors and domestic attendees. The key security concerns for police leaders at such events include crime against visitors who may be exposed to potential offenses ranging from fraud to more serious crimes. Foreign visitors and nationals from local and external areas are a potential crime target (Botterill & Jones, 2010; Horn & Breetzke, 2009, p. 28). Major public order offenses are also another concern. Mapping crime and the movement of potential offenders is of particular importance to police planners; however, as the riots of August 2011 in the UK have demonstrated, unpredicted patterns of crime and antisocial behavior can potentially be caused by unrelated incidents that can catch the police off guard (National Police Improvement Agency, 2009, p. 7; Wain, 2012).

In addition, the prevention of terrorism is a primary concern of government and planners of the Olympic Games. Britain has become a priority target of Islamic fundamentalist terrorist groups, illustrated by the attacks across London in July 2005 (Silke, 2011). Even more worrying is the unpredictability and characteristics of some forms of modern terrorism as witnessed by the actions of Andres Brevik in Norway, and more recently in the killing of soldier Lee Rigby (Silke, 2012; Whitehead, 2013), both incidents involving lone wolf perpetrators. Moreover, the sheer size of the Olympic event and the activities which it is comprised of, their geographical dispersion, and the large attendance clearly create unique challenges for the organizing authorities. Some observers have described the scale of the Olympic Games as akin to the simultaneous staging of seven athletic world championships, or in policing terms, the largest scale peacetime security operations ever mounted (Jennings & Lodge, 2012).

The security objectives for the OPGs were led by the UK Home Office and government departments and statutory bodies with security-related responsibilities, which included the Ministry of Transport, Immigration authorities, the police and intelligence services, and armed forces via the Office of Security and Counter-Terrorism, and the Assistant Commissioner for Special Operations (Home Office, 2012, p. 11). Also involved in the strategic development were those with direct responsibilities for the staging of the Games such as the UK Department of Culture, Media and Sport, the London Organising Committee for the Olympic Games (LOCOG), and the Olympic Delivery Authority (ODA), responsible for the building and infrastructure program (Olympic and Paralympic Security Strategy Home Office, 2012).

The strategy was based on the interorganizational partnership approach of the "CONTEST" counter-terrorist model introduced in 2006 to defend Britain and its interests abroad from attacks (Home Office, 2013; Weston, 2011), and consists of five main areas of activity highlighted in Table 13.1. *Protect* addresses matters such as the safeguarding of athletes, coaching staff, attendees, VIPs, OPG officials, and venues, to include actions to reduce the likelihood of biological and chemical threats. *Prepare* covers the designing

Table 13.1 Key Elements of Safety and Security Strategy

Protect	Prepare	Identify	Command, Control, Plan, and Resource
People	• Olympic resilience	• Olympic intelligence	**Command and Control**
• Personnel security	• Specialist response	• Covert	• National coordination
• Accreditation	• COSI	• Serious and organized crime	• Operational control
• VIP protection		• Volume crime	• Infrastructure
Venue		• Automatic number	• Airwave
• Site and venue		• Plate recognition	**Resources**
• Security			• Demand and resource
• CBRNE			• Training
Non-venue			• Operational logistics infrastructure
• Transport security			
• Border security			
• CCTV			

Engage
International relations
Community relationships
Prevent
Industry

Source: Home Office, (2012), *Olympic Security and Safety Strategy*, London: Home Office. p. 14.

and planning of a range of contingencies to counter potential disruption, such as major critical incidents or terrorist attacks. *Identify and disrupt* is the general rubric for all intelligence gathering activities involving human and technological means supported by investigative responses. The final element, *Command and Control,* refers to the key task of senior leaders in the management, coordination, and communication processes, and the overall resourcing of the strategy. Linking all these dimensions of the strategy was *Engage,* which addresses the communication element and relations between OPG planners and domestic and international stakeholders (Home Office, 2012, p. 14). The budget awarded to the police and other stakeholder partners for delivering the additional security measures associated with the OPG in line with the strategy was a maximum of £600 million, this being only a part of the entire security costs (Home Office, 2012, p. 22).

Police Leadership

Leaders play a crucial role in organizational life in the ability to achieve goals, and none more as important as in state policing, which constitutes such an essential function in the workings of governance, the legitimacy of the state, and in the lives of citizens and local communities through the response to everyday matters, critical incidents, and major events (Reiner 1991; Stanislas, 2014). Leadership in police organizations can be generally categorized as operating at three broad areas of governance and strategy, tactics, and implementation (Peeters, 2013), which is loosely aligned with the British command and control structure for police operations, commonly referred to as the "Gold, Silver, and Bronze" model (NPIA, 2009, pp. 15–20; Weston, 2011, p. 192).

Police leadership roles share core requirements which include: communicating priorities, providing support and resources (Neyroud, 2011; Peeters, 2012; Stanislas, 2014), shaping work standards, and monitoring performance and professional conduct (Adebayo, 2005; Neyroud, 2011, pp. 113–117; Webster et al., 1994). Leaders also play a critical function in developing and motivating personnel (Adebayo, 2005; Stanislas, 2014; Wright, Alison, & Crego, 2008).

How police leaders carry out their roles and the various approaches they use have been the subject of much theorizing under the rubric of leadership styles (Adebayo, 2005, p. 115; Wright et al., 2008, pp. 59–63). For Peeters (2013), the immediate task environment or situational context in which police leaders are expected to operate determines selection decisions and information collection options. For instance, types of relevant work experiences, personal qualities individuals should have, the means used to assess these things, as well as the training, preparation, and support required in order to perform effectively, would all play critical roles. In British policing, the route to formal leadership roles is based on work experience, appropriate support, the level of skill, knowledge, and aptitude, and the passing of relevant assessment tests (Neyroud, 2011). A fundamental component in preparing police personnel for basic and more specialist roles, including formal leadership responsibilities, includes passing mandatory training courses (Stanislas, 2013, pp. 3–5).

Responding effectively to critical incidents has become a mandatory element of British police leadership and management training at the intermediate and senior levels. An example of this is the Hydra training system, designed by Professor Jonathan Crego and his colleagues, based on dynamic real-time computer-based critical incident simulations (see Alison & Crego, 2008). The importance of Hydra and similar approaches to the training is that it replicates many of the processes that have to be used in a potentially changing scenario, and thereby calling on trainees to respond in realistic ways. The development and enhancement of senior police leaders has been achieved through *command* training courses, where participants are taught issues involving supervision, leadership, strategic and tactical planning, decision making, resource management, effective communication, partnership working, and working with the media inter alia (see Neyroud, 2011). According to the National Police Improvement Association (NPIA), the heart of senior command training involves the core skill areas of command, business, and professional *skills*, which are illustrated in Figure 13.1. While the model in Figure 13.1 can be said to be conceptual and is not a precise reflection of the training and education presently received, it is useful in the context of the current discussion in identifying the core resources required for leading and managing mega events such as the OPG, since it illustrates a comprehensive and multifaceted approach.

Police Leadership of the OPG

Given the significance of a mega event, the selection of the individual to lead and coordinate security is extremely important. One of the key risk avoidance decisions, and likely the most pressing, is the caliber of the individual who is given that responsibility (Leonard & Hewitt, 2012). This can be viewed in the context of the preparations for the 2007 Cricket World Cup in St. Lucia and the appointment of Superintendent Errol Alexander (promoted to assistant commissioner) to lead what turned out to be the largest, most important, and successful international sporting event ever held in the small Caribbean country. Alexander was a highly regarded officer among his peers, and more importantly in the eyes of his commissioner (Stanislas, 2013), and given the history of political interference in governmental

Figure 13.1 NPIA model of senior officer education and training.

decision making in St. Lucia, his appointment enjoyed the backing of key stakeholders within the government and the private sector who had invested unprecedented amounts of money to ensure the event's success (Stanislas, forthcoming).

The overall leadership of the security of particular mega events can be expected to be given to the most experienced, well-trained, and successful operational law enforcement executives (Leonard & Hewitt, 2012, p. 25), which is reflected in the formal appointment of Assistant Commissioner Chris Allison of the London Metropolitan Police in 2008 as the National Olympic Security Coordinator (NOSC) (Weston, 2011, p. 187). The appointment process for the role was conducted by the Metropolitan Police Authority, after having approached and entered discussions with both the Home Office and the Association of Chief Police Officers. While appointed in 2009, Alison did not take up this role full time until January 2011, which involved him preparing for the task on an interim basis, while carrying out most of his usual policing duties as a chief officer in one of the country's busiest and largest cities. The role of NOSC was largely one of national coordination, leaving operational command decision making to local police agencies. It also involved providing support to "Gold" and other commanders in implementing the strategy, and communicating with numerous domestic and international stakeholders, such as foreign embassies, the media, inter alia (Home Office, 2012, p. 9).

At the time of his appointment to the role, Chris Allison had 25 years of experience in the Metropolitan Police, starting as a constable and ultimately drawn to public order policing. He played an important role in the development of operational forward intelligence teams and spent many years as a member of the Territorial Support Group, before becoming a member of the Advanced Public Order Cadre (APOC), responsible for the most important public events and incidents in 1996.* Since joining the APOC, Allison has played an important leadership role in every major public event in London, and was the Gold Commander for the policing response to the London 2005 terrorist bombings (Alexander, 2012). In detailed terms, Allison has received every level and type of training available within the British policing system, right through to his Senior Command Course, in preparing for his role as NOSC. Recognized as one of the best and most important police leaders in London, Allison's experience, knowledge, technical skills, and accomplishments have many of the characteristics of high-performing officers that eventually attained the ultimate leadership position of police commissioner (see Neyroud, 2011; Reiner, 1991).

While policing the OPG represents an unprecedented strategic, operational, and organizational challenge, it also provided a unique once in a lifetime opportunity for the individual selected to lead this area of work to draw on the sum of their career experiences, and personal resources, and to demonstrate their abilities on the largest possible stage (Leonard & Hewitt, 2012, p. 25). The NOSC describes the type of intrinsic motivation that such an opportunity represents:

> Without knowing it, I have been training for 25 years for this job before I got it.

An important criterion for appointing the NOSC was working experience at the Association of Chief Police Officer (ACPO) level and the ability to command the support and respect of senior police colleagues nationally (Reiner, 1991, p. 350). Allison had worked for many years as the ACPO lead officer on alcohol-related policy matters. One of the first things that Allison did in his new role was to establish the OPG Coordinating Team (Weston, 2011, p. 187), which played a critical role in the planning of the Olympic Games nationally. An early responsibility of the NOSC was to become familiar with many of the key personnel that he would have to rely on in order to effectively carry out his role. Fortunately for Allison, he was relatively well-known among national

---

* Metropolitan Police Authority Public Order Review 2007.

colleagues, which made his task somewhat easier. Given the history of the British police and the special status of the Metropolitan Police, its influence on world policing (Emsley, 2010; Mason, 2004), its size and remit for the capital, and close association and proximity to the Home Secretary, tensions and rivalries with other regional police forces could be viewed as being inevitable.

One of the major obstacles to effective leadership involving multiple organizations is the potential for conflict and interagency competition. At a bare minimum, leaders must not exacerbate these differences (Weston, 2011, pp. 182–183). Despite ACPO support, this did not guarantee that the planning for the OPG would not be without its difficulties at the lower levels of decision making (Simon, 1976), as the NOSC explains:

> There was a bit of anti-Met feeling among some of the other forces….that that we are big, bold, and brash, and that type of stereotype, and early on, I discovered a couple of Olympic meetings were held by other forces which I knew nothing about.

An important practice of effective leaders in overcoming the type of problems described by the NOSC is by reaffirming core institutional values (Leonard & Hewitt, 2012, p. 29; Sherif, 1958). In the context of the OPG, the reduction of interorganizational tensions was achieved by the NOSC by appealing to the service ethic of the police:

> One of my first jobs was to convince everyone that this was for the service and not just the Met, and we were not trying to steal any glory here. We were a team and would have to work like one for the service and country.

A feature of the leadership of the OPG across all domains of activity was the development of a strong ethos which called on higher values to motivate and discipline the massive workforce, which included approximately 70,000 volunteers and auxiliary police officers. This ethos contributed in creating a form of what Bull, Ridley-Duff, Foster, & Seanor (2010) termed *ethical capital*, that is, a higher set of ethical standards or purpose, described by some as the "Olympic effect," which will be more thoroughly examined later (see National Audit Office, 2012). This environment promoted a sense of meaningful participation to something larger than the individual, which could involve international ramifications and where national pride was at stake.

Preparation and Training

Training constitutes the backbone of most aspects of police work and routinely consumes a significant amount of the police budget (Stanislas, 2013, pp. 4–7). It was to play a particularly important role in the OPG human resource strategy, and its relevance was recognized through the establishment of The Olympic Safety and Security and Testing and Exercising Board (OSTEB) (Home Office, 2012, p. 22). Testing and exercising was a vital component in preparing partner agencies to effectively work together in responding to a diverse range of emergency scenarios (see Alison & Crego, 2008). While the police have worked and trained with some emergency services, the large number of partners involved in the OPG meant many participating agencies had little joint working experiences (see Weston, 2011, pp. 182–183). The NOSC sums up the importance of training in this context:

> You don't want to learn to dance at the dance. You want to learn before the dance and know who your dance partner is, and know they can also dance, and they need to know you can dance.

While OSTEB identified the key areas of training required in supporting the strategy, Exercise Control designed its content and organized its delivery. This resulted in holding three of the largest command post exercises ever held, which involved approximately 5000 people at each. Conducting drills is not a risk-free activity and can be potentially very threatening, in that the deficiencies of particular agencies and individuals can be exposed in front of partners (Weston, 2011, p. 194). The comprehensive nature of the training received in terms of the scenarios it addressed has been described by the NOSC:

> Exercise Control threw at us literally everything you could possibly imagine that could happen. A fire, for example, suddenly starts at a big waste disposal facility in the East End of London, its pumping toxic stuff out, and the fire service can't get it under control, and the wind plume is sending it over Olympic Park just as the closing ceremony is about to take place. That actually happened. We ended up with a fire on the last day of the Games in the East End.

This training built on previous preparation meetings, which involved briefings by the Canadian Winter Olympics Senior Command team (who were flown to Britain), the use of desktop exercises, and the utilization of computer-based tri-service packages that detailed the Olympic Games schedule and venues and the respective expectations of each agency, such as the fire and ambulance services. A training package was designed and delivered by the National Police Improvement Association on the use of the Airwaves Communication System (Home Office, 2012, p. 14; Weston, 2011, p. 190). Similar briefings and packages were used for Bronze level police commanders and their local partners responsible for venues. One agency with which the police do not work together regularly is the military. According to the NOSC, the planned use of the armed forces at the

OPG eventually required military trainers to help develop a joint response to various threat scenarios:

> We had the marines and police training together, practising boarding boats on the river, and simulations of terrorists blowing up a train.

Resourcing the Strategy

The Olympic Security and Safety Strategy was developed by a partnership of government departments, agencies, and organizations operating across five broad domains of activity. Its key objectives were to ensure that participants and spectators were safe from a range of potential threats. The roles of the NOSC and other key players in the security strategy were part of a broader Safety and Concept of Operations framework that had specifically detailed their roles and responsibilities (Home Office, 2012, p. 19). In the case of Chris Allison, his job involved overseeing the strategic planning to cover the 12 Olympic areas across the country where activities were being held (Home Office, 2012; Weston, 2011); as well as ensuring that all forces were working together in a coordinated way to manage the Olympic Torch (the iconic symbol of the Games) as it made its way around and across the country. A very important aspect of the strategy was the requirement for a national coordinated approach to ensure the type of police coverage required without undermining the ethos of the Olympic Games. The NOSC explains:

> What we did not want was if you went to Dorset, it was being policed by two PCSOs,* and then you then travel to London and find it is being protected by a ring of steel of armed officers. What we needed was a consistent look and feel and a welcoming look and feel, which at the same time clearly delivered the type of security required.

The challenge the NOSC faced in avoiding some of the worse features of securitization can be appreciated and contextualized by the fact the preparation for the Games took place for the first time in a severe security threat environment where the temptation to overpolice could be viewed as being reasonable (Home Office, 2012, p. 12). The placement of military surface-to-air missiles on the roofs of residents' homes in East London, near Olympic Park, demonstrated how serious the Government took the threat assessment (Gibson, 2012). A very important dimension of the work of contemporary law enforcement executives consists of operating in an international

---

* Police Community Support Officers.

environment and was highlighted in Neyroud's model of police senior officer education and training. This can consist of transnational criminal investigations, as commonly carried out by the detectives in the Serious and Organised Economic Crime Unit and other police specialty units (Bowling & Sheptycki, 2012, p. 53). In the context of the Games, the NOSC's role involved communicating with key international stakeholders and informing them about the types of policing and security arrangements which he describes:

> Our international strategy consisted of speaking to foreign countries and embassies and reassuring them about the safety of the Games and the preparations made, stressing that the police and not the military would manage the public streets. It also included managing the media and responding to negative reports and that kind of thing.

In this specific instance the type of security arrangements and environment they contributed to were a worry for some countries, the British Government, and the Olympic organizers (Home Office, 2012, p. 7). Another problem was obtaining sufficient personnel to police the OPG for the entire 122 days of its duration, against the background of the police having little experience of such a large and lengthy event. The largest event normally held in Britain is the two day annual Notting Hill Carnival held in London involving over a million people, started by Caribbean immigrants in the 1950s, which has become an important testing ground for the development of police public order expertise, after several major disturbances and fatalities over the years (Batty, Desyllas, & Duxbury, 2003; Ramadin, 1987). How to deploy police personnel constituted another challenge for the NOSC and his colleagues, given the essential management task of balancing priorities (Stanislas, 2013, p. 3). The NOSC conveyed:

> Policing still had to continue throughout the rest of the UK. We couldn't say to the people of Lincolnshire, could you wait until two weeks when we will have police officers available before you dial 999. So we were forced to do a bit of clever thinking about how we policed the country while ensuring we had adequate cover for the Games.

While the coordination and planning of police deployment is largely a technical and managerial matter, it raises important questions about an age old issue in British policing history about the locus of accountability and legitimacy (in crude terms who pays and controls), and how citizens in many parts of the country may feel about their law enforcement resources being used for sporting or similar events (ACPO, 2010*; Reiner 1991, pp. 264–266). Obtaining staff for the OPG took place against a background of budget cuts

---

* See Paying the Bill (2010) ACPO/APA Guidance on Charging for Police Services. Accessed February 12, 2014, www.acpo.police.co.uk.

and reduction in training, which were even more pressing for the NOSC in the short-term given the traditional practice of reducing specialist staff, crucial to the planning and delivery of the Games, in an effort to save money (Wakefield & Button, 2013):

> I made a plea to my colleagues; if they were going to make cuts in specialists could they do it after the Games, which for the most part colleagues did. (p. 256)

The requirement for specialists and appropriately qualified staff was a major problem given the high value placed on them by their own departments and their limited numbers, and despite the importance of the OPG, advertised vacancies for Olympic Games related positions could only be filled by short-term appointments, which is not attractive to people already engaged in other areas of work. The importance of having appropriately qualified people serves two functions as the NOSC elucidates:

> Everybody who we utilise in key positions in the policing of major events has to be appropriately qualified, not only for the obvious reasons that they need to know what they are doing, but also have to be seen as doing things properly. I am thinking of worse case outcomes and talking about public inquiries, and that sort of thing, where the service is placed under very forensic scrutiny, and the Taylor Report* is just one of which comes immediately to mind.

The NOSC was able to obtain the personnel required to resource the strategy with the assistance of the ACPO OPG Coordinating Team in making personnel available across the 43 police forces in England and Wales by canceling leave and training and through the use of funding from the government for overtime payments (Home Office, 2012, p. 21). Planning the deployment of personnel across the country against perceived need was constantly reviewed by the NOSC in conjunction with the OPG Coordinating Team, and required ongoing communication between local Gold Commanders and the central command (Peeters, 2013, pp. 96–98). An important mechanism for assessing daily resource needs took the form of planning meetings prior to daily briefings at local venues. A large mobile reserve of officers was formed to rapidly deploy to parts of London, and potentially elsewhere, in the event of a major incident, which also demonstrated police leaders' sensitivity of being caught off guard, and the possible political fallout from such an occurrence. However, this contingency was not required. In addition, the crime rate leading up to and throughout the OPG period had been in decline in London and other parts of the country.[†]

---

* Final Report of Inquiry by Lord Justice Taylor into the Hillsborough Stadium Disaster (1989), Home Office, London.
[†] Olympic Games Impact Study, University of East London, Economic and Social Research Council, Final Report (2010).

Key Elements of a Successful Strategy

An important legacy of the London Games was the success of its policing and security arrangements. While important factors which contributed to this outcome are only partially influenced by the police, such as national crime rates,[*] they were influential in shaping outcomes in many areas crucial to the strategy's success. Reflecting on the police's performance, the NOSC identified evidence of their accomplishment:

> Terrorists were unable to get through; there were no serious incidents or major crimes. A very good example which is not much in the public domain is the Operation Podium Team,[†] whose work in serious and organised economic crime was so effective that we did not find one counterfeit ticket in the 11 Million available for the Games.[‡]

Apart from preventative policing goals, the strategy also contained softer goals in terms of complementing the broader London Olympic ethos in how they related to the public, which reflected similar challenges faced by Peel's police in staging the Great Exhibition (Emsley, 2010; BBC 2, 2009). Success in this area is highlighted by the NOSC:

> All you have to do is look at the positive response and applause the police and soldiers and the G4S received at the various search points and at Olympic Park to show I think we got that balance just right.

Careful and detailed planning, coordination, and number of professional policing and business skills, as called for by Neyroud (2011) and illustrated in Figure 13.1, were crucial to the success of the OPG. This is illustrated by the controversy that engulfed the preparation of the Olympic Games, when it was revealed that the private security company G4S was unable to supply sufficient staff, and concerns about the quality of training received by those hired (Wakefield & Button, 2013, p. 264). This was addressed by the government and the NOSC utilizing a contingency backup of police and armed forces personnel who took over some of the planned functions of G4S staff at many venues. An invaluable feature in the success of the policing of the OPG was the institutional experience of staging prior large-scale events, which in the case of the British police has been considerable (Leonard & Hewitt, 2010; Weston, 2011, p. 191), and the ability to not stray from tried

---

[*] Olympic Games Impact Study (2010, p. 52).

[†] Operation Podium is an initiative of the Serious Organised Economic Crime Unit of the Metropolitan Police.

[‡] The work of the Operation Podium Team during the lead-up and throughout the OPG will be the focus of a forthcoming publication.

and trusted practices despite the uniqueness of the Olympic events. As in any strategy, there is the potential for unintended consequences (Simons, 1976). Fortunately for the police, the need to reduce their resource requirements created opportunities for unexpected benefits. The NOSC conveyed:

> Officers had the space and time to interact with the public and rediscover their public and to interact meaningfully with them, which lack of time normally does not allow, which was a really nice bonus.[*]

An important source of motivation for those leaders in the various domains of activity for the OPG (such as transport, events, safety, and security) has been described as the "Olympic effect," that derived from national pride, and the competitive desire in wanting to stage an event which was better than previous Olympic experiences, that was highlighted in a documentary entitled "Building the Olympic Dream" (BBC, 2009). In this regard, while risk avoidance is an important motivator (Jennings & Lodge, 2012), the aforementioned is equally important for domain leaders given the positive reputational consequences (Parker & Pagalia, 2012). This ethos contributed to the creation of strong partnership teams, which were vital to the success of the event (see National Audit Office, 2012). The NOSC describes the importance of this environment for the performance and working relations between key partners responsible for the Games:

> It was successfully delivered because of a lot of people and organisations came together to put together spectacular games. There was the work done by Peter Hendy of Transport for London in ensuring that, despite what everybody thought would happen, that the roads and public transport could not cope. In fact everything worked like a dream. We had the Mayor's Office and Neil Coleman who made sure London looked right and was dressed right and London operated properly throughout the Games, and the safety and security domain, which I was privileged to lead, and it was about us all coming together with one common vision of putting on a fantastic Olympic event.

The role of the NOSC in helping to bring about such a successful Olympic Games event was officially recognized when Assistant Commissioner Allison was awarded the Commander of the British Empire (CBE) medal in the Queen's 2013 Birthday's Honours List, along with his colleague Commissioner of Transport for London Sir Peter Hendy, who received a knighthood for his leadership of the transport domain.[†] The success of the OPG domain leaders

---

[*] Former Inspector Chris Alcott of Leicestershire Police highlighted an important consideration in the quality of interaction police officers had with the public was the significant numbers of police deployed to the OPG from smaller regional forces, who traditionally rely on more face-to-face policing methods in the forms of community and neighborhood policing unlike larger metropolitan forces. Personal communication, December 19, 2013.

[†] Accessed February 12, 2014, www.gov.uk (June 14, 2013).

and government in the staging of the Games is particularly impressive when considering that its national focal point, Olympic Park, and some of the major events were held in the East London inner city London boroughs of Hackney/ Stratford with heavy concentrations of socioeconomic disadvantage, and a history of police and ethnic tensions within some parts of the community, and very similar in character to some of the areas that experienced wide-spread rioting in 2011 (Stanislas, 2011; Wain & Joyce, 2012). As the Olympic Games Impact Study carried out by the University of East London (2010) has indicated, the peaceful nature of the OPG was not simply accidental but a product of skilful planning, evaluation, and research into many of the critical factors that contribute to social discord and forms of intervention to alleviate them where possible. This demonstrates the unprecedented levels of success-ful state management involved in the planning and delivery of the Games.

Problems and Constraints

While the experience, specialist background, and senior command training of the NOSC prepared him well for his coordination role and other leadership aspects of the post, and positively reflect the existing police career develop-ment process, its limitations were highlighted in the area of program man-agement (see Figure 13.1), reinforcing an important criticism of the existing system (Neyroud, 2011). By the same token, the strengths of Allison are what his appointees believed to be the most important aspects of his role, which critics may suggest is a potentially outdated view of contemporary leadership requirements. This knowledge and skill deficiency represented an important challenge for the NOSC given his career background in predominantly oper-ational police work and the requirements for accessing Home Office funds allocated for the Games. He describes the processes involved:

> Government put in place a fairly strong programme management structure; so £600 million wasn't given to me. I was told there was a £600 million envelope and through the use of business cases and commissioning we had to apply for that money going through a fairly rigorous approval process.

A problem experienced with the program management process is that it is operated in a manner contrary to the way operational police leaders plan in holistic terms. For example, an event such as the Notting Hill Carnival is con-ceptualized as a whole event by the Gold Commander developing a strategy for policing it. The Home Office however required costing of specific themes of activity across all Olympic forces, for example, cost of ANR, CCTV, and communication systems, and so forth. Despite initial difficulties, the NOSC was able to achieve his objectives of accessing appropriate funding. However, contrary to a view outlined in Neyroud (2011), his lack of background with program management matters was not seen as a training deficiency or did not prove to be an insurmountable obstacle. The NOSC remarked:

> I gained a better understanding of the programme management processes which is something that we, as senior police officers, don't do much of. There are a small number of police officers who, given the nature of their work, do use programme management,* but my personal view is that the role of police leaders is to lead the men and women of the service, and things like programme management in my view doesn't really sit with that.

While the NOSC holds a relatively traditional view of police leadership, his ability to resolve the challenges with the program management process gives some support to his view. Those who promote greater professionalization of the police see improvements in education and the introduction of mandatory qualifications for senior leaders as part of their senior command training as the solution in improving their all-round capabilities (Peeters, 2013; Neyroud, 2011). Another way around this route is making expert resources available in-house or via partners in assisting them in particular areas of activity.† The NOSC was able to draw on the experiences of personnel from partner agencies, such as the Home Office, to improve his understanding and competence in order to achieve his objectives within the government's program management process that were important to the success of the whole enterprise, albeit unappreciated until required. This suggests that the problem-solving capacity of chief officers and the ability to use available resources may be more important in specific instances than the reforms being called for.

Another basic problem was the amount of money and staff available to cover additional costs associated with securing the Games. The police and

---

* Examples of this are senior managers involved in matters such as purchasing entire ITC systems and other hardware. However there is an implicit tension between the remedies called for by Neyroud and those calling for greater civilianization and the opening up of the police organization as championed by the Winsor Report (Stanislas 2013, pp. 66–67). In the former model improving the levels of senior police education and training to encompass more discipline areas, by extension reduces the need for civilian specialists or the type of police organization envisaged by Winsor. Moreover, there is the question of how much procurement activity actually takes place in the average small police force in England and Wales, compared to the mega forces such as the Greater Manchester Police. With the de facto regionalization and amalgamation of many forces the number of people engaged in procurement and program management activities in theory is reduced.

† This is the route the Chief Constable of Bedfordshire Police adopted when employing the writer, and his preferred means of bringing in specialist expertise, preferably from a generic policing background, into the force to provide support for him and his senior command team. A chief constable sits at the apex of a massive resource network across entire cities and regions and is able to obtain expertise and support relatively easily; for example, from chief executives of local authorities. The Chief Constable of Bedfordshire viewed his role in very traditional terms not dissimilar to that of the NOSC and took the view that the basic role of police officers was mastering the core aspects of the ever-evolving areas of policing, such as new categories of offenses, patterns of crime, legislation, and public concern.

other partners had potentially £600 million available to them; however this has to be placed in the context of the London region being granted over £500 million to carry out its various security duties. Disagreements over money constituted an area of difficulty for the NOSC and called for some tough negotiating as he recalls:

> Of course, the government was trying to constantly reduce our estimates with me, but I had to tell them that often I can't reduce the cost any lower than that because of the safety and risk.

The funding formula agreed to by the government provided no additional monies for police officers who were already expected to be working in their local police areas. Government funding was used for overtime payments or to pay officers where they would not be normally working. The police reserves (unpaid trained volunteers), that is, the Special Constabulary, and Police Community Support Officers played an invaluable role in providing an important labor resource to communities, thereby ensuring that there were sufficient personnel to undertake routine policing, as well as securing the OPG venues (Crisp, 2013).

Conclusion

Mega events such as the Olympic Games represent an unprecedented challenge to policing, security, and other government authorities responsible for the safety of those involved. The London 2012 OPG highlighted this, particularly given that unlike any other Olympic event, the related international Paralympic Games were staged shortly after, creating a policing and security task unparalleled in the history of the Olympic Games. The environment in which the OPG was held was also important in terms of the threat assessment level which shaped leaders' planning. In short, the intrinsic nature of the task of leading the policing of these events and the circumstances in which they took place created considerable challenges for the National Olympic Security Coordinator.

The appointment of Assistant Commissioner Allison to the role throws important light on the strengths of the Metropolitan Police and British police's systems for selecting and nurturing highly experienced, well-trained specialist leaders to successfully take on major and unparalleled tasks which the OPG represented. This achievement by the NOSC raises important issues in the ongoing debate about the future of senior police leadership development and the direction it will take. But more broadly, the OPG and its successful staging clearly reflects effective government leadership and coordination capabilities, and highlights the potential of various institutions, which included a vast number of public and private partners and volunteers in a way that have rarely been observed to successfully tackle a major and complex problem that involves such global ramifications, and in which the police, security services, and their emergency response partners were critical lead players. Key to the success of the Olympic Games in London, and highlighted in the work of the NOSC, was the national approach adopted by government and the requirement for central coordination, which drew upon the resources of all 43 individual police forces across England and Wales and brought them under a unified command structure. The entire coordinated effort of the British police, the military, rescue services, other government and private organizations, and the numerous volunteers has proven again that critical planning and effective interagency deployment can lead to a successful, safe and secure event, even if exceptionally large and spread over a sizable area over a long period of time.

References

ACPO. (2010). Paying the Bill. ACPO/APA Guidance on Charging for Police Services. Retrieved February 12, 2014 from: www.acpo.uk

Adebayo, D. (2004). Perceived workplace fairness, transformational leadership and motivation in the Nigeria Police: Implications for change. *International Journal of Police Science & Management*, (2), 110–121.

Alexander, D. (2012). The London Bombings of July 7, 2005. In Hesloot, I., Boin, A. Jacobs, B., & Comfort, L. (Eds.), *Mega-crises, understanding the prospects, nature, characteristics and effects of cataclysmic events*. Springfield: Charles C Thomas Publishers Ltd.

Alison, L., & Crego, J. (2008). *Policing critical incidents, leadership and critical incident management*. Devon: Willan Publishing.

Batty, M., Desyllas, J., & Duxbury, E. (2003). Safety in numbers? Modelling crowds and designing control for Notting Hill carnival. *Urban Studies, 40*(8), 1573–1590.

Botterill, D., & Jones, T. (Eds.). (2010). *Tourism and crime: Key themes*. Oxford: Goodfellow Publishers.

Bowling, B., Marks, A., & Murphy, C. (2008). Crime Control Technologies: Towards an Analytical Framework and Research Agenda. In Brownsword R., & Yeung, K. (Eds.), *Regulating technologies: Legal futures, regulatory frames and technological fixes*. Oxford: Hart Publishing.

Bowling, B., & Sheptycki, J. (2012). *Global policing*. London: Sage.

Brownword, R., & Yeung, K. (Eds.). (2008). *Regulating technologies*. Portland, OR: Hart Publishing.

Bull, M., Ridley-Duff, R., Foster, D., & Seanor, P. (2010). Conceptualising ethical capital in social enterprises. *Social Enterprise Journal, 6*(3), 250–264.

Crisp, A. (2013). Getting Back to Peel: PCSO Training in England and Wales. In P. Stanislas (Ed.), *International perspectives on police education and training*. Abingdon: Routledge.

Davenport, J. (June 21, 2012). London 2012 Olympics: Foreign crime gangs target Games visitors. *The Standard*. Retrieved December 2, 2013 from: www.standard.co.uk

Emsley, C. (2005). The Birth and Development of the Police. In T. Newburn (Ed.), *Handbook of policing*. Devon, UK: Willan Publishing.

Emsley, C. (2010). *The Great British Bobby, the history of British policing from 1829 to the present*. London: Quercus Books.

Evans, D. (2011). The Role of the Private Sector. In Richards, A., Fussey, P., & Silke, P. (Eds.), *Terrorism and the Olympics*. London: Routledge.

French, S., & Disher, M. (1997). Atlanta and the Olympics, a one-year retrospective. *Journal of the American Planning Association, 63*(3), 379–392.

Fussey, P. (2011). Surveillance and the Olympics. In A. Richards, P. Fussey, & P. Silke (Eds.), *Terrorism and the Olympics: Major event security and lessons for the future*. London: Routledge.

Gibson, O. (July 3, 2012). London 2012 missile deployment goes ahead despite protests. *The Guardian*. Retrieved January 8, 2014 from: www.theguardian.com

Hesloot, I., Boin, A. Jacobs, B., & Comfort, L. (Eds.). (2012) *Mega-crises, understanding the prospects, nature, characteristics and effects of cataclysmic events*. Springfield, IL: Charles C Thomas Publishers Ltd.

Horn, A., & Breetzke, G. (2009). Informing a crime strategy for FIFA 2010 World Cup: A case study for the Loftus Versfeld Stadium in Tshwane, South Africa. *Urban Forum, 20*, 19–32.

Jennings, W. (2011). Governing the Games in the Age of Uncertainty: The Olympics and Organisational Responses to Risk. In A. Richards, P. Fussey, & P. Silke (Eds.), *Terrorism and the Olympics: Major event security and lessons for the future*. London: Routledge.

Jennings, W., & Lodge, M. (2012). The Olympic Games: Coping with Risk and Vulnerabilities of a Mega-Event. In Hesloot, I., Boin, A. Jacobs, B., & Comfort, L. (Eds.), *Mega-crises, understanding the prospects, nature, characteristics and effects of cataclysmic events*. Springfield, IL: Charles C Thomas Publishers Ltd.

Leonard, H., & Hewitt, A. (2012). Leading in Crisis: Observations on the Political and Decision-Making Dimension of Response. In Hesloot, I., Boin, A. Jacobs, B., & Comfort, L. (Eds.), *Mega-crises, understanding the prospects, nature, characteristics and effects of cataclysmic events*. Springfield, IL: Charles C Thomas Publishers Ltd.

Mason, G. (2004). *The official history of the Metropolitan Police*. London: Carlton Books Ltd.

McIntrye, T., & Scott, C. (2008). Internet Filtering: Rhetoric, Legitimacy, Accountability and Responsibility. In R. Brownword, & Yeung, K. (Eds.), *Regulating technologies*. Portland, OR: Hart Publishing.

O'Malley, P. (1997). Policing, politics and postmodernity. *Social and Legal Studies, 8*(3), 363–381.

Parker, C., & Paglia, E. (2012). Hurricane Katrina: The Complex Origins of a Mega-Disaster. In Hesloot, I., Boin, A. Jacobs, B., & Comfort, L. (Eds.), *Mega-crises, understanding the prospects, nature, characteristics and effects of cataclysmic events*. Springfield, IL: Charles C Thomas Publishers Ltd.

Peeters, H. (2013). Constructing Comparative Competency Profiles: The Netherlands Experience. In P. Stanislas (Ed.), *International perspectives on police education and training*. Abbingdon: Routledge.

Ramadin, R. (1987). *The making of the black working class in Britain*. London: Wildwood Press.

Rayner, G., & Marsden, S. (August 12, 2012). Olympics saw crime fall in London. *Telegraph*. Retrived December 2, 2013 from: www.telegraph.co.uk

Reiner, R. (1991). *Chief constables*. Oxford: Oxford University Press.

Sherif, M. (1958). Subordinate goals in the reduction of intergroup conflict. *The American Journal of Sociology*, *63*, 349–356.

Silke, A. (2011). Understanding Terrorist Target Selection. In A. Richards, P. Fussey, & P. Silke (Eds.), *Terrorism and the Olympics: Major event security and lessons for the future*. London: Routledge.

Simon, H. (1976*). Administrative behavior* (3rd ed.) New York: The Free Press.

Stanislas, P. (2011). Post 80s black leadership, the family and crime. *Safer Communities*, *11*(3), 134–144.

Stanislas, P. (Ed.). (2013). *International perspectives in police education and training*. Abbingdon: Routledge.

Stanislas, P. (2014). Interview with the Commissioner of the Royal Bahamas Police. In Baker, B., & Das, D. (Eds.), *Trends in policing: interviews with police leaders across the globe*. Boca Raton, FL: CRC Press.

Stanislas, P. (forthcoming). *Reconceptualizing Former Colonial Police Organization: The Challenges of Modernization and Professionalization and the Royal St. Lucia Police Force*.

Swain, S. (2011). Securing the Transport System. In A. Richards, P. Fussey, & P. Silke (Eds.), *Terrorism and the Olympics: Major event security and lessons for the future*. London: Routledge.

Wain, P., & Joyce, P. (2012). Disaffected communities, riots and policing in Manchester 1981–2011. *Safer Communities*, *11*(3), 125–134.

Wakefield, A. & Button, M. (2013). New Perspectives on Police Education and Training: Lessons from the Private Security Sector.

Weston, A. (2011). The Challenge of Inter-Agency Collaboration. In A. Richards, P. Fussey, & P. Silke (Eds.), *Terrorism and the Olympics: Major event security and lessons for the future*. London: Routledge.

Whitehead, T. (November 29, 2013). Lee Rigby murder trial: Solider was killed in "cowardly" and "callous" attack in Woolwich. *The Telegraph*. Retrived December 17, 2013 from: www.telegraph.co.uk

Wright, A., Alison, L., & Crego, J. (2008). The Current State of Police Research. In L. Alison, & J. Crego (Eds.), *Policing critical incidents*. Devon: Willan Publishing.

Reports

Charted Institute of Building. (2008). *Crime in the Construction Industry*. Charted Institute of Building.

Home Office. (2012). *Olympic Security and Safety Strategy*. London: Home Office.

National Audit Office. (2012). *London 2012 Olympic and Paralympic Games: Post Games Review*.

National Police Improvement Agency (NPIA). (2009). *Guidance on Command and Control*.

Neyroud, P. (2011). *Review of Police Leadership and Training*, Vol 1. London: Home Office.

University of East London. (2010). *Olympic Games Impact Study*. London: Economic and Social Research Council, Final Report.

About the Author

Dr. Perry Stanislas is a professor of Criminal Justice in the Department of Applied Social Sciences at De Montfort University in Leicester, UK.

Planning for Major Events on Aboriginal Lands in Canada

14

RICK PARENT

Contents

Introduction

This chapter discusses the unique setting of Aboriginal communities and the importance of strategic initiatives that facilitate a successful police response to events on tribal lands. A community-based policing approach will be presented: one that engages the Aboriginal community prior to a major event, that mobilizes community members, and that establishes positive relationships and a network of support. In addition, the importance of involving Aboriginal and nonindigenous community members, as well as local leaders, groups, government, business, and industry representatives, will be presented.

This chapter will also outline the Ontario Provincial Police "Framework Approach" to event planning, which delineates specific instructions on how police are to respond to incidents occurring on Aboriginal lands. By way of open dialog and mediation, the cooperation of all parties should be sought by police as a means to avoid unlawful or violent activities, preventing injury or harm, and avoiding potential conflict.

Aboriginal Communities and the Police

Relations between Aboriginal peoples and the police, historically and in contemporary times, have often been characterized by a high degree of mutual suspicion and hostility. In addition, Aboriginal communities confront a variety of social and policing problems that are distinctive and typically more serious than those in nontribal communities. The rural, isolated nature of most Aboriginal communities and the disproportionate presence of poverty, as well as associated social problems create a distinctive geographic and community context for Aboriginal law enforcement officials.

In many Aboriginal communities, the typical criminal justice oriented and crime control model of policing has resulted in reportedly unacceptable levels of incarceration of Aboriginal peoples. This *criminalization* has failed to adequately resolve the crime and public security problems of many Aboriginal communities.

In response, most Aboriginal communities have expressed the desire for a different style of policing that would include an alternative model of community justice that is different from the conventional model offered by U.S. and Canadian criminal justice systems. The values expressed can generally be described as restorative and integrative, rather than retributive and exclusionary, and community-based rather than simply criminal justice oriented (Linden, Clairmont, & Murphy, 2001, p. 39). In this regard, Aboriginal community justice with a restorative community-based focus requires the police to play a broad law enforcement and public service role and to utilize alternative policing techniques and methods.

In Canada, numerous government task forces and commissions of inquiry conducted over the past two decades have also documented instances in which police officers acted in a discriminatory fashion against Aboriginal peoples. This has led to initiatives on the part of various law enforcement agencies to improve the training and cultural sensitivity of police officers, to establish better lines of communication with Aboriginal communities, and to support Aboriginal police forces that have been created.

In conjunction, several Aboriginal lands have developed community-based criminal justice services and programs that are designed to address the specific needs of community residents, victims, and offenders. These initiatives have often been developed as part of a process of cultural and community revitalization and are part of the increasing efforts by Aboriginal peoples and communities to reassert their authority over all facets of community life (Griffiths & Hamilton, 1996). These trends have also provided the opportunity for Native American peoples in the United States and Canada to create autonomous police services and to establish partnerships between Aboriginal and nontribal police services.

Aboriginal Policing

A unique feature of the North American policing landscape involves the existence of "autonomous" Aboriginal police forces, which have developed over the past decades. Typically known as "Tribal Police" in the United States and "First Nations Police" in Canada, these Aboriginal law enforcement entities are emerging within the context of Aboriginal self-government. In Canada, the First Nations Policing Policy (FNPP) is a tripartite agreement negotiated among the federal government, provincial or territorial governments, and the specific First Nations. The agreements are cost-shared and, depending on the resources available, the Native American tribes may develop and administer its own police service.

In other instances, the First Nation may enter into a Community Tripartite Agreement (CTA) in which the tribal land has its own dedicated contingent of officers from an existing police service (such as the Royal Canadian Mounted Police or the Provincial Police in Ontario or Quebec). Every effort is made by these police services to have the department staffed by members directly from the First Nations community.

In 2008, there were 405 Aboriginal communities in Canada, with dedicated police services employing 1217 police officers, most of whom are of Aboriginal descent. In the province of Ontario, there are 92 First Nations communities policed by eight self-directed services. For communities without self-directed police services, the Ontario Provincial Police administers policing for 20 communities under the Ontario First Nations Policing Agreement and provides direct services to 22 other communities.

Among the larger Aboriginal police forces is the Nishnawbe-Aski Police Service, providing policing to 35 communities, the Six Nations Tribal Police in Ontario policing a population of 10,000 people, and the Amerindian Police Council in Quebec. These police forces have been established through negotiations and cost-sharing arrangements involving the federal government, the provincial governments, and First Nations communities.

Officers in Aboriginal police departments generally have full powers to enforce the *Criminal Code of Canada*, federal and provincial statutes, as well as tribal by-laws on Native American reserve lands. The activities of tribal police agencies are overseen by reserve-based police commissions or by the local tribal ("band") council. There are also band constables who are appointed under provisions of the *Indian Act* and who are responsible for enforcing tribal by-laws. Band constables are not fully sworn police officers and their powers are limited (Whitelaw & Parent, 2014, p. 24).

Mobilizing and Engaging the Aboriginal Community: Prior to an Event

In 2010, the Ontario Association of Chiefs of Police introduced a policing model known as the Ontario's Mobilization and Engagement Model of Community Policing (see Figure 14.1). This model is designed to deliver

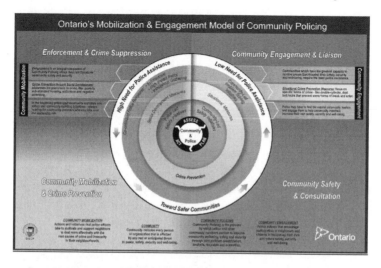

Figure 14.1 Ontario's mobilization and engagement model of community policing. (From Ontario Association of Chiefs of Police, OACP, 2010, *Ontario's Mobilization and Engagement Model of Community Policing,* Retrieved from: http://oacp-b2b.ca/article/community-policing-is-what-we-do/.)

policing services to the unique needs of a community. The model also serves as a diagnostic tool in which both the police and community leaders assess how much support is required to achieve a safer neighborhood. The model is broken down into four key areas:

- Enforcement and crime suppression
- Community mobilization and crime prevention
- Community safety and consultation
- Community engagement and liaison

The mobilization and engagement concepts are key to event planning as it requires police officers to meet with Aboriginal community leaders and determine how the specific area rates across these four dimensions. Specific policing strategies are identified that will assist in maintaining or improving overall community safety. For example, police may be required to stabilize neighborhood problems and to begin developing community capacity (ability) to take ownership for many problems that had led to feelings of insecurity.

The goal for both the police and the Aboriginal residents is to move away from a community requiring a high need for law enforcement assistance to one requiring a lower level of public safety services. In this regard, police must establish partnerships by identifying Aboriginal leaders who are able to sustain and build on positive accomplishments and to continually engage the Aboriginal community to address many of its crime and disorder problems. Over time, through the application of community-based policing strategies, the community is better equipped to manage its own problems and consequently lessen its reliance on the police (Whitelaw & Parent, 2013, pp. 309–311).

Even more importantly, this strategic approach to policing engages the Aboriginal community and their leaders prior to a major event, thereby establishing positive relationships. If and when required, the community can be further mobilized to respond in a proactive fashion with event planning and other public safety issues.

A "Framework Approach" to Confronting Incidents on Aboriginal Lands

In Canada, the Ontario Provincial Police (OPP) utilizes a "Framework Approach" in defining and guiding the police response to various incidents that can occur on Aboriginal lands. It provides flexibility in how to manage individual conflict situations while establishing consistency and meeting policing core duties as well as statutory and common law responsibilities. The Framework Approach also provides for accommodation and mutual respect for differences, positions, and interests of involved Aboriginal and nontribal communities and the police. The strategies that are developed support the minimal use of force by police to the fullest extent possible.

> Critical incidents are often avoidable. The benefits of the Framework are maximized if put to use before an issue becomes a critical incident. Identifying, establishing and maintaining open and transparent relationships with all stakeholders are vital to maximized public safety.
>
> ... the Framework provides a guideline for police response to conflict and has applicability to both Aboriginal and non-Aboriginal issue-related conflict. ... Its focus on negotiation and mediation applies to police-related matters during a conflict. The Framework is recognized as a best practice for police response to an Aboriginal critical incident. (OPP, 2013, pp. 11–13)

The Framework Approach

The Framework Approach identifies three stages of potential conflict that can occur: preincident, incident, and post-incident. Actual incidents occurring on Aboriginal lands are further defined:

- A *major incident* is an occurrence that, by circumstance, requires employees, equipment, and resources beyond those required for normal police service delivery; for example, civil disturbances or disasters such as an airplane crash.
- A *critical incident* is a high-risk incident requiring mobilization of an integrated emergency response; for example, an active shooter, a hostage taking, or a barricaded person. Typically, in these instances, a tactical team will be deployed in conjunction with an incident commander and crisis negotiators.
- An *Aboriginal critical incident* is any critical or major incident where the source of conflict may stem from assertions of inherent, Aboriginal, or treaty rights; or that is occurring on a First Nation territory; or involving an Aboriginal person(s), where the potential for significant impact or violence may require activation of an integrated emergency response unit. (OPP, 2013, pp. 4–6)

The OPP Framework Approach also provides guidance for police engagement. The uniqueness of Aboriginal occupations and protests are underscored as they are often complex in nature and qualitatively different from single-issue labor or political disputes. Emphasis is placed upon the awareness of related Aboriginal historical and cultural factors. These factors should be considered in determining what police resources may be required to peacefully resolve the incident.

Emphasis is placed upon the importance of understanding what is at issue and the complexities involved; the various positions being taken; the range of interested and influential parties—both Aboriginal and nontribal, with the potential to impact the achievement of a peaceful resolution of the Aboriginal critical incident.

A measured and flexible police response that employs the use of negotiation and mediation has the greatest potential to achieve success. This process provides the greatest benefit when these skills and tactics are utilized prior to the incident escalating into a larger-scale issue. Relationship building and open communication with all of the involved parties are the keys to the success of the Framework Approach (OPP, 2013, pp. 4–5).

> The Framework Approach emphasizes peacekeeping as a means to minimize violence, keep and restore public order, maintain neutrality, facilitate rights and work toward trusting relationships. Equally important, the Framework establishes that the OPP will investigate and take appropriate action in response to civil disobedience and unlawful acts, using discretion, a carefully measured approach and only the level of force necessary to ensure the safety of all citizens and to maintain/restore peace, order and security. The use of force is always a last resort. In keeping with the objectives of peacekeeping, police may exercise considerable discretion with respect to how and when enforcement initiatives are undertaken. (OPP, 2013, p. 5).

Specialized Police Training and Organizational Sustainability

In 2009, the OPP created the Provincial Liaison Team (PLT) program with the mandate to establish and maintain open and transparent lines of communication with all stakeholders who may be affected, directly or indirectly, by major events. PLT members are specially trained, experienced police officers who operate openly as part of a police response to major events. These officers receive intensive, two-week training on building trust, enhancing relationships, effective communication, mediation and negotiation, as well as relevant, regular, ongoing training in specialized areas (OPP, 2013, p. 7).

Under the objective of sustainability, the OPP also ensures that there is a mandated element of training for all uniformed police personnel with regard to the Framework Approach. This includes recruit training, which now involves the presentation and detailed discussions about the Framework Approach. These concepts and strategies are further embedded within the training provided to Major Critical Incident Command management, specialty teams such as tactics and rescue units, emergency response teams, and other specialty support services, including public order units and crisis negotiators. OPP policy and operational planning for major incidents additionally incorporate the Framework Approach, while reinforcing the need to proactively establish strong relationships; to communicate, mediate, and negotiate police-related interests; and to work to maintain and restore relationships following an event or incident. This would include community outreach initiatives, undertaken proactively and in response to requests, providing information about and explaining the Framework Approach to area constituents. The recipients may include Aboriginal and nontribal community members and leaders, groups, government, business and industry representatives, and activists. By way of open dialog and mediation, cooperation of all parties is sought by police as a means to avoid unlawful or violent activities, preventing injury or harm, and avoiding potential conflict (OPP, 2013, pp. 9–11).

In sum, an embedded organizational commitment must be made by the police agency to engage in a flexible, consistent, and professional approach to policing Aboriginal areas, and more so when major critical incidents are involved. In order to be effective, this approach must be sustainable, transparent, and wide reaching, to both Aboriginal and nontribal members of the community. Mutual respect for differences must be acknowledged, while resolving conflict and managing crisis situations with minimal force.

A Framework Toward Peaceful Resolution

A key aspect of the Framework Approach is the emphasis and use of observations made by police personnel, prior to the event, during the event, and upon conclusion of the event. The Framework Approach incorporates signs, behaviors, and cues that may be present at each stage of the three-stage "conflict cycle" with suggested resolution techniques on how to avoid, de-escalate, or appropriately manage a situation (OPP, 2013, pp. 14–16). The observations and concerns by police personnel and the resolution opportunities that may be available are outlined as follows:

1. The pre-event: Police observations and concerns:
   - Real or perceived inequities in privilege or power with the community or between the community and contemporary society
   - An initiative or event being planned that could lead to conflict
   - High probability that an ongoing initiative or event could lead to conflict or crisis
   - Words and images used to describe an initiative or event that could generate negative emotions, dissension, disagreement, or conflict
   - Involved persons stating that if an initiative or event is not dealt with sensitively, a conflict or crisis will ensue

The police response may include the following activities or actions:

- Be informed and consult with Aboriginal elected councils, First Nations/Tribal Police, community members, groups, and other levels of Aboriginal leadership
- Remain informed of the positions and the impact of non-Aboriginal stakeholders
- Consider the policing implications of the local issues identified
- Develop and display respect for all concerned by active listening
- Always be honest: overt and consistent honesty is the best way to earn trust
- Build positive trusting relationships with members of all communities, First Nations/Tribal Police officers, and other agencies
- Be open and available to all parties, and engage and begin a dialog
- Encourage individuals to come together around issues and activities where agreement and common ground exist
- Consult with elected and traditional leaders of the community if an issue arises that may precipitate a dispute or conflict
- Consult with community leaders on potentially conflicting issues using existing opportunities for dialog
- Identify community and agency representatives who can serve as resource persons or mediators
- Review the local emergency plan to ensure it adequately addresses potential conflict situations including diversion routes as well as possible blockade locations

2. The actual event: Police observations and concerns should include:

- Involved persons expressing a perception that their concerns are not being satisfactorily addressed
- Comments about the incident increasing in frequency or intensity, indicating greater likelihood of crisis
- Communicated positions becoming entrenched and polarized
- Involved persons becoming increasingly vocal, forceful, and threatening
- Increasing media coverage with potential to further divide positions
- Persons or agencies not directly involved, taking public positions concerning the dispute
- Individuals from the Aboriginal community, including leaders, looking for police personnel of Aboriginal ancestry to assist as a point of contact

The police response may include:

- From an operational perspective, the police agency should consider using an incident commander for the duration of the incident, who would be responsible for the overall command and control of an integrated response that may include tactical team deployment and the use of skilled negotiators

- Ensure that all parties to the incident have the opportunity to contribute to resolution strategies
- Provide options that are transparent to the parties in conflict to promote a safe resolution; police should state their position and interests clearly so as to be understood by all, which may defuse an incident and lead to a safe resolution
- Establish the policing interest as it relates to the dispute at hand, for example, explain that the police intend to maintain an orderly flow of traffic while allowing participants to lawfully demonstrate; and where possible attempt to reroute traffic in order to avoid confrontation and minimize impact
- Emphasize that negotiations will be used at every opportunity
- Acknowledge the existence of underlying factors within the incident
- Communicate to disputants that all demonstrators and other members of the public will be treated with dignity, respect, and fairness—consider the values, traditions, and interests of the affected communities
- Seek out common ground between all stakeholders and aspects of the dispute where agreement exists and take every opportunity to facilitate productive communication
- Establish with disputants a means by which information and progress will be communicated to media
- Consider the impact of decisions on the safety of police officers, demonstrators, and other members of the public
- Respond to conflict with the minimal use of force
- Explain that a cooling off period and its length, if needed and possible, will be jointly agreed to
- Ensure that police personnel on the ground are kept informed

3. The post-event: Police observations and concerns:
- The emotional and physical exhaustion of participants
- Differing perceptions of the incident by those involved
- Stakeholders wanting to reflect on what has occurred, discuss lessons learned, and identify peace-building actions

The police response may include:
- Operational debriefings to review and assess operations and seek lessons learned
- Develop and implement a strategy to restore relationships with all involved communities
- Consider general objectives, responsibilities, and potential activities to restore relationships and be adapted to specific circumstances as necessary (OPP, 2013, pp. 14–16)

Examples: Applying the Framework to Conflict on Aboriginal Lands in Ontario

Case Example One: First Nation Opposition to Harmonized Sales Tax in Ontario—2009

In late 2009, the Governments of Ontario and Canada signed a Memorandum of Agreement to create the Harmonized Sales Tax (HST). First Nations people and political leaders across Ontario immediately opposed this new tax as there was no consultation with First Nations as to how harmonization would impact them and there were no provisions in place to ensure the existing Point of Sale tax exemption would continue.

Frustration boiled over in the form of protests and other organized events across the province for many months. Following the Framework Approach to dealing with events, the Ontario Provincial Police (OPP) began outreach to First Nations leaders and commenced research into the new legislation (pre-incident stage). Proactive efforts during this pre-incident stage positioned the OPP well and ensured a consistent and coordinated response to planned events as they happened (incident stage).

Each police detachment was provided an operational plan template to be completed, followed, and filed with the Emergency Management Unit. Using one template ensured that the Framework was embedded in each operational plan, making it necessary for all OPP members associated to an event to understand it. Weekly conference calls were implemented with representation from OPP regions and units, the Emergency Management Unit, the Aboriginal Critical Incident Command, and Corporate Communications to maintain a consistent and knowledgeable approach to events associated to the tax (HST) implementation.

On July 1, 2010, the HST was implemented, while at the same time the provincial and federal governments announced that an agreement was in place to continue the existing Point of Sale tax exemption for First Nations.

Across Ontario, there were 25 protests involving more than 30 communities over a six-month period. Local detachment commanders and Provincial Liaison Team (PLT) members continued to work with individuals and First Nation communities, after the fact, in efforts to maintain relationships that had been established (post-incident stage).

Case Example Two: An Integrated Response on First Nation Territory—2010

In 2010, Ontario Provincial Police (OPP) officers were deployed as part of an Integrated Response to assist "Treaty Three" First Nations Police with a barricaded person situation on a tribal territory. The suspect eventually surrendered to police and was arrested without incident. The OPP Provincial Liaison Team (PLT) followed up, after the successful resolution of the call, to explain and answer concerns from community members about the OPP presence, the different resources used, and the number of officers deployed to the incident.

Members of the Tribal Council had concerns and questions about the number of officers responding to the incident and the different (green) uniforms worn by some of the officers at the scene. The explanations and information provided served to assure the leadership and community members that the incident was managed with the overall safety of the officers involved and the security of the community and its members as priorities. Further follow-up was provided in response to a community request for a presentation about the OPP Emergency Response Team (ERT). (OPP, 2013, pp. 17–18)

Discussion

The case examples involving the Ontario Provincial Police show how the Framework approach, if followed properly, can "minimize the use of force to the fullest extent possible." Several key components of the Framework Approach were used effectively in the cases presented, demonstrating relationship building with the Aboriginal peoples, an open and honest dialog, proactive engagement (OPP, 2013, pp. 17–19).

Prior to an event occurring, the police agency must dedicate the necessary resources to build capacity to respond to events occurring on and involving Aboriginal communities. The police strategy must emphasize the development of communication networks and trusting relationships with Aboriginal peoples before, during, and after an event or crisis occurs. This process emphasizes the need for ongoing communication, collaboration, and partnerships with Aboriginal leaders and the communities that they represent.

More importantly, day-to-day policing activities in Aboriginal communities should be based upon a "cultural foundation" thereby establishing and enhancing trust and transparency. Police officers who understand Aboriginal issues and work closely with Native American communities will be better prepared to identify and defuse potentially violent confrontations. As a direct result, the police agency will be more effective and the Aboriginal community is more likely to view the public safety activities as having legitimacy (Ipperwash, 2007, pp. 179–180).

In this regard, there is a need to place greater emphasis upon training police personnel to utilize those communication and tactical skills that are associated with crisis intervention. The components of this training also need to emphasize Aboriginal history, customs, legal issues, and community dynamics. Police officers require training that will allow them to interact in a calm and controlled manner when confronting individuals that may be angry or emotional due to the complexities associated with Aboriginal issues. An informed and comprehensive front-line intervention strategy will have a greater chance of successfully resolving face-to-face confrontation in a peaceful manner.

Aboriginal protests and occupations should be considered a separate and unique form of dissent. As demonstrated by the Ontario Provincial Police Framework Approach, there is a need for specific strategies and responses to Aboriginal related events including a dedicated and specially trained police response. The objectives of the police service and the agency command staff during the event must be to minimize the potential for violence, facilitate constitutional rights, and to restore public order. Also key to the resolution of the event is the need to maintain and facilitate positive and trusting relationships with individuals in both the Aboriginal and nontribal communities.

> Canadian police forces have generally shown a preference for cautious engagement. On one hand they can be criticized for not upholding the law, but on the other, they are accustomed to being society's front line in cases of ambiguous justice. Interposing themselves between angry and riotous citizens is neither fun nor safe, yet police are asked to do this somewhere every month. In the case of Indian lands, they have learned that a strict constructionist approach to law enforcement is a recipe for danger and public obloquy. (Swain, 2010, pp. 191–192)

References

Ipperwash Inquiry Report. (2007). Commissioner Sidney B. Linden. Ottawa: Government of Ontario. Volume 2.

Linden, R., Clairmont, D., & Murphy, C. (2001). *Aboriginal Policing in Manitoba. A Report to the Aboriginal Implementation Commission.* Manitoba Government. Retrieved from: http://www.ajic.mb.ca/policing.pdf

Ontario Association of Chiefs of Police. (2010). *Ontario's Mobilization and Engagement Model of Community Policing.* Retrieved from: http://oacp-b2b.ca/article/community-policing-is-what-we-do/

Ontario Provincial Police (OPP). (2013). *Annual Report on the Framework Approach 2007–2012.* A Framework for the Police Preparedness for Aboriginal Critical Incidents. Retrieved from: http://www.scribd.com/doc/199455930/OPP-Aboriginal-Critical-Incidents

Swain, H. (2010). *Oka: A political crisis and its legacy.* Vancouver, Canada: Douglas and McIntyre.

Uniform Crime Reports (2010). *Crime in the United States. Federal Bureau of Investigation.* Washington, DC: U.S. Department of Justice. Retrieved from: http://www.fbi.gov/about-us/cjis/ucr/ucr

Whitelaw, B., & Parent, R. (2014). *Community-based strategic policing in Canada* (4th ed.). Toronto: Nelson.

About the Author

Dr. Rick Parent is an assistant professor at Simon Fraser University, School of Criminology—Police Studies. Dr. Parent completed 30 years of service as a police officer in the Vancouver area. He is also a former police recruit instructor at the Justice Institute of British Columbia, and spent over eight years as a crisis negotiator assigned to a regional Emergency

Response Team. His research and expertise is in the police use of lethal force, including the phenomena of suicide by cop. Dr. Parent is the coauthor of the book entitled *Community-Based Strategic Policing in Canada*, 4th Edition, and the subject matter expert/author of the Canadian Police Knowledge Network course entitled "Police Ethics and Accountability." He is also a senior researcher for the Canadian Network for Research on Terrorism, Security, and Society (TSAS). Dr. Parent can be contacted via: rparent@sfu.ca or www.rickparent.ca.

Conclusion, Discussion, and Policy Implications

The issues explored in the preceding chapters highlight how the political, economic, legal, and social contexts of the various countries represented shape the experiences of all stakeholders in relation to the policing of major events. Despite these differences, there were at least seven key themes that have been discussed here that have repeatedly surfaced in both explicit and implicit references: communication and information technology; shared understanding; policing culture and reform; public perceptions of police; civility, equity, and rights-based orientations; contextual awareness and social change; and the relevance of effective planning and coordinated inter-agency response. We would argue that further contextualizing these seven themes are two key social forces that complicate any analysis of the work involved in policing major events: legislative frameworks and the media representations of events.

Communication and Information Technology

All of the chapters highlight the need for more opportunities for meaningful exchanges of ideas and information among academics, researchers, law enforcement personnel, and other stakeholders in developing more collaborative, effective, and sustainable strategies to respond to the challenges of policing major events. There needs to be more attention paid to global and local lessons learned through the creation of more innovative, accessible, and sustainable strategies for knowledge transfer among all stakeholders. Importantly, this need for more inclusive communicative partnerships comes at a time when a number of policing jurisdictions are becoming more restrictive in providing access to information that would support more evidence-based approaches to policing.

In part, these restrictions may be a reaction to greater public scrutiny facilitated by greater use and accessibility of technology including cell phone cameras and social media making the average citizen a critical cog in the dissemination of information and consequently police forces have become more guarded in their relationships with the public and more particularly the mainstream media.

Shared Understanding of Key Issues

Associated with the need for improved communication is the need and consequent challenges associated with developing shared understandings of concepts, strategies, and even desired outcomes. How many situations associated with policing major events are aggravated by unclear and insufficient definitions of threat and risk even as stakeholders in various contexts acknowledge the fundamental importance of risk assessment in managing major events. There are instructive questions about the similarities and differences between codes of conduct and measures of police performance in a time characterized by increasing demands for more transparent mechanisms of accountability. Further evidence of this need to develop shared understandings continues to surface in discussions about community policing. It has become increasingly clear that differing perceptions about the efficacy and/or role of community policing may be grounded in differing definitions of what community policing means rather than in the underlying principles associated with those definitions.

Connors' (2007) report for the U.S. Department of Justice on Planning and Managing Security for Major Special Events is one of the few reports that emphasizes the role community policing can play in managing major events:

> The city of Portland, Oregon, which has its share of protest movements, also has a strong community policing history. The police department emphasizes a community policing approach for negotiating with protesters and, as a result, preventing disruptions. The event commander seeks out and initiates meetings with protest organizers who apply for march permits or are otherwise known to police—such as representatives of unions or police accountability groups—and with others who are not yet known, such as anarchists. In August 2003, Portland police successfully employed a community policing approach to aid in managing protesters whose leadership appeared to be anarchist. The site was a park, which was near a University of Portland facility that was being visited by the President of the United States. A total of about 3000 people assembled in the park for this event.
>
> The anarchists did not obtain a march permit but, a few days before the event, they did send a liaison to meet with the police department's liaison to the crowd. At the meeting, the police discussed the "rules of engagement," determined what most wanted (media coverage and a good viewing area), and suspected that there might be other elements in the crowd who would be interested in more aggressive outcomes, like breaching barricades and stopping the motorcade. Police made decisions that gave the larger, less threatening group most of what it wanted. This separated out the more dangerous group, and the police were able to control it. (p. 72)

As various forms of community policing become more prominent in the planning and execution of security for major events, more traditional and in many cases antiquated modes of policing will come under increasing scrutiny.

Policing Culture and Reform

There are numerous critiques of both the characteristics and consequences of more traditional, "closed-shop" reactive and top-down police organizations. In response to what appears to be a general agreement that this model is neither desirable nor effective, there are various efforts to change the culture of policing through: different leadership models; recruitment strategies; in-service training; postsecondary education opportunities; and, perhaps most importantly greater, or in some cases, any transparency. While many authors in this volume allude to some of the challenges associated with police reform, it is clear that there need to be more conversations about the resistance to these changes that is fueled by the very culture that many are trying to reform.

Despite such resistance, this transformation from a more traditional hierarchical and paramilitary structure to a more communicative and collaborative model has been underway for quite some time. Critics fear that such a transformation impairs the ability of police to respond to police major events and intervene when crowds turn unruly, while proponents point to the successes experienced when less confrontational methods are employed.

Noakes, Klocke, and Gillham (2005) argue that toward the end of the 20th century, police shifted to a more negotiated management model:

> In effect, negotiated management entails altering the "rules of the game" to allow greater police discretion in facilitating protests and in interacting with protest groups. This trend away from "king's police" approaches toward an emphasis on community policing maps onto a coherent police philosophy relating to legitimacy and democracy. (p. 189)

This sentiment is echoed by Gorringe and Rosie (2008) who discuss the move away from coercive heavy-handed policing of public protests to more progressive models emphasizing cooperation and dialog:

> This new style of policing protest was based on the premise that police could better achieve their two primary goals of minimizing public disorder and increasing the predictability of protest events by ceding temporary and partial control of public spaces to demonstrators. Police would underenforce the law and negotiate with protest groups prior to a demonstration in an effort to establish mutually agreeable terms and conditions under which the demonstrations would be held. (p. 239)

Internationally, there is agreement that the culture of policing must continue to evolve in a manner that supports more inclusive, community-based models of problem solving with respect to a wide range of law enforcement and broader public policy issues. Importantly, these shifts are likely to encourage increasingly positive relations with the general public.

Public Perceptions of Police

The importance of public perceptions of police is a key thread that is woven throughout this book and the broader literature. These discussions are grounded in dramatically different contexts than would be expected given the diversity of countries represented; however, the common themes that were foundational to the importance of public perceptions were instructive. These commonalities are found in conversations about police corruption in various jurisdictions; media representations of crowd control at major events; police tactics in riot situations; and the reluctance of citizens to report crimes due to perceptions of insensitivity or because of expectations, particularly evident in countries experiencing significant transitions, that the police were not to be trusted and perhaps even feared. All of these issues connect public perceptions of police with greater or lesser latitude for police interventions.

The Greater Manchester Police Authority's review (2011) of policing of major events highlighted the importance of public perceptions of police by addressing several scenarios including high profile events, protests, and football matches (where crowds in excess of 70,000 are not uncommon). Several of the key factors linked to successful policing of major events were connected to police–public relations including: partnerships, public expectations and experiences, human rights and civil liberties, and inclusive planning.

To an extent this could be considered an incident driven analysis as it comes on the heels of a highly publicized event:

> The events which transpired during and following the G20 summit protests in London in April 2009 resulted in national implications for the policing of protests. The national media coverage of the protests, how they were policed and, most notably, the death of Ian Tomlinson provoked a widespread negative reaction on the part of the public. (p. 15)

This report as well as many other "postmortems" of major events emphasize that high-visibility policing enhances both public confidence and the sense of being in a safe city.

Civility, Equity, and Rights-Based Orientations

A meaningful discussion about the concept of civility as it relates to police action necessitates a more critical and creative approach to definitions of civility and order maintenance. Ideas about the potential for a police approach grounded in civility, equity, and rights-based discourse include human rights advisors working more closely with police during protests, the screening and training of private security, and a range of community-based preventative programs. All of these examples and countless others emphasize the role of civil society in progressive policing.

Constitutional rights, case law, civil liberties groups, litigation, policy makers, and police have all worked to change the landscape of crowd control moving to a more progressive and less confrontational approach to policing major events. Having said that, there are situations that necessitate a more aggressive, law and order approach, and more than a few policing agencies question whether in these times they are adequately equipped for the paradigm shift.

Contextual Awareness and Social Change

It is impossible to have meaningful conversations about any of the issues captured in these chapters without understanding the diversity of socio-political frameworks within which all stakeholders are seeking remedies. There is a need to think more critically about the causes and indeed appropriate interventions in relation to the historical, cultural, social, political, and economic realities that contextualize these events and circumstances. This need for a more contextual and structural awareness is illustrated throughout this volume including discussions of football fan violence as an extension of political unrest, political protest as a necessary expression of community discontent, and the growing role of private security.

Effective Planning and Coordinated Interagency Response

Clearly by combining a better understanding and appreciation of the above factors with a protocol that incorporates effective planning and coordinated interagency response, the police and partner agencies can enhance public safety and security, while also increasing public confidence in law enforcement and government officials. Whether planning for a large demonstration or a major sporting event, or responding to a natural or man-made disaster, it is critical that officials incorporate lessons learned and recommended best practices into organizational procedure and protocol. And routine and comprehensive training must be a mandatory organizational practice to enhance individual and agency professionalism and effectiveness, and to ensure public confidence and trust.

Summary

So many of the issues and examples examined in this book demonstrate how often the legal, political, economic, and social policies purportedly implemented to address various public issues have little hope of any meaningful success because they are not grounded in valid theoretical frameworks. It is not unique to policing that there is incongruence between the policies invoked and the issues they are designed to address.

All of the chapter contributions illustrate the fundamental importance of appreciating the context in which communities are policed, and most importantly promote social change in the circumstances that are most significant in contributing to public disorder in all of its forms.

Interestingly, at the same time that the editors were contemplating the themes, concepts, and issues for this textbook, many law enforcement agencies in the Western world were dealing with one of the most interesting and high-profile examples of policing a major event: the Occupy movement, back in 2011. The unpredictable and media-saturated nature of the event made policing it incredibly complex. The make-up of the participants was impossible to anticipate as the internal demographics were changing dramatically from day to day and location to location. What could be more challenging than strategizing to control and contain a protest that included elected public officials, labor leaders, activists, environmentalists, First Nations members, curious onlookers, street people, drug dealers, self-described anarchists, and disgruntled youth, many looking for trouble?

The unique challenges these situations presented to law enforcement resulted in a diminished capacity to develop intelligence and engage in effective and strategic pre-event planning. The economic conditions that, to one extent or another, precipitated the multiple occupations and related disorder are unlikely to improve anytime soon. Furthermore, poor economic forecasts may have the effect of not just energizing follow-up occupation movements, but validating them in the eyes of many. In particular, poor employment prospects for youth will likely kickstart another round of occupation demonstrations in the years to come. A key distinction between the occupation demonstrations and other significant and often violent responses at the scene of economic summits or even major sporting events is that the latter have start and end dates. The former, meanwhile, need not be attached to any such scheduled event. Further complications arise when one considers the occupation movements have not been jurisdictionally specific. A perimeter fence or barricade to keep the protesters out of a particular city block or venue has often had no impact on a sporadic demonstration that may be so fluid and mobile that targeting a particular location will be of little importance. While specific experiences or lessons learned in dealing with crowds at major sporting events, global economic conferences, and political protests are not necessarily transferable to the Occupy movement, it would appear that the movement toward a more collaborative, problem-solving approach is more conducive than a harsher law and order mentality. This new era of uncertainty and unpredictability, in conjunction with diminishing economic resources to provide law and order at major public events and gatherings, suggests that today's best practices may need to be revisited soon.

There will continue to be new iterations and subsequent policing challenges associated with major events, however, we argue that shifts toward more progressive policing models and the associated enhancements in public confidence, conflict management strategies, attentiveness to the civility of policing, and finally knowledge transfer of lessons learned will ensure more positive and effective response to future events and incidents.

References

Connors, Edward. (2007). U.S. Department of Justice, Office of Community Oriented Policing Services. Planning and Managing Security for Major Special Events—Guidelines for Law Enforcement. Retrieved from: http://www.cops.usdoj.gov/files/ric/Publications/e07071299_web.pdf

Gorringe, H., & Rosie, M. (2008). It's a long way to Auchterarder! "Negotiated management" and mismanagement in the policing of G8 protests. *The British Journal of Sociology, 59*(2), 187–205.

Greater Manchester Police Authority. (2011). Preserving the Peace—The Policing of Major Events in Greater Manchester. Retrieved from: http://www.manchester.gov.uk/egov_downloads/6c._Policing_of_Major_Events.pdf

Noakes, J. A., Klocke, B. V., & Gillham, P. F. (2005). Whose streets? Police and protester struggles over space in Washington. *Policing & Society, 15*(3), 235–254.

International Police Executive Symposium (IPES), www.ipes.info

The International Police Executive Symposium was founded in 1994. It enjoys a Special Consultative status with the United Nations. The aims and objectives of the IPES are to provide a forum to foster closer relationships among police researchers and practitioners globally, to facilitate cross-cultural, international and interdisciplinary exchanges for the enrichment of the law enforcement profession, and to encourage discussion and published research on challenging and contemporary topics related to the profession.

One of the most important activities of the IPES is the organization of an annual meeting under the auspices of a police agency or an educational institution. Every year since 1994, annual meetings have been hosted by such agencies and institutions all over the world. Past hosts have included the Canton Police of Geneva, Switzerland; the International Institute of the Sociology of Law, Onati, Spain; Kanagawa University, Yokohama, Japan; the Federal Police, Vienna, Austria; the Dutch Police and Europol, The Hague, The Netherlands; the Andhra Pradesh Police, India; the Center for Public Safety, Northwestern University, USA; the Polish Police Academy, Szczytno, Poland; the Police of Turkey (twice); the Kingdom of Bahrain Police; a group of institutions in Canada (consisting of the University of the Fraser Valley, Abbotsford Police Department, Royal Canadian Mounted Police, the Vancouver Police Department, the Justice Institute of British Columbia, Canadian Police College, and the International Centre for Criminal Law Reform and Criminal Justice Policy); the Czech Police Academy, Prague; the Dubai Police; the Ohio Association of Chiefs of Police and the Cincinnati Police Department, Ohio, USA; the Republic of Macedonia and the Police of Malta. An annual meeting on the theme of "Policing Violence, Crime, Disorder, and Discontent: International Perspectives" was hosted in Buenos Aires, Argentina on June 26–30, 2011. The 2012 annual meeting was hosted at the United Nations in New York on the theme of "Economic Development, Armed Violence, and Public Safety" on August 5–10. The Ministry of the Interior of Hungary and the Hungarian National Police hosted the meeting in 2013 in Budapest on August 4–9 on the theme of "Contemporary Global

Issues in Policing." The 2014 meeting on "Crime Prevention and Community Resilience" took place in Sofia, Bulgaria on July 27–31.

There have also been occasional special meetings of the IPES. A special meeting was cohosted by the Bavarian Police Academy of Continuing Education in Ainring, Germany, University of Passau, Germany, and the State University of New York, Plattsburgh, USA in 2000. The second special meeting was hosted by the police in the Indian state of Kerala. The third special meeting on the theme of "Contemporary Issues in Public Safety and Security" was hosted by the commissioner of police of the Blekinge region of Sweden and the president of the University of Technology on August 10–14, 2011. The most recent special meeting was held in Trivandrum (Kerala, India) on "Policing by Consent" on March 16–20, 2014.

The majority of participants of the annual meetings are usually directly involved in the police profession. In addition, scholars and researchers in the field also participate. The meetings comprise both structured and informal sessions to maximize dialogue and exchange of views and information. The executive summary of each meeting is distributed to participants as well as to a wide range of other interested police professionals and scholars. In addition, a book of selected papers from each annual meeting is published through CRC Press/Taylor & Francis Group, Prentice Hall, Lexington Books, and other reputed publishers. A special issue of *Police Practice and Research: An International Journal* is also published with the most thematically relevant papers after the usual blind review process.

IPES Board of Directors

The IPES is directed by a board of directors representing various countries of the world (listed below). The registered business office is located at Norman Vale, 6030 Nott Road, Guilderland, NY 12084, and the registered agent is National Registered Agents, 200 West Adams Street, Chicago, IL 60606.

President
Dilip Das, Norman Vale, 6030 Nott Road, Guilderland, NY 12084. Tel: 802-598-3680. Fax: 410-951-3045. E-mail: dilipkd@aol.com.

Vice President
Etienne Elion, Case J-354-V, OCH Moungali 3, Brazzaville, Republic of Congo. Tel: 242-662-1683. Fax: 242-682-0293. E-mail: ejeej2003@yahoo.fr.

Treasurer/Secretary
Paul Moore, 125 Kenny Lane, West Monroe, LA 21294. Tel: 318-512-1500. E-mail: paul@ipes.info.

Directors

Rick Sarre, GPO Box 2471, Adelaide, 5001, South Australia. Tel: 61-8-83020889. Fax: 61-8-83020512. E-mail: rick.sarre@unisa.edu.au.

Tonita Murray, 73 Murphy Street, Carleton Place, Ontario K7C 2B7 Canada. Tel: 613-998-0883. E-mail: tonita_murray@hotmail.com.

Snezana (Ana) Mijovic-Das, Norman Vale, 6030 Nott Road, Guilderland, NY 12084. Tel: 518-452-7845. Fax: 518-456-6790. E-mail: anamijovic@yahoo.com.

Andrew Carpenter, The Pier, 1 Harborside Place, Apt 658, Jersey City, NJ 07311. Tel: 917-367-2205. Fax: 917-367-2222. E-mail: carpentera@un.org.

Paulo R. Lino, 111 Das Garcas St., Canoas, RS, 92320-830, Brazil. Tel: 55-51-8111-1357. Fax: 55-51-466-2425. E-mail: paulino2@terra.com.br.

Rune Glomseth, Slemdalsveien 5, Oslo, 0369, Norway. E-mail: rune.glomseth@phs.no.

Maximilian Edelbacher, Riemersgasse 16/E/3, A-1190 Vienna, Austria. Tel: 43-1-601-74/5710. Fax: 43-1-601-74/5727. E-mail: edelmax@magnet.at.

A.B. Dambazau, P.O. Box 3733, Kaduna, Kaduna State, Nigeria. Tel: 234-80-35012743. Fax: 234-70-36359118. E-mail: adambazau@yahoo.com.

IPES Institutional Supporters

IPES is guided and helped in all the activities by a group of Institutional Supporters around the world. These supporters are police agencies, universities, research organizations, and similar instiutions.

African Policing Civilian Oversight Forum (APCOF; Sean Tait), 2nd floor, The Armoury, Buchanan Square, 160 Sir Lowry Road, Woodstock, Cape Town 8000, South Africa. E-mail: sean@apcof.org.za.

Australian Institute of Police Management, Collins Beach Road, Manly, NSW 2095, Australia (Connie Coniglio). E-mail: cconiglio@aipm.gov.au.

Baker College of Jackson, 2800 Springport Road, Jackson, MI 49202 (Blaine Goodrich). Tel: 517-841-4522. E-mail: blaine.goodrich@baker.edu.

Cyber Defense & Research Initiatives, LLC (James Lewis), P.O. Box 86, Leslie, MI 49251. Tel: 517-242-6730. E-mail: lewisja@cyberdefenseresearch.com.

Defendology Center for Security, Sociology and Criminology Research (Valibor Lalic), Srpska Street 63, 78000 Banja Luka, Bosnia and Herzegovina. Tel and Fax: 387-51-308-914. E-mail: lalicv@teol.net.

Fayetteville State University (Dr. David E. Barlow, Professor and Dean), College of Basic and Applied Sciences, 130 Chick Building, 1200 Murchison Road, Fayetteville, NC, 28301. Tel: 910-672-1659. Fax: 910-672-1083. E-mail: dbarlow@uncfsu.edu.

Kerala Police (Mr. Balasubramanian, Director General of Police), Police Headquarters, Trivandrum, Kerala, India. E-mail: jpunnoose@gmail.com.

Molloy College, The Department of Criminal Justice (contact Dr. John A. Eterno, NYPD Captain-Retired), 1000 Hempstead Avenue, P.O. Box 5002, Rockville Center, NY 11571-5002. Tel: 516-678-5000, Ext. 6135. Fax: 516-256-2289. E-mail: jeterno@molloy.edu.

Mount Saint Vincent University, Department of Psychology (Stephen Perrott), 166 Bedford Highway, Halifax, Nova Scotia, Canada. E-mail: stephen.perrott@mvsu.ca.

National Institute of Criminology and Forensic Science (Kamalendra Prasad, Inspector General of Police), MHA, Outer Ring Road, Sector 3, Rohini, Delhi 110085, India. Tel: 91-11-275-2-5095. Fax: 91-11-275-1-0586. E-mail: director.nicfs@nic.in.

National Police Academy, Police Policy Research Center (Naoya Oyaizu, Deputy Director), 183-8558: 3- 12- 1, Asahi-cho Fuchu-City, Tokyo, Japan. Tel: 81-42-354-3550. Fax: 81-42-330-1308. E-mail: PPRC@npa.go.jp.

North Carolina Central University, Department of Criminal Justice (Dr. Harvey L. McMurray, Chair), 301 Whiting Criminal Justice Building, Durham, NC 27707. Tel: 919-530-5204/919-530-7909. Fax: 919-530-5195. E-mail: hmcmurray@nccu.edu.

Royal Canadian Mounted Police (Helen Darbyshire, Executive Assistant), 657 West 37th Avenue, Vancouver, BC V5Z 1K6, Canada. Tel: 604-264 2003. Fax: 604-264-3547. E-mail: helen.darbyshire@rcmp-grc.gc.ca.

Edith Cowan University, School of Psychology and Social Science, Social Justice Research Centre (Prof. S. Caroline Taylor, Foundation Chair in Social Justice), 270 Joondalup Drive, Joondalup, WA 6027, Australia. E-mail: c.taylor@ecu.edu.au.

South Australia Police, Office of the Commissioner (Commissioner Mal Hyde), 30 Flinders Street, Adelaide, SA 5000, Australia. E-mail: mal.hyde@police.sa.gov.au.

University of the Fraser Valley, Department of Criminology & Criminal Justice (Dr. Irwin Cohen), 33844 King Road, Abbotsford, British Columbia V2 S7 M9, Canada. Tel: 604-853-7441. Fax: 604-853-9990. E-mail: irwin.cohen@ufv.ca.

University of Maribor, Faculty of Criminal Justice and Security, (Dr. Gorazd Mesko), Kotnikova 8, 1000 Ljubljana, Slovenia. Tel: 386-1-300-83-39. Fax: 386-1-2302-687. E-mail: gorazd.mesko@ fvv.uni-mb.si.

University of Maine at Augusta, College of Natural and Social Sciences (Mary Louis Davitt, Professor of Legal Technology), 46 University Drive, Augusta, ME 04330-9410. E-mail: mldavitt@maine.edu.

University of New Haven, School of Criminal Justice and Forensic Science (Dr. Richard Ward), 300 Boston Post Road, West Haven, CT 06516. Tel: 203-932-7260. E-mail: rward@newhaven.edu.

University of South Africa, College of Law, School of Criminal Justice (Prof. Kris Pillay, Director), Preller Street, Muckleneuk, Pretoria, South Africa. E-mail: cpillay@unisa.ac.za.

University of South Africa, Department of Police Practice, Florida Campus (Setlhomamaru Dintwe), Christiaan De Wet and Pioneer Avenues, Private Bag X6, Florida, 1710 South Africa. Tel: 011-471-2116. Fax: 011-471-2255. E-mail: dintwsi@unisa.ac.za.

Index

CRC Press and the International Police Executive Symposium Co-Publications

The International Police Executive Symposium (IPES) was awarded special consultative status with the United Nations in 2011. IPES brings together leading police researchers and practitioners to facilitate cross-cultural, international, and interdisciplinary exchanges for the enrichment of the policing profession. It encourages dynamic discussions and writing on challenging topics of contemporary importance through an array of initiatives, including conferences and publications. For more information, please visit **http://www.ipes.info/**.

Now Available from CRC Press in Cooperation with the International Police Executive Symposium

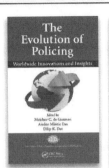

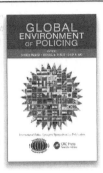

CRC Press and the International Police Executive Symposium Co-Publications

Police **P**ractice **&** **R**esearch
An International Journal

Published		Forthcoming

Strategic Responses to Crime

Thinking Locally, Acting Globally
Edited by
Melchor de Guzman,
Aiedeo Mintie Das, and
Dilip K. Das
Catalog no. 76698, October 2011
365 pp., ISBN: 978-1-4200-7669-1

Effective Crime Reduction Strategies

International Perspectives
Edited by
James F. Albrecht and
Dilip K. Das
Catalog no. 78380, February 2011
650 pp., ISBN: 978-1-4200-7838-1

Contemporary Issues in Law Enforcement and Policing

Edited by
Andrew Millie and Dilip K. Das
Catalog no. 72153, May 2008
248 pp., ISBN: 978-1-4200-7215-0

Global Trafficking in Women and Children

Edited by
Obi N.I. Ebbe and Dilip K. Das
Catalog no. 59432
December 2007
272 pp., ISBN: 978-1-4200-5943-4

Criminal Abuse of Women and Children

An International Perspective
Edited by
Obi N.I. Ebbe and Dilip K. Das
Catalog no. 88033, July 2009
396 pp., ISBN: 978-1-4200-8803-8

Urbanization, Policing, and Security

Global Perspectives
Edited by
Gary Cordner, AnnMarie Cordner,
and Dilip K. Das
Catalog no. 85573
December 2009
475 pp., ISBN: 978-1-4200-8557-0

Police Without Borders

The Fading Distinction Between Local and Global
Edited by
Cliff Roberson, Dilip K. Das, and
Jennie K. Singer
Catalog no. K10281, July 2010
328 pp., ISBN: 978-1-4398-0501-5

Police Reform

The Effects of International Economic Development, Armed Violence, and Public Safety
Edited by
Garth den Heyer and
Dilip K. Das
Catalog no. K21383,
June 2014, c. 400 pp.
ISBN: 978-1-4822-0456-8

Policing Major Events

Perspectives from Around the World
Edited by
Martha Christine Dow, Darryl Plecas, and Dilip K. Das
Catalog no. K20365
August 2014, c. 450 pp.
ISBN: 978-1-4665-8805-9

Global Issues in Contemporary Policing

Edited by
John A. Eterno, Aiedeo Mintie Das, and Dilip K. Das
Catalog no. K23677
March 2015, c. 350 pp.
ISBN: 978-1-4822-4852-4

Most titles also available as eBook

CRC Press
Taylor & Francis Group

*To order these or other titles,
please visit our website at*
www.crcpress.com